STUDIES OF CONTEMPORARY POETS

STUDIES OF CONTEMPORARY POETS

By

MARY C. STURGEON

REVISED AND ENLARGED

KENNIKAT PRESS
Port Washington, N. Y./London

STUDIES OF CONTEMPORARY POETS

First published in 1916
Revised edition published in 1920
Revised edition reissued in 1970 by Kennikat Press
Library of Congress Catalog Card No: 78-105839
ISBN 0-8046-1055-X

Manufactured by Taylor Publishing Company   Dallas, Texas

Preface

IN issuing a new edition of this book a word
may be said which perhaps should have
been said at first. It is a study of Contemporary Poetry using the word *contemporary* in
its full sense—that is to say, poetry which is of our
time not alone in the mere date of its appearance,
but in its spirit and form ; poetry which, for good
or evil, draws its breath from the more vital forces
of its age.

That is not to make any absolute claim for the
poets in this group, either as to their art or thought ;
nor to try to enthrone mere modernity. Still less
would one attempt to appraise the poets relatively
to each other or to the poets of earlier times. One
sees simply that, despite faults, their work has much
beauty and deep significance.

It follows from the plan of the work that a good
deal of poetry which is being written contemporaneously is necessarily excluded, as, for one
example only, that of Sir William Watson. The
plan also explains why, in 1914, when the first
edition was written, the greater figures of the
group which is now added (and which is placed,
for convenience, at the end of this volume)
were not then included. Neither Mr Hardy nor

5

Contemporary Poets

Mr Yeats were producing poetry at that time, but both have since published volumes which are different in character from their previous work and which are clearly signed of the new spirit; and the most exciting work of Michael Field did not appear till quite recently.

It was my belief when, before the War, this book was first planned, that a renaissance of poetry was quietly coming; and one wished to serve, however humbly, the travail of that event. It appeared that an Age of Minstrels had dawned and was gathering power; and I looked for that minstrel age to prepare the way for the great poet, and eventually to bring him forth. Then came the War, when hope of all kinds sickened; and as the storm swept away one after another of the singers, one trembled for poetry. But, the immense night now over, one peeps out again and is rejoiced to see that the young upspringing spirit of poetry is not destroyed. By some miracle it is thriving lustily.

MARY C. STURGEON

December 1919

Acknowledgment

THE author begs to offer warm thanks to the following poets and their publishers for the use of the quotations given in these studies :

Mr Masefield, Anna Wickham, " John Presland " (Mrs Skelton), and Anna Bunston (Mrs de Bary) ; Mr John Lane for the work of Mr Abercrombie, Mrs Woods, Olive Custance, and Helen Parry Eden ; Messrs Sidgwick and Jackson for the work of Miss Macaulay, Rupert Brooke and Mr John Drinkwater ; Mr A. C. Fifield and Mr Elkin Mathews for the work of Mr W. H. Davies ; Mr A. H. Bullen for the work of Mr W. B. Yeats, from the *Collected Works*, published by the Shakespeare Head Press ; Mr T. Fisher Unwin for " The Lake Isle of Innisfree," from *Poems*, by W. B. Yeats ; Messrs Constable for the work of Mr De la Mare ; Mr Elkin Mathews, *New Numbers*, and the Samurai Press for the work of Mr W. W. Gibson ; the Poetry Bookshop for the work of Mr Hodgson ; Messrs Max Goschen, Ltd., for the work of Mr Ford Madox Hueffer ; Mr Secker for the work of Mr J. C. Squire ; Messrs Maunsel and Co., Ltd., for the work of the members of " An Irish Group " and of Mr Stephens ; the Samurai Press and the Poetry Book-

7

shop for the work of Mr Monro; Mr William Heinemann for the work of Mrs Naidu; Messrs G. Allen and Unwin, Ltd., for the work of Miss Margaret M. Radford; Messrs Macmillan and Co. for the work of Mr Thomas Hardy; Mr Sturge Moore, Mr Eveleigh Nash, and the Poetry Bookshop for the work of Michael Field.

Thanks are also due to *The Englishwoman* for permission to reprint the chapter on " Contemporary Women Poets," and the author wishes to acknowledge especially the kind help she received from Miss Alida Klementaski in preparing the Bibliography.

Contents

Lascelles Abercrombie

IN the sweet chorus of modern poetry one may hear a strange new harmony. It is the life of our time, evoking its own music: constraining the poetic spirit to utter its own message. The peculiar beauty of contemporary poetry, with its fresh and varied charm, grows from that; and in that, too, its vitality is assured. Its art has the deep sanction of loyalty: its loyalty draws inspiration from the living source.

There is a fair company of these new singers; and it would seem that there should be large hope for a generation, whether in its life or letters, which can find such expression. Listening carefully, however, some notes ring clearer, stronger, or more significant than others; and of these the voice of Mr Abercrombie appears to carry the fullest utterance. It is therefore a happy chance that the name which stands first here, under a quite arbitrary arrangement, has a natural right to be put at the head of a group of the younger moderns.

But that is not an implicit denial to those others of fidelity to their time. It is a question of degree and of range. Every poet in this band will be found to represent some aspect of our complex life—its awakened social conscience or its frank joy in the

world of sense: its mysticism or its repudiation
of dogma, in art as in religion: its mistrust of
materialism or keen perception of reality: its
worship of the future, or assimilation of the heritage
of the past to its own ideals: its lyrical delight
in life or dramatic re-creation of it: its insistence
upon the essential poetry of common things, or its
discovery of rare new values in experience and
expression.

This poetry frequently catches one or another
of those elements, and crystallizes it out of a mere
welter into definite form and recognizable beauty.
But the claim for Mr Abercrombie is that he has
drawn upon them more largely: that he has made
a wider synthesis: that his work has a unity more
comprehensive and complete. It is in virtue of
this that he may be said to represent his age so fully;
but that is neither to accuse him of shouting with
the crowd, nor to lay on the man in the street the
burden of the poet's idealism. He is, indeed, in a
deeper sense than politics could make him, a
democrat: perhaps that inheres in the poetic
temperament under its shyness. But intellectuality and vision, a keen spirit and a sensuous equipment at once delicate and bountiful, are not to be
leashed to the common pace. That is a truism, of
course: so often it seems the destiny of the poet

Lascelles Abercrombie

to be at one with the people and yet above them.
But it needs repetition here, because it applies
with unusual force. This is a poet whose instinct
binds him inescapably to his kind, even when his
intellect is soaring where it is sometimes hard to
follow.

One is right, perhaps, in believing that this
affinity with his time is instinctive, for it reveals
itself in many ways, subtler or more obvious,
through all his work. As forthright avowal it
naturally occurs most in his earlier poems. There
is, for example, the humanitarianism of the fine
" Indignation " ode in his first volume, called
Interludes and Poems. This is an invocation of
righteous anger against the deplorable conditions
of the workers' lives. A fierce impulse drives
through the ode, in music that is sometimes
troubled by its own vehemence.

> Wilt thou not come again, thou godly sword,
> Into the Spirit's hands ?
>
> .   .   .   .   .
>
> Against our ugly wickedness,
> Against our wanton dealing of distress,
> The forced defilement of humanity,
>
> .   .   .   .   .
>
> And shall there be no end to life's expense
> In mills and yards and factories,

> With no more recompense
> Than sleep in warrens and low styes,
>   And undelighted food ?
> Shall still our ravenous and unhandsome mood
> Make men poor and keep them poor ?—

In the same volume there is a passage which may be said to present the obverse of this idea. It occurs in an interlude called " An Escape," and is only incidental to the main theme, which is much more abstract than that of the ode. A young poet, Idwal, has withdrawn from the society of his friends, to meditate about life among the hills. All the winter long he has kept in solitude, his spirit seeking for mastery over material things. As the spring dawns he is on the verge of triumph, and the soul is about to put off for ever its veil of sense, when news reaches him from the outer world. His little house, from which he has been absent so long, has been broken into, and robbed, by a tramp. The friend who comes to tell about it ends his tale by a word of sympathy—" I'm sorry for you "— and Idwal replies :

> It's sorry I am for that perverted tramp,
> As having gone from being the earth's friend,
> Whom she would have at all her private treats.
> Now with the foolery called possession he
> Has dirtied his own freedom, cozen'd all

His hearing with the lies of ownership.
The earth may call to him in vain henceforth,
He's got a step-dame now, his Goods. . . .

Evidence less direct but equally strong is visible in the later work. It lies at the root of the tragedy of *Deborah*, a heroine drawn from fisherfolk, who in the extremity of fear for her lover's life cries :

> O but my heart is dying in me, waiting :
>
> .   .   .   .   .
>
> For us, with lives so hazardous, to love
> Is like a poor girl's game of being a queen.

And it is found again, gathering materials for the play called *The End of the World* out of the lives of poor and simple people. Here the impulse is clear enough, but sometimes it takes a subtler form, and then it occasionally betrays the poet into a solecism. For his sense of the unity of the race is so strong that natural distinctions sometimes go the way of artificial ones. He has so completely identified himself with humanity, and for preference with the lowly in mind and estate, that he has not seldom endowed a humble personality with his own large gifts. Thus you find Deborah using this magnificent plea for her sweetheart's life :

. . . there's something sacred about lovers.

.   .   .   .   .

For there is wondrous more than the joy of life
In lovers ; there's in them God Himself
Taking great joy to love the life He made :
We are God's desires more than our own, we lovers,
You dare not injure God !

Thus, too, a working wainwright suddenly startled
into consciousness of the purpose of the life-force
muses :

Why was I like a man sworn to a thing
Working to have my wains in every curve,
Ay, every tenon, right and as they should be ?
Not for myself, not even for those wains :
But to keep in me living at its best
The skill that must go forward and shape the world,
Helping it on to make some masterpiece.

And with the same largesse a fiddling vagabond,
old and blind, thief, liar, and seducer, is made to
utter a lyric ecstasy on the words which are the
poet's instrument :

Words : they are messengers from out God's heart.
Intimate with him ; through his deed they go,
This passion of him called the world, approving
All of fierce gladness in it, bidding leap
To a yet higher rapture ere it sink.
                                    . . . There be

Lascelles Abercrombie

Who hold words made of thought. But as stars slide
Through air, so words, bright aliens, slide through
   thought,
Leaving a kindled way.

Now, since Synge has shown us that the poetry
in the peasant heart does utter itself spontaneously,
in fitting language, we must be careful how we
deny, even to these peasants who are not Celts, a
natural power of poetic expression. But there is a
difference. That spontaneous poetry of simple
folk which is caught for us in *The Playboy of the
Western World* or *The Well of the Saints*, is generally
a lyric utterance springing directly out of emotion.
It is not, as here, the result of a mental process,
operating amongst ideas and based on knowledge
which the peasant is unlikely to possess. One may
be justified, therefore, in a show of protest at the
incongruity; we feel that such people do not talk
like that. The poet has transferred to them too
much of his own intellectuality. Yet it will probably be a feeble protest, proportionate to the degree
that we are disturbed by it, which is practically
not at all. For as these people speak, we are
convinced of their reality : they live and move
before us. And when we consider their complete
and robust individuality, it would appear that
the poet's method is vindicated by the dramatic

17

force of the presentment. It needs no other
vindication, and is no doubt a reasoned process.
For Mr Abercrombie makes no line of separation
between thought and emotion ; and having entered
by imagination into the hearts of his people, he
might claim to be merely interpreting them—
making conscious and vocal that which was already
in existence there, however obscurely. There is a
hint of this at a point in *The End of the World* where
one of the men says that he had *felt* a certain thought
go through his mind—" though 'twas a thing of
such a flight I could not read its colour." And in
this way Deborah, being a human soul of full
stature, sound of mind and body and all her being
flooded with emotion, would be capable of feeling
the complex thought attributed to her, even if no
single strand of its texture had ever been clear in
her mind. While as to the fiddling lyrist, rogue
and poet, one sees no reason why the whole argument
should not be closed by a gesture in the direction
of Heine or Villon.

We turn now to the content of thought in Mr
Abercrombie's poetry—an aspect of his genius
to be approached with diffidence by a writer
conscious of limitations. For though we believed
we saw that his affinity with the democratic
spirit of his age is instinctive, deeply rooted

Lascelles Abercrombie

and persistent, his genius is by no means ruled by instinct. It is intellectual to an extreme degree, moving easily in abstract thought and apparently trained in philosophic speculation. Indeed, his speculative tendency had gone as far as appeared to be legitimate in poetry, when he wisely chose another medium for it in the volume of prose *Dialogues* published in 1913.

It must not be gathered from this, however, that the philosophic pieces are dull or difficult reading. On the contrary, they are frequently cast into the form of a story with a dramatic basis ; and although the torrent of thought sometimes keeps the mind astretch to follow it, it would be hard to discover a single obscure line. An astonishing combination of qualities has gone to produce this result : subtlety with vigour, delicacy with strength, and loftiness with simplicity. Things elusive and immaterial are caught and fixed in vivid imagery ; and often charged with poignant human interest. No other of the younger poets expresses thought so abstract with such force, or describes the adventures of the voyaging soul with such clarity. It is a combination which suggests high harmony in the development of sense and spirit : it explains how it happens that a rapture of delight in the physical world can coexist with spiritual exaltation : while it hints a reason for the poet's preoccupation with the duality in human life, and his vision of an ultimate union of the rival powers.

We may note in passing how this reacts upon the form of his work. It has created a unique vocabulary (enriched from many sources but derived from no single one), which is nervous, flexible, vigorous, impassioned : assimilating to its grave beauty not only the wealth and dignity of our language, but words homely, colloquial, and quaint.

Again, rather curiously, this complex thought has tended toward the dramatic form. At first glance that form would seem to be unsuitable for the expression of a prevailing reflectiveness. Yet here is a poet whose dominant theme might be defined, tritely, as the development of the soul; and he hardly ever writes in any other way.

The fact sends us back to the contrast with the Victorians. The representative poet then, musing about life and death and the evolution of the soul, felt himself impelled to the elegiac form. But the nature of the thought itself has changed. The representative poet now does not stand and lament, however exquisitely, because reality has shattered dogma ; neither does he try to create an epic out of the incredible theme of a perfect soul. He accepts reality ; and then he

perceives that the perfect soul *is* incredible, besides
being poor material for his art. But on the other
hand, while he takes care to seize and hold fast
truth : while it does not occur to him to mourn
that she is implacable : he resolutely denies to
phenomena, the appearance of things, the whole of
truth. That is to say, he has transcended at once
the despair of the Victorians and their materialism.
He has banished their lyric grief for a dead past,
along with their scientific and religious dogmas.
That was a bit of iconoclasm imperatively demanded
of him by his own soul ; but from the fact that
he is a poet, it is denied to him to find final satisfaction in the region of sense and consciousness.

Thus there arises a duality, and a sense of conflict, which would account for the manner of this
poet's expression, without the need to refer it to
the general tendency of modern poetry toward
the dramatic form. Doubtless, however, that also
has been an influence, for the virility of his genius
and the positive strain in his philosophy would lead
that way.

One can hardly say that there are perceptible
stages in Mr Abercrombie's thought. He appears
to be one of the few poets with no crudities to
repent, either artistic or philosophic. Yet there
is a poem in his first volume, a morality called

"The New God"; and there is another piece called
"The Sale of St Thomas," first published in 1911,
which are relatively simple. Here he is content
to take material that is traditional, both to poetry
and religion, and infuse into it so much of modern
significance as it will carry. The first re-tells the
mediæval legend of a girl changed by God into his
own likeness in order to save her from violence.
There is, apt to our present study, but too long to
give in full, at least one passage that is magnificent
in conception and imagery alike. It is the voice of
God, answering the girl's prayer that she may be
saved by the destruction of her beauty. The voice
declares that the petition is sweet and shall be granted,
that he will quit the business of the universe, that
he will "put off the nature of the world," and become

> God, when all the multitudinous flow
> Of Being sets backward to Him ; God, when He
> Is only glory. . . .

The "Sale of St Thomas" also treats a legend,
with originality and power. This remarkable poem
is already well known: but one may at least call
attention to the fitness and dignity with which the
poet has placed the modern gospel upon the lips
of the Christ. Thomas has been intercepted by
his master, as he is about to run away for the second
time from his mission to India.

Lascelles Abercrombie

Now, Thomas, know thy sin. It was not fear ;
Easily may a man crouch down for fear,
And yet rise up on firmer knees, and face
The hailing storm of the world with graver courage.
But prudence, prudence is the deadly sin,
And one that groweth deep into a life,
With hardening roots that clutch about the breast.
For this refuses faith in the unknown powers
Within man's nature ; shrewdly bringeth all
Their inspiration of strange eagerness
To a judgment bought by safe experience ;
Narrows desire into the scope of thought.
But it is written in the heart of man,
Thou shalt no larger be than thy desire.
Thou must not therefore stoop thy spirit's sight
To pore only within the candle-gleam
Of conscious wit and reasonable brain ;

.   .   .   .   .

But send desire often forth to scan
The immense night which is thy greater soul ;
Knowing the possible, see thou try beyond it
Into impossible things, unlikely ends ;
And thou shalt find thy knowledgeable desire
Grow large as all the regions of thy soul,
Whose firmament doth cover the whole of Being,
And of created purpose reach the ends.

Perhaps the thought here is not so simple as the
pellucid expression makes it to appear : yet the
conventional material on which the poet is working
restrains it to at least relative simplicity. When,

however, his inspiration is moving quite freely, unhampered by tradition either of technique or of theme, the result is more complex and more characteristic.

The tragedy called "Blind", in his first volume, is an example. The plot of this dramatic piece is probably unique. If one gave the bald outline of it, it might seem to be merely a story of crude revenge. It is concerned with rude and outlawed people: it springs out of elemental passions—fierce love turned to long implacable hatred, and then reverting to tenderness and pity and overwhelming remorse. And yet the three characters who enact this little tragedy are very subtly studied—the woman who has reared her idiot son to be the weapon to avenge her wrongs upon the father he has never known; the blind son himself; and his father, the same fiddling tramp whom we have already noted. There are points in the delineation of all three which are quite brilliantly imagined: the change in the woman when she meets at last the human wreck who had once been her handsome lover; the idiot youth hungering to express the beauty which is revealed to him, through touch, in a child's golden hair, the warmth of fire, the mysterious presence of the dark:

24

Lascelles Abercrombie

. . . . like a wing's shelter bending down.
I've often thought, if I were tall enough
And reacht my hand up, I should touch the soft
Spread feathers of the resting flight of him
Who covers us with night, so near he seems
Stooping and holding shadow over us,
Roofing the air with wings.   It's plain to feel
Some large thing's near, and being good to us.

But, above all, there is the character of the fiddler.
At first glance, the phenomenon looks common
enough and all its meaning obvious.   " A wastrel "
one would say, glibly defining the phenomenon ; and
add " a *drunken* wastrel," believing that we had
explained it.   But the poet sees further, apprehends
more and understands better.   Drunken indeed,
but an intoxication older and more divine than that
of brandy began the business ; and much brandy
had not quenched the elder fire.   It flamed in him
still, mostly a sinister glow, fed from his bad and
sorrowful past, but leaping on occasion to clear
radiance, as in the talk with his unknown son, when
some magnetic influence drew the two blind men
together and made them friends before they had
any knowledge of relationship.   Of the many finer
touches in this poem, none is more delicate and
none more moving than the suggestion of unconscious affinity between these two: the idiot,

25

with his half-awake mind, groping amidst shadows
of ideas which to the older man are quick with
inspiration.

> Son.   What are words ?
> Tramp.   God's love !   Here's a man after my own
>   heart ;
> We must be brothers, lad.

But besides his dramatic and psychological interest, the fiddler is important because he seems to
represent the poet's philosophy in its brief icono-
clastic phase. For we find placed in his lips a
destructive satire of the old theological doctrine
of Good and Evil. The passage is too long to quote,
and it would be unfair to mutilate it. Incidentally
we may note, however, the keen salt humour of it,
and how that quality establishes the breadth and
sanity of the poet's outlook. The point of peculiar
interest at the moment is that this phase passes
with the particular poem—an early one ; and thenceforward it is replaced by more constructive thought.
We come to "The Fool's Adventure," for instance,
and find the "Seeker" travelling through all the
regions of mind and spirit to find God, and the
nature and cause of sin. His quest brings him first
to the Self of the World, and he believes that this
is God. But the Sage corrects him :

26

Lascelles Abercrombie

> . . . Poor fool,
> And didst thou think this present sensible world
> Was God ? . . .
>
> .   .   .   .   .
>
> It is a name, ; . . . .
> The name Lord God chooses to go by, made
> In languages of stars and heavens and life.

And when, finally, he has won through to a certain palace at the " verge of things," he cries his question to the unseen king within.

> SEEKER.   Then thou art God ?
> WITHIN.   Ay, many call me so.
> And yet, though words were never large enough
> To take me made, I have a better name.
> SEEKER.   Then truly, who art thou ?
> WITHIN.   I am Thy Self.

Another aspect of the same idea, caught in a more lyrical mood, will be found in the poem called "The Trance." The poet is standing upon a hill-side alone at night, watching the " continual stars " and overawed by the vastness and " fixt law " of the universe. Then, in a sudden revelation of perhaps a fraction of a minute :

> I was exalted above surety
> And out of time did fall.
> As from a slander that did long distress,
> A sudden justice vindicated me
> From the customary wrong of Great and Small.

I stood outside the burning rims of place,
Outside that corner, consciousness.
Then was I not in the midst of thee
Lord God ?

That, however, is the triumphant ecstasy of a
moment. More often he is preoccupied with the
duality in human nature, and in "An Escape" there
is a fine simile of the struggle :

Desire of infinite things, desire of finite.
. . . 'tis the wrestle of the twain makes man.
—As two young winds, schooled 'mong the slopes and
   caves
Of rival hills that each to other look
Across a sunken tarn, on a still day
Run forth from their sundered nurseries, and meet
In the middle air. . . .
And when they close, their struggle is called Man,
Distressing with his strife and flurry the bland
Pool of existence, that lay quiet before
Holding the calm watch of Eternity.

The incidence of finite and infinite is felt with
equal force : sense is as powerful as spirit, and therein
of course lives the keenness of the strife. In "Soul
and Body " there is a passage—only one of many,
however—in which the rapture of sensuous beauty
is expressed. The spirit is imagined to be just
ready to put off sense, to be for ever caught out of

" that corner, consciousness." And the body reminds it :

> Thou wilt miss the wonder I have made for thee
> Of this dear world with my fashioning senses,
> The blue, the fragrance, the singing, and the green.
>
> .   .   .   .   .
>
> Great spaces of grassy land, and all the air
> One quiet, the sun taking golden ease
> Upon an afternoon :
> Tall hills that stand in weather-blinded trances
> As if they heard, drawn upward and held there,
> Some god's eternal tune ;

We may take our last illustration of this subject from a passage at the end of the volume called *Emblems of Love*. It is from a poem so rich in beauty and so closely woven, that to quote from it is almost inevitably to do the author an injustice. But the same may be said about the whole book : while single poems from it will disclose high individual value, both as art and philosophy, their whole effect and meaning can only be completely seized by reading them as a sequence, and in the light of the conception to which they all contribute.

The book is designed to show, in three great movements representing birth, growth, and perfection, the evolution of the human spirit in the

world. The spirit, which is here synonymous with
love, is traced from the instant which is chosen to
mark its birth (the awakening sense of beauty in
primitive man), through its manifold states of excess
and defect, up to a transcendent union which draws
the dual powers into a single ecstasy. The greatness of the central theme is matched by the dignity
of its presentment, while the dramatic form in
which it is embodied saves it from mere abstraction.
We see the dawn of the soul in the wolf-hunter,
suddenly perceiving beauty in nature and in women:
the vindication of the soul by Vashti, magnificently
daring to prove that it is no mere vassal to beauty:
and the perfecting of the soul in the terrible
paradox of Judith's virginity. But it is in one
of the closing pieces, called fittingly "The Eternal
Wedding," that the poet attains the summit of his
thought along these lines ; prefiguring the ultimate
union of the conflicting powers of life in one perfect
rapture.

> . . . I have
> Golden within me the whole fate of man :
> That every flesh and soul belongs to one
> Continual joyward ravishment . . .
> That life hath highest gone which hath most joy.
> For like great wings forcefully smiting air
> And driving it along in rushing rivers,

Lascelles Abercrombie

Desire of joy beats mightily pulsing forward
The world's one nature. . . .

                 . . . . so we are driven
Onward and upward in a wind of beauty,
Until man's race be wielded by its joy
Into some high incomparable day,
Where perfectly delight may know itself,—
No longer need a strife to know itself,
Only by its prevailing over pain.

That is the topmost peak that his philosophy
has gained—for just so long as to give assurance that
it exists. But no one supposes that he will dwell
there: it is altogether too high: the atmosphere is
too rare. It was reached only by the concentration
of certain poetical powers, chiefly speculative imagination, which carried him safely over the chasms
of a lower altitude. But when other powers are
in the ascendant, as for instance in *The End of the
World*: when he is recalled to actuality by that
keen eye for fact which is so rare a gift to genius
of this type, the terror of those lower chasms is revealed. Here is one of the characters reflecting on
the thought of the end of the world, which he
believes to be imminent from an approaching comet:

Life, the mother who lets her children play
So seriously busy, trade and craft,—
Life with her skill of a million years' perfection
To make her heart's delighted glorying

31

Of sunlight, and of clouds about the moon,
Spring lighting her daffodils, and corn
Ripening gold to ruddy, and giant seas,
And mountains sitting in their purple clothes—
O life I am thinking of, life the wonder,
All blotcht out by a brutal thrust of fire
Like a midge that a clumsy thumb squashes and smears.

That passage will serve to point the single comment on technique with which this study must close. It has not been selected for the purpose, and therefore is not the finest example that could be chosen. It is, however, typical of the blank-verse form which largely prevails in this poetry, and which, in its very texture, reveals the same extraordinary combination of qualities which we have observed in the poet's genius.

We have already seen that spiritual vision is here united with intellectuality as lucid as it is powerful: that the mystic is also the humanitarian: that imagination is balanced by a good grip on reality; and that the sense-impressions are fine as well as exuberant. We have seen, too, that this diversity and apparent contrast, although resulting in an art of complex beauty, do not tend towards confusion or ob curity. There has been a complete fusion of the elements, and the molten stream that is poured for us is of glowing clarity.

Lascelles Abercrombie

Exactly the same feature is discernible in the style of this verse. Look at the last passage for a moment and consider its effect. It is impossible to define in a single word, because of its complexity. The mind, lingering delightedly over the metaphor of life the mother, is suddenly awed by the magnitude of the idea which succeeds it. The æsthetic sense is taken by the light and colour of the middle lines, and then, as if the breath were caught on a half-sob, a wave of emotion follows, pensive at first, but rising abruptly to a note that is as rough as a curse. There are more shades of thought, lightly reflective or glooming with prescience; and there are more degrees of emotion, from tenderness to wrath, than we have time to analyze. The point for the moment is the manner in which they are conveyed, and the adequacy of the instrument to convey them.

The texture of the verse itself will provide evidence of this. Here are barely a dozen lines of our English heroic verse; and they will be found to contain the maximum of metrical variety. Probably only two, or at most three of them (it depends upon scansion, of course) are of the regular iambic pentameter: that is to say, built up strictly from the iamb, which is the unit of this form. All the others are varied by the insertion at some point

33

in the line, and frequently at two or three points, of a different verse-unit, dactyl, anapæst, trochee or spondee; and no two lines are varied in exactly the same way.

But, besides the range of the instrument, there is the exquisite harmony of it with mood or idea. The strong down-beat of the trochee summons the intellect to consider a thought: the dactyl will follow with the quick perception of a simile: the iamb will punctuate rhythm: anacrusis will suggest the half-caught breath of rising emotion, and turbulent feeling will pour through spondee, dactyl, and anapæst. And so with the diction. Just as we find a measure which is both vigorous and light, precise and flexible, easily bending law to beauty; so in the language there is a corresponding union of strength and grace, homeliness and dignity. Could a great conception be stated in a simpler phrase than that of the two first lines?

> Life, the mother who lets her children play
> So seriously busy, trade and craft—

and yet this phrase, simple and lucid as it is, conveys a sense of boundless tenderness and pity, playing over the surface of a deeper irony. Doubtless its strength and clarity come from the fact that each word is of the common coin of daily life; but its

34

atmosphere, an almost infinite suggestiveness of familiar things brooded over in a wistful mood, comes partly at least through the colloquial touch.

Mr Abercrombie has no fear to be colloquial, when that is the proper garment of his thought, the outer symbol of the inner reality. Nor is he the least afraid of fierce and ugly words, when they are apt. The last line of our passage illustrates this. Taken out of its setting, and considering merely the words, one would count a poet rash indeed who would venture such a harsh collocation. But repeat the line aloud, and its metrical felicity will appear at once: put it back in its setting, as the culmination of a wave of feeling that has been gathering strength throughout: remember the idea (of beauty annihilated by senseless law and blind force), which has kindled that emotion ; and then we shall marvel at the art which makes the line a growl of impotent rage.

All of which is merely to say that the spirit of this poetry has evolved for itself a living body, wearing its beauty delightedly, rejoicing in its own vitality, and unashamed either of its elemental impulse or its transcendent vision.

Rupert Brooke

Born at Rugby on August 3, 1887;
Died at Lemnos on April 23, 1915

PROBABLY most English people who love their country and their country's greatest poet have at some time taken joy to identify the spirit of the two. England and Shakespeare : the names have leapt together and flamed into union before the eyes of many a youngster who was much too dazzled by the glory to see how and whence it came. But returning from a festival performance on some soft April midnight, or leaning out of the bedroom window to share with the stars and the wind the exaltation which the play had evoked, the revelation suddenly shone. And thenceforward April 23 was by something more than a coincidence, the day both of Shakespeare and St George.

Reason might come back with the daylight to rule over fancy ; and the cool lapse of time might remove the moment · far enough to betray the humour of it. But the glow never quite faded ; or if it did it only gave place to the steadier and clearer light of conviction. One came to see how the poet, by reason of his complete humanity,

36

Rupert Brooke

stood for mankind ; and how, from certain sharp
characteristics of our race, he stood pre-eminently
for English folk. And coming thence to the
narrower but firmer ground of historical fact, one
saw how shiningly he represented the Elizabethan
Age, with its eager, inquisitive, and adventurous
spirit ; its craving to fulfil to the uttermost a gift
of glorious and abundant life.

Now precisely in that way, though not of course
in the same superlative degree, one may see Rupert
Brooke standing for the England of his time. And
when this poet died at Lemnos on April 23, 1915,
those who knew and loved his work must have felt
the tragic fitness of the date with the event. If the
gods of war had decreed his death, they had at least
granted that he might pass on England's day. In
him indeed was manifested the poetic spirit of the
race, warm with human passion and sane with
laughter : soaring on wings of fire but nesting always
on the good earth. And though one does not claim
to find in him the highest point or the extremest
advance to which the thought of his day had gone,
he stands pre-eminently for that day in the steel-
clear light of his gallant spirit.

The title of Rupert Brooke's posthumous book
—*1914*—signifies that moment of English history
which is reflected in his work. He is the symbol

of that year in a double sense. He represents the calamitous political event of it in his voluntary service to the State, and the manner of his death. Thus by the accident of circumstance which made him eminent and vocal, he serves to speak for the silent millions of English men and women who splendidly sprang to duty. But in his poetry there is a closer and deeper relation to that tragic year. Incomplete as it may be : youthful and prankish as some of it is, the thought and manner of the time are imaged there. A certain level of humane culture had been reached, a certain philosophy of life had been evolved, and a definite attitude to reality taken. Lightly but clearly, these things which reflect the colour of our civilization at August 1914 are crystallized in Rupert Brooke's poetry to that date. But at that point the image, like the whole order of which it was the reflection, was shattered by the clash of arms ; and the few poems which he wrote subsequently are preoccupied with the spiritual crisis which the war precipitated.

Most of the admirers of this poet have seen only in his last pieces the singular identity of his spirit with the spirit of his country. And that is so noble a concord that it cannot be missed. For when England plunged into the greatest war of history, she flung off in the act several centuries of her age.

Rupert Brooke

Priceless things, slowly and patiently acquired, went overboard as mere impedimenta ; but in the relapse, the slipping backward to an earlier time and consequent recovery of youth, with its ardour and passion, its recklessness and generosity and courage, the optimist saw a reward for all that was lost. So with the poetry of Rupert Brooke. Those few last sonnets, as it were the soul of rejuvenated England, seem to the same hopeful eye a complete compensation, not only for the wasted individual life, but for the beauty and significance of the age for which he stood, now irrevocably lost.

Blow out, you bugles, over the rich Dead !
    There's none of these so lonely and poor of old,
    But, dying, has made us rarer gifts than gold.
These laid the world away ; poured out the red
Sweet wine of youth ; gave up the years to be
    Of work and joy, and that unhoped serene,
    That men call age ; and those who would have been,
Their sons, they gave, their immortality.

Blow, bugles, blow ! They brought us, for our dearth,
    Holiness, lacked so long, and Love, and Pain.
Honour has come back, as a king, to earth,
    And paid his subjects with a royal wage ;
And Nobleness walks in our ways again ;
    And we have come into our heritage.

Before that renunciation one can only stand with

bowed head, realizing perhaps more clearly than the giver did, the splendour of the gift. But he too, being representative of his age, had weighed in full the value of the life that he was casting away. It was to him a " red sweet wine," precious for the " work and joy " it promised, and the sacred seed of immortality. It is this, above all, that his poetry signifies ; a rich and exuberant life, keenly conscious of itself, and fully aware of the realities by which it is surrounded. Its nature grows from that—sensuous and spiritual, passionate and intellectual, ingenuous and ironic, tragic and gay. Not even in Donne, whom, perhaps, as some one has suggested, he does resemble—was such intensity of feeling coupled with such merciless clarity of sight : mental honesty so absolute, controlling a flame of ardour.

From the fusion of those two powers comes the distinctive character of this poetry : the peculiar beauty of its gallant spirit. They are constant features of it from first to last, but they are not always perfectly fused nor equally present. In the earlier poems, to find which you must go back to the volume of 1911 and begin at the end of the book, they enter as separate and distinct components. One would expect that, of course, at this stage ; and we shall not be surprised, either, if we discover that there is here a shade of excess

in both qualities : a touch of self-consciousness
and relative crudity. The point of interest is that
they are so clearly the principal elements from
which the subtle and complex beauty of the later
work was evolved. Thus, facing one another on
pages 84 and 85, are two apt examples. In "The
Call" sheer passion is expressed. The poet's great
love of life, taking shape for the moment as love of
his lady, is here predominant.

> Out of the nothingness of sleep,
>   The slow dreams of Eternity,
> There was a thunder on the deep :
>   I came, because you called to me.
>
> I broke the Night's primeval bars,
>   I dared the old abysmal curse,
> And flashed through ranks of frightened stars
>   Suddenly on the universe !
>
> .   .   .   .   .
>
> I'll break and forge the stars anew,
>   Shatter the heavens with a song ;
> Immortal in my love for you,
>   Because I love you, very strong.

But on the opposite page, the sonnet called "Dawn"
swings to the extremest point from the magniloquence
of that. It is realistic in a literal sense : a bit of
wilful ugliness. Yet it springs, however distortedly,
from the root of mental clarity and courage which

was to produce such gracious blossoming thereafter. It is engaged with an exasperated account of a night journey in an Italian train : all the discomfort and weary irritation of it venting itself upon two unfortunate Teutons.

. . . . .

> One of them wakes, and spits, and sleeps again.
>   The darkness shivers. A wan light through the rain
> Strikes on our faces, drawn and white.   Somewhere
>   A new day sprawls ; and, inside, the foul air
> Is chill, and damp, and fouler than before. . . .
> Opposite me two Germans sweat and snore.

It is not long, however, before we find that the two elements are beginning to combine ; and we soon meet, astonishingly, with a third quality of the poet's genius. It is strange that imagination always has this power to surprise us. No matter if we have taught ourselves that poetry cannot begin to exist without it : no matter how watchful and alert we think we are, it will spring upon us unaware, taking possession of the mind with amazing exhilaration. That is especially true of the quality as it is found in Rupert Brooke's poetry. For, however you have schooled yourself, you are not looking for imaginative power of the first degree in alliance with sensuous joy so keen, and irony so acute. Yet in a piece called " In Examina-

Rupert Brooke

tion " the miracle is wrought. This, too, is an early poem, which may be the reason why one can disengage the threads so easily; whilst a notable fact is that the delicate fabric of it is woven directly out of a commonplace bit of human experience. The poet is engaged with a scene that is decidedly unpromising for poetical treatment—all the stupidity of examination, with its dull, unhappy, " scribbling fools."

> Lo ! from quiet skies
> In through the window my Lord the Sun !
> And my eyes
> Were dazzled and drunk with the misty gold,
>
> .   .   .   .   .
>
> And a full tumultuous murmur of wings
> Grew through the hall ;
> And I knew the white undying Fire,
> And, through open portals,
> Gyre on gyre,
> Archangels and angels, adoring, bowing,
> And a Face unshaded . . .
> Till the light faded ;
> And they were but fools again, fools unknowing,
> Still scribbling, blear-eyed and stolid immortals.

There are at least two poems, " The Fish " and " Dining-Room Tea," in which imaginative power prevails over every other element ; and if imagination be the supreme poetic quality, these are Rupert

43

Brooke's finest achievement. They are, indeed, very remarkable and significant examples of modern poetry, both in conception and in treatment. In both pieces the subjects are of an extremely difficult character. One, that of "The Fish," is beyond the range of human experience altogether ; and the other is only just within it, and known, one supposes, to comparatively few. The imaginative flight is therefore bold : it is also lofty, rapid, and well sustained. In "The Fish" we see it creating a new material world, giving substance and credibility to a strange new order of sensation :

> In a cool curving world he lies
> And ripples with dark ecstasies.
> The kind luxurious lapse and steal
> Shapes all his universe to feel
> And know and be ; the clinging stream
> Closes his memory, glooms his dream,
> Who lips the roots o' the shore, and glides
> Superb on unreturning tides.

.   .   .   .   .

> But there the night is close, and there
> Darkness is cold and strange and bare ;
> And the secret deeps are whisperless ;
> And rhythm is all deliciousness ;
> And joy is in the throbbing tide,
> Whose intricate fingers beat and glide

Rupert Brooke

In felt bewildering harmonies
Of trembling touch ; and music is
The exquisite knocking of the blood.
Space is no more, under the mud ;
His bliss is older than the sun.
Silent and straight the waters run.
The lights, the cries, the willows dim,
And the dark tide are one with him.

We see, all through this poem (and the more
convincingly as the whole of it is studied) the
" fundamental brain-stuff " : the patient constructive power of intellect keeping pace with fancy
every step of the way. So, too, with " Dining-Room
Tea." Imagination here is busy with an idea that
is wild, elusive, intangible : on the bare edge, in
fact, of sanity and consciousness. It is that momentary revelation, which comes once in a lifetime
perhaps, of the reality within appearance. It
comes suddenly, unheralded and unaccountable :
it is gone again with the swiftness and terror of a
lightning-flash. But in the fraction of a second
that it endures, æons seem to pass and things un-
utterable to be revealed. Only a poet of undoubted
genius could re-create such a moment, for on any
lower plane either imagination would flag or intellect would be baffled, with results merely chaotic.
And only to one whose quick and warm humanity

held life's common things so dear could the vision shine out of such a homely scene. But therein Rupert Brooke shows so clearly as the poet of his day : that through the familiar joys of comradeship and laughter : through the simple concrete things of a material world—the " pouring tea and cup and cloth," Reality gleams eternal.

> When you were there, and you, and you,
> Happiness crowned the night ; I too,
> Laughing and looking, one of all,
> I watched the quivering lamplight fall
>
> .   .   .   .   .
>
> Flung all the dancing moments by
> With jest and glitter. . . .
>
> Till suddenly, and otherwhence,
> I looked upon your innocence.
> For lifted clear and still and strange
> From the dark woven flow of change
> Under a vast and starless sky
> I saw the immortal moment lie.
> One instant I, an instant, knew
> As God knows all.   And it and you
> I, above Time, oh, blind ! could see
> In witless immortality.

But the precise characteristic of this poetry is not one or other of these individual gifts. It is an intimate and subtle blending of them all, shot

through and through with a gallant spirit which resolutely and gaily faces truth. From this brave and
clear mentality comes a sense of fact which finds its
artistic response in realism. Sometimes it will be
found operating externally, on technique ; but more
often, with truer art, it will wed truth of idea and
form, in grace as well as candour. From its detachment and quick perception of incongruity
comes a rare humour which can laugh, thoughtfully
or derisively, even at itself. It will stand aside,
watching its own exuberance with an ironic smile,
as in "The One Before the Last." It will turn
a penetrating glance on passion till the gaudy thing
wilts and dies. It will pause at the height of
life's keenest rapture to call to death an undaunted
greeting :

> Breathless, we flung us on the windy hill,
>> Laughed in the sun, and kissed the lovely grass.
>> You said, " Through glory and ecstasy we pass ;
> Wind, sun, and earth remain, the birds sing still,
> When we are old, are old. . . ." " And when we die
>> All's over that is ours ; and life burns on
> Through other lovers, other lips," said I,
> —" Heart of my heart, our heaven is now, is won ! "
>
> " We are Earth's best, that learnt her lesson here.
>> Life is our cry. We have kept the faith ! " we said ;
>> " We shall go down with unreluctant tread
> Rose-crowned into the darkness ! " . . . Proud we were,

47

And laughed, that had such brave true things to say.
—And then you suddenly cried, and turned away.

Perception keen and fearless, piercing readily through the half-truths of life and art, has its own temptation to mere cleverness. Thence come the conceits of the sonnet called " He Wonders Whether to Praise or Blame Her," a bit of the deftest juggling with ideas and words. Thence, too, the allegorical brilliance of the " Funeral of Youth " ; and the merry mockery of the piece called " Heaven." This is an excellent example of the poet's wit, as distinct from his richer, more pervasive, humour. It is very finely pointed and closely aimed in its satire of the Victorian religious attitude. And if we put aside an austerity which sees a shade of ungraciousness in it, we shall find it a richly entertaining bit of philosophy :

> Fish say, they have their Stream and Pond ;
> But is there anything Beyond ?
> This life cannot be All, they swear,
> For how unpleasant, if it were !
> One may not doubt that, somehow, Good
> Shall come of Water and of Mud ;
> And, sure, the reverent eye must see
> A Purpose in Liquidity.
> We darkly know, by Faith we cry,
> The future is not Wholly Dry.

Rupert Brooke

Mud unto Mud !—Death eddies near—
Not here the appointed End, not here !
But somewhere, beyond Space and Time,
Is wetter water, slimier slime !

.   .   .   .   .

And in that Heaven of all their wish,
There shall be no more land, say fish.

But, on the whole, one loves this work best when
its genius is not shorn by the sterile spirit of derision.
Its charm is greatest when the creative energy of it is
outpoured through what is called personality. Never
was a poet more lavish in the giving of himself,
yielding up a rich and complex individuality with
engaging candour. And poems will be found in
which all its qualities are blended in a soft and
intricate harmony. Passion is subdued to tenderness : imagination stoops to fantasy : thought, in
so far as it is not content merely to shape the form
of the work, is bent upon ideas that are wistful,
or sad or ironic. Humour, standing aloof and quietly
chuckling, will play mischievous pranks with people
and things. A satirical imp will dart into a line
and out again before you realize that he is there ;
and all the time a clear-eyed, observing spirit will
be watching and taking note with careful accuracy.

Of such is "The Old Vicarage, Grantchester," in

which the poet is longing for his home in Cambridge-
shire as he sits outside a café in Berlin.   The poem
is therefore a cry of homesickness, a modern " Oh,
to be in England ! "   But there is much more in it
than that ; it is not merely a wail of emotion.   The
lyrical reverie which recalls all the sweet natural
beauty that he is aching to return to is closely woven
with other strands.   So that one may catch half a
dozen incidental impressions which pique the mind
with contrasting effects and yet contribute to the
prevailing sense of intolerable desire for home.
Thus, when the poet has swung off into a sunny
dream of the old house and garden, the watching
sense of fact suddenly jogs him into consciousness
that he is not there at all, but in a very different
place.   And that wakens the satiric spirit, so that
an amusing interlude follows, summing up by
implication much of the contrast between the
English and German minds :

> . . . *there* the dews
> Are soft beneath a morn of gold.
> Here tulips bloom as they are told ;
> Unkempt about those hedges blows
> An English unofficial rose ;
> And there the unregulated sun
> Slopes down to rest when day is done,
> And wakes a vague unpunctual star,
> A slippered Hesper ; and there are

Rupert Brooke

Meads towards Haslingfield and Coton
Where *das Betreten*'s not *verboten*.

εἴθε γενοίμην . . . would I were
In Grantchester, in Grantchester !—

He slips back again into the softer mood of memory,
not of the immediate home scenes only, but of their
associations, historical and academic. Always, however, that keen helmsman steers to the windward
of sentimentality : better risk rough weather, it
seems to say, than shipwreck on some lotus-island.
And every time the boat would appear to be making
fairly for an exquisite idyllic haven, she is headed
into the breeze again. But though she gets a
buffeting, and even threatens to capsize at one
moment in boisterous jest, she comes serenely into
port at last.

> Say, do the elm-clumps greatly stand
> Still guardians of that holy land ?
> The chestnuts shade, in reverend dream,
> The yet unacademic stream ?
> Is dawn a secret shy and cold
> Anadyomene, silver-gold ?
> And sunset still a golden sea
> From Haslingfield to Madingley ?
> And after, ere the night is born,
> Do hares come out about the corn ?
> Oh, is the water sweet and cool,
> Gentle and brown, above the pool ?

And laughs the immortal river still
Under the mill, under the mill ?
Say, is there Beauty yet to find ?
And Certainty ? and Quiet kind ?
Deep meadows yet, for to forget
The lies, and truths, and pain ? . . . oh ! yet
Stands the Church clock at ten to three ?
And is there honey still for tea ?

William H. Davies

I SHOULD think that the work of Mr Davies is the nearest approach that the poetic genius could make to absolute simplicity. It is a wonderful thing, too, in its independence, its almost complete isolation from literary tradition and influence. People talk of Herrick in connexion with this poet ; and if they mean no more than to wonder at a resemblance which is a surprising accident, one would run to join them in their happy amazement. But there is no evidence of direct influence, any more than by another token we could associate his realism with that of Crabbe. No, this is verse which has " growed," autochthonic if poetry ever were, unliterary, and spontaneous in the many senses of that word.

From that fact alone, these seven small volumes of verse are a singular phenomenon. But they teem with interest of other kinds too. First and foremost there is, of course, the preciousness of many of the pieces they contain, as pure poetry, undimmed by any other consideration whatsoever. That applies to a fair proportion of this work ; and it is a delightsomeness which, from its very independence of time and circumstance, one looks quite soberly to last the centuries through ; and if it lapse at all from

Contemporary Poets

favour, to be rediscovered two or three hundred years hence as we have rediscovered the poets of the seventeenth century.

It has, however, inherent interest apart from this æsthetic joy, something which catches and holds the mind, startling it with an apparent paradox. For this poetry, with its solitariness and absence of any affiliation ancient or modern, with its bird-note bubbling into song at some sweet impulse and seemingly careless of everything but the impelling rapture, is at the same time one of the grimmest pages out of contemporary life. In saying that, one pauses for a moment sternly to interrogate one's own impression. How much of this apparent paradox is due to knowledge derived from the author's astounding autobiography ? Turn painfully back for a moment to the thoughts and feelings aroused by that book : recall the rage against the stupidity of life which brings genius to birth so carelessly, endowing it with appetites too strong for the will to tame and senses too acute for the mind to leash until the soul had been buffeted and the body maimed. And admit at once that such a tale, all the more for its quiet veracity, could not fail to influence one's attitude to this poetry. No doubt it is that which gives assurance, certainty, the proof of actual data, to the human record adumbrated

54

William H. Davies

in the poems. But the record itself is no less present there. It often exists, implicit or explicit, in that part of the verse which sings because it must and for sheer love of itself. And in that other part of the work where the lyric note is not so clear : in the narrative poems and queer character-studies and little dramatic pieces, the record lives vivid and almost complete. Perhaps it is the nature of the record itself which denies full inspiration to those pieces : perhaps Mr Davies' lyric gift cannot find its most fitting expression in themes so grim : in any case it is clear that these personal pieces are not equal to the lighter songs.

Now if one's conscience were supple enough to accept those lighter songs as Mr Davies' complete work : if we could conveniently forget the auto-biography, and when visualizing his output, call up some charming collected edition of the poems with the unsatisfactory ones carefully deleted, we could go on with our study easily and gaily. We might pause a moment to marvel at this 'isolated phe-nomenon' : we might even remark upon his detachment, not only from literature, but almost as completely from the ordinary concerns of life. That done, however, we should at once take a header into the delicious refreshment of the lyrics. Such a study would be very fascinating ; and from the standpoint of Art as Art, it might not be inadequate. But it would totally lack significance. Even from the point of view of pure poetry, the loss would be profound—not to realize that behind the blithest of these trills of song is a background as stormy as any winter sky behind a robin on a bare bough. There is this one, for example, from the volume called *Foliage* :

> If I were gusty April now,
>   How I would blow at laughing Rose ;
> I'd make her ribbons slip their knots,
>   And all her hair come loose.
>
> If I were merry April now,
>   How I would pelt her cheeks with showers ;
> I'd make carnations rich and warm,
>   Of her vermilion flowers.
>
> Since she will laugh in April's face,
>   No matter how he rains or blows—
> Then O that I wild April were,
>   To play with laughing Rose.

The gaiety of that, considered simply in its lightness of heart, its verbal and metrical felicity, is a delightful thing. And it recurs so frequently as to make Mr Davies quite the jolliest of modern poets. So if we are content to stop there, if we are not teased by an instinct to relate things, and see all round them, we may make holiday pleasantly enough with this part of the poet's work. The method is not really satisfying, however, and the inclusion of the more personal pieces adds a deeper value to the study. Not merely because the facts of a poet's life are interesting in themselves, but because here especially they are illuminating, explanatory, suggestive : connecting and unifying the philosophical interest of the work, and supplying a background, darkly impressive, for the bright colours of its art.

For that reason one would refuse to pass over in silence Mr Davies' first book of poems, *The Soul's Destroyer*, published in 1907. Not that it is perfect poetry : indeed, I doubt whether one really satisfying piece could be chosen from the whole fourteen. But it has deep human interest. The book is slim, sombre, almost insignificant in its paper wrappers. But its looks belie it. It is, in fact, nothing less than a flame of courage, a shining triumph of the spirit of humanity. Mr Shaw has made play with the facts of this poet's life, partly because ' it is his nature so to do,' and partly, one suspects, to hide a deeper feeling. But play as you will with the willing vagabondage, the irresponsibility, the excess and error of exuberant youth, you will only film the surface of the tragedy. Underneath will remain those sullen questions—what is life about, what are our systems

Contemporary Poets

and our laws about, that a human creature and one with the miraculous spark of genius in him, is chased hungry and homeless up and down his own country, tossed from continent to continent and thrown up at last, broken and all but helpless, to be persecuted by some contemptible agent of charity and to wander from one crowded lodging-house to another, seeking vainly for a quiet corner in which to make his songs. The verses in *The Soul's Destroyer* were written under those conditions ; and by virtue of that it would seem that the drab little volume attains to spiritual magnificence.

The themes in this book and those of *New Poems*, published in the same year, are of that personal kind of which we have already spoken. But you will be quite wrong if you suppose that they are therefore gloomy. On the contrary, though there is an occasional didactic piece, like that which gives its title to the first volume, there is more often a vein of humour. Thus we have the astonishing catalogue of lodging-house humanity in " Saints and Lodgers " with the satirical flavour of its invocation :

> Ye saints, that sing in rooms above,
> Do ye want souls to consecrate ?

And there is " The Jolly Tramp," a scrap of autobiography, perhaps not very much coloured :

58

William H. Davies

I am a jolly tramp : I whine to you,
Then whistles till I meet another fool.
I call the labourer sir, the boy young man,
The maid young lady, and the mother I
Will flatter through the youngest child that walks.

In " Wondering Brown " there is surely something
unique in poetry : not alone in theme, and the
extraordinary set of circumstances which enabled
such a bit of life to be observed, by a poet, from the
inside ; but in the rare quality of it, its sympathetic
satire, the genial incisiveness of its criticism of life :

There came a man to sell his shirt,
   A drunken man, in life low down ;
When Riley, who was sitting near,
   Made use of these strange words to Brown.

" Yon fallen man, that's just gone past,
   I knew in better days than these ;
Three shillings he could make a day,
   As an adept at picking peas."

.   .   .   .   .

" You'd scarcely credit it, I knew
   A man in this same house, low down,
Who owns a fish-shop now—believe
   Me, or believe me not," said Brown.

" He was a civil sort of cove,
   But did queer things, for one low down :
Oft have I watched him clean his teeth—
   As true as Heaven's above ! " cried Brown.

This humorous quality is the most marked form of an attitude of detachment which may be observed in most of the personal pieces. So complete is this detachment sometimes, as in " Strange People " or " Scotty Bill " or " Facts," that one is tempted to a heresy. Is it possible, in view of this lightness of touch, this untroubled pace and coolness of word and phrase, that the poet did not see the implications of what he was recording, or seeing them, was not greatly moved by them ? Now there are certain passages which prove that that doubt *is* a heresy : that the poet did perceive and feel the complete significance of the facts he was handling. Otherwise, of course, he were no poet. There is evidence of this in such a poem as " A Blind Child," from which I quote a couple of stanzas :

> We're in the garden, where are bees
> And flowers, and birds, and butterflies ;
> There is one greedy fledgling cries
> For all the food his parent sees !

> I see them all : flowers of all kind,
> The sheep and cattle on the leas ;
> The houses up the hills, and trees—
> But I am dumb, for she is blind.

There is, too, the last stanza of " Facts," a narrative piece which relates the infamous treatment by workhouse officials of an old and dying man :

William H. Davies

Since Jesus came with mercy and love,
  'Tis nineteen hundred years and five :
They made that dying man break stones,
  In faith that Christ is still alive.

A hideous scrap of notoriety for A.D. 1905 !—and
proof enough to convince us of our author's
humanity. At the same time, however, it is the
fact that there is little sign of intense emotion in
this work. One comes near it, perhaps, in a passage
in " The Forsaken Dead," where the poet is musing in
the burial-place of a deserted settlement, and breaks
into wrath at the tyranny which drove the people
out :

Had they no dreamer who might have remained
To sing for them these desolated scenes ?
One who might on a starvèd body take
Strong flights beyond the fiery larks in song,
With awful music, passionate with hate ?

But that is a rare example. Deep emotion is not
a feature of Mr Davies' poetry : neither in the
poems of life, which might be supposed to awaken
it directly ; nor, stranger still, in the infrequent
love poems ; nor in the lyrics of nature. It would
be interesting to speculate on this, if there were
any use in it—whether it is after all just a sign of
excessive feeling, masked by restraint ; whether it
may be in some way a reaction from a life of too

much sensation ; or whether it simply means that
emotion is nicely balanced by objective power.
Perhaps an analysis would determine the question
in the direction of a balance of power ; but the fact
remains that though sensibility has a wide range,
though it is quick, acute and tender, it is not
intense.

It would be unfair, however, to suggest that these
earlier volumes are only interesting on the personal
side. The pure lyric note is uttered first here :
once or twice in a small perfect song, as " The
Likeness " and " Parted " ; but oftener in a snatch
or a broken trill, as

> He who loves Nature truly, hath
> His wealth in her kind hands ; and it
> Is in safe trust until his death,
> Increasing as he uses it.

Or a passage from " Music," invoking the memory
of childhood :

> O happy days of childhood, when
> We taught shy Echo in the glen
> Words she had never used before—
> Ere Age lost heart to snmmon her.
> Life's river, with its early rush,
> Falls into a mysterious hush
> When nearing the eternal sea :
> Yet we would not forgetful be,

William H. Davies

In these deep, silent days so wise,
Of shallows making mighty noise
When we were young, when we were gay,
And never thought Death lived—that day.

Or a fragment from "The Calm," when the poet
has been thinking of his "tempestuous past," and
contrasts it with his present well-being, and the
country joys which he fears will be snatched away
again :

But are these pleasant days to keep ?
Where shall I be when Summer comes ?
When, with a bee's mouth closed, she hums
Sounds not to wake, but soft and deep,
To make her pretty charges sleep ?

The love of Nature which supplies the theme
here is a characteristic that persists throughout the
subsequent volumes. It recurs more and more
frequently, until the autobiographical element is
almost eliminated ; and just as it is the main motive
of the later poetry, so it is its happiest inspiration.
It is rather a pagan feeling, taking great joy in the
beauty of the material world, revelling in the
impressions of sight and scent, sound and taste and
touch. It is humane enough to embrace the whole
world of animal life ; but it seeks no spirit behind
the phenomena of Nature, and cares precisely
nothing about its more scientific aspect. Its gay

63

lightsomeness is a charming thing to watch, an amazing thing to think about :

> For Lord, how merry now am I !
> Tickling with straw the butterfly,
> Where she doth in her clean, white dress,
> Sit on a green leaf, motionless,
> To hear Bees hum away the hours.

Or again, from " Leisure," in *Songs of Joy* :

> What is this life if, full of care,
> We have no time to stand and stare.
>
> .   .   .   .   .
>
> No time to see, when woods we pass,
> Where squirrels hide their nuts in grass.
>
> No time to see, in broad daylight,
> Streams full of stars, like skies at night.
>
> .   .   .   .   .
>
> A poor life this if, full of care,
> We have no time to stand and stare.

And a " Greeting," from the volume called *Foliage* :

> Good morning, Life—and all
> Things glad and beautiful.
> My pockets nothing hold,
> But he that owns the gold,
> The Sun, is my great friend—
> His spending has no end.

William H. Davies

Hail to the morning sky,
Which bright clouds measure high ;
Hail to you birds whose throats
Would number leaves by notes ;
Hail to you shady bowers,
And you green fields of flowers.

The poet does not claim to be learned in nature lore : indeed he declares in one place that he does not know ' the barley from the oats.' But he has a gift of fancy which often plays about his observation with delightful effect. One could hardly call it by so big a name as imagination : that suggests a height and power of vision which this work does not possess, and which one would not look for in this type of genius. It is a lighter quality, occasionally childlike in its naïveté, fantastical, graceful, even quaint. It is seen in simile sometimes, as this from *The Soul's Destroyer*, describing the sky :

It was a day of rest in heaven, which seemed
A blue grass field thick dotted with white tents
Which Life slept late in, though 'twere holiday.

Or this account of the origin of the Kingfisher, from " Farewell to Poesy " :

It was the Rainbow gave thee birth,
And left thee all her lovely hues ;
And, as her mother's name was Tears,
So runs it in thy blood to choose

65

For haunts the lonely pools, and keep
In company with trees that weep.

Or a fancy about the sound of rain from *Nature Poems* :

> I hear leaves drinking rain ;
>   I hear rich leaves on top
> Giving the poor beneath
>   Drop after drop ;
> 'Tis a sweet noise to hear
> Those green leaves drinking near.

It plays an important part too in the poems upon other favourite themes, on a woman's hair, on her voice, on music. Such are " Sweet Music " and "A Maiden and her Hair " in *Nature Poems*: as well as " The Flood," from which I quote. It will be found in *Songs of Joy* :

> I thought my true love slept ;
> Behind her chair I crept
>   And pulled out a long pin ;
> The golden flood came out,
> She shook it all about,
>   With both our faces in.
>
> Ah ! little wren I know
> Your mossy, small nest now
>   A windy, cold place is :
> No eye can see my face,
> Howe'er it watch the place
>   Where I half drown in bliss.

William H. Davies

A development of technique in the later work lends ease and precision to the poet's use of his instrument. Little faults of metre and of rhyme are corrected : banalities of phrase and crudities of thought almost disappear, so that the verse acquires a new grace. It gains, too, from a wider variety of form : for the verses may be as short as one foot, or as long as five : and there may be stanzas of only two lines, or anything up to eight. There are even pieces written in the closed couplet and in blank verse. But Mr Davies is by no means an innovator in his art, as so many of his contemporaries are. The variety we have noted is, after all, only a modification of traditional form and not a departure from it ; and always as its basis, the almost constant unit is the iamb. Very rarely is any other measure adopted ; and so well does the iamb suit the simple and direct nature of this work in thought, word and phrase, that one would not often alter it. One of the perfect examples of its fitness is in " The Battle," from *Nature Poems*:

> There was a battle in her face,
>   Between a Lily and a Rose :
> My Love would have the Lily win
>   And I the Lily lose.
>
> I saw with joy that strife, first one,
>   And then the other uppermost ;

Contemporary Poets

> Until the Rose roused all its blood,
> And then the Lily lost.
>
> When she's alone, the Lily rules,
> By her consent, without mistake :
> But when I come that red Rose leaps
> To battle for my sake.

Occasionally, however, and especially in the longer poems, the regular recurrence of the iamb is a little monotonous. Then a wish just peeps out that Mr Davies were more venturous : that he had some slight experimental turn, or that he did not stand quite so far aloof from the influences which, within his sight and hearing, are shaping a new kind of poetic expression. But the regret may be put aside. The fresh forms which those others are evolving are valid for them—for life as they conceive it—for the wider range and the more complex nature of the experience out of which they are distilling the poetic essence. For him, however, the lyric mood burns clear and untroubled, kindling directly to the beauty of simple and common things. And instinctively he seeks to embody it in cadence and measure which are sweetly familiar. When some exhilarating touch quickens and lightens his verse with a more tripping measure, as in "The Laughers" (from *Nature Poems*) its gay charm is irresistible.

William H. Davies

Mary and Maud have met at the door,
　Oh, now for a din ; I told you so :
They're laughing at once with sweet, round mouths,
　Laughing for what ? does anyone know ?

Is it known to the bird in the cage,
　That shrieketh for joy his high top notes,
After a silence so long and grave—
　What started at once those two sweet throats ?

Is it known to the Wind that takes
　Advantage at once and comes right in ?
Is it known to the cock in the yard,
　That crows—the cause of that merry din ?

Is it known to the babe that he shouts ?
　Is it known to the old, purring cat ?
Is it known to the dog, that he barks
　For joy—what Mary and Maud laugh at ?

Is it known to themselves ?　It is not,
　But beware of their great shining eyes ;
For Mary and Maud will soon, I swear,
　Find cause to make far merrier cries.

It is hard to close even a slight study of Mr Davies'
work without another glance at his originality. One
hesitates to use that word, strained and tortured
as it often is to express a dozen different meanings.
It might be applied, in one sense or another, to
nearly all our contemporary poets, with whom it
seems to be an article of artistic faith to avoid like

the plague any sign of being derivative. So, although their minds may be steeped in older poetry, they deliberately turn away from its influence, seeking inspiration in life itself. There is no doubt that they are building up a new kind of poetry, with values that sound strange perhaps to the unfamiliar ear, but which bid fair to enlarge the field for the poetic genius and enrich it permanently. But the crux of the question for us at this moment is the fact of effort, the deliberate endeavour which is made by those poets to escape from tradition. No sign of such an effort is visible in Mr Davies' work, and yet it is the most original of them all—the newest, freshest, and most spontaneous.

The reason lies, of course, in the qualities we have already noted. It is not entirely an external matter, as the influence of his career might lead us to believe. That has naturally played its part, making the substance of some of his verse almost unique ; and, more important still, guarding him from bookishness and leaving his mind free to receive and convey impressions at first hand. From this come the bracing freshness of his poetry, its naïveté of language, its apparent artlessness and unconscious charm. But the root of the matter lies deeper than that, mainly I think in the sincerity and simplicity which are the chief qualities of his genius.

70

William H. Davies

Both qualities are fundamental and constant, vitalizing the work and having a visible influence upon its form. For, on the one hand, we see that simplicity reflected not only in the thought, and themes, but in the language and the technique of this poetry ; while on the other hand there is a loyalty which is absolutely faithful to its own experience and the laws of its own nature.

Walter De La Mare

THERE is one sense in which this poet has never grown up, and we may, if we please, recapture our own childhood as we wander with him through his enchanted garden. And if it be true, as John Masefield says, that " the days that make us happy make us wise," it is blessed wisdom that should be ours at the end of our ramble. For see what a delightful place it is ! Not one of your opulent, gorgeous gardens, with well-groomed lawns and flower-beds teeming with precious nurselings ; but a much homelier region, and one of more elusive and delicate charm. Boundaries there are, for order and safe going, but they are hidden away in dancing foliage : and there are leafy paths which seem to wind into infinity, and corners where mystery lurks.

> Some one is always sitting there,
>   In the little green orchard ;
>
> .   .   .   .
>
> When you are most alone,
> All but the silence gone . . .
> Some one is waiting and watching there,
>   In the little green orchard.

Flowers grow in the sunny spaces, and all the wild

Walter De La Mare

things that children love—primrose and pimpernel,
darnel and thorn ;

> Teasle and tansy, meadowsweet,
> Campion, toadflax, and rough hawksbit ;
> Brown bee orchis, and Peals of Bells ;
> Clover, burnet, and thyme. . . .

It is mostly a shadowy place however, not chill
and gloomy, but arched with slender trees, through
whose thin leafage slant the warm fingers of the sun,
picking out clear, quickly-moving patterns upon
the grass. The air is soft, the light is as mellow
as a harvest moon, and the sounds of the outer
world are subdued almost to silence. Nothing
loud or strenuous disturbs the tranquillity : only
the remote voices of happy children and friendly
beasts and kind old people. Wonder lives here,
but not fear ; smiles but not laughter ; tenderness
but not passion. And the presiding genius of the
spot is the poet's " Sleeping Cupid," sitting in the
shade with his bare feet deep in the grass and the dew
slowly gathering upon his curls : a cool and lovesome
elf, softly dreaming of beauty in a quiet place.

So one might try to catch into tangible shape the
spirit of this poetry, only to realize the impossibility
of doing anything of the kind. But mere analysis
would be equally futile ; for the essence of it is as

subtle as air and as fluid as light ; and one is finally
compelled, in the hope of conveying some impression
of the nature of it, to fall back upon comparison.
It is a clumsy method however, frequently doing
violence to one or both of the poets compared ; and
even when used discreetly, it often serves only to indicate a more or less obvious point of resemblance. But
we must take the risk of that for the moment, and call
out of memory the magical effect that is produced
upon the mind by the reading of " Kubla Khan,"
or " Christabel" or " The Ancient Mariner." Very
similar to that is the effect of Mr de la Mare's
poetry. There is a difference, and its implications
are important ; but the chief fact is that here,
amongst this modern poetry of so different an order,
you find work which seems like a lovely survival
from the age of romance.

That is why one has the feeling that this poet
has never grown up. Partly from a natural in-
clination, and partly from a deliberate plan (like
that of Coleridge) to produce a certain kind of art,
he has created a faëry, twilight world, a world of
wonder and fantasy, which is the home of perpetual
youth. He has never really lost that time when,
as a little boy, he says that he listened to Martha
telling her stories in the hazel glen. Martha, of
' the clear grey eyes ' and the ' grave, small,

Walter De La Mare

lovely head' is surely a veritable handmaid of
romance :

> 'Once . . . once upon a time . . .'
> Like a dream you dream in the night,
> Fairies and gnomes stole out
> In the leaf-green light.
>
> And her beauty far away
> Would fade, as her voice ran on,
> Till hazel and summer sun
> And all were gone :—
>
> All fordone and forgot ;
> And like clouds in the height of the sky,
> Our hearts stood still in the hush
> Of an age gone by.

That hush, invoking a sense of remoteness in space
and time, lies over all his work. It is as though,
walking in the garden of this verse, a child flitted
lightly before us with a finger raised in a gesture
of silence. And it is not for nothing that his principal book is called *The Listeners*. Footfalls are light,
and voices soft, and the wind is gentle : the noise
of life is filtered to a whisper or a rustle or a sleepy
murmur. It is a device, of course, as we quickly
see if we peer too curiously at it : just a contrivance
of the romantic artist to create ' atmosphere.'
But it is so cunningly done that you never suspect

75

the contriving ; and if you would gauge the skill of the poet in this direction, you should note that he is able to produce the desired effect in the broad light of day as well as in shadow and twilight. It is a more difficult achievement, and much rarer. Evening is the time that the poets generally choose to work this particular spell : though moonlight or starlight, dawn, sunset, and almost any degree of darkness will serve them. Sunlight alone, wide-eyed, penetrating and inquisitive, is inimical to their purpose. Yet Mr de la Mare, in a poem called "The Sleeper," succeeds in spinning this hush of wondering awe out of the full light of a summer day. A little girl (Ann, a charming and familiar figure in this poetry : at once a symbol of childhood and a very human child) runs into the house to her mother, and finds her asleep in her chair. That is all the ' plot ' ; and it would be hard to find an incident slighter, simpler and more commonplace. But out of this homespun material the poet has somehow conjured an eerie, brooding, impalpable presence which steals upon us as it does upon the child in the quiet house until, like her, we want to creep quickly out again.

A sense of the supernatural, that constant component of the romantic temperament, is of the essence of this poetry. The manifestation of it is something more than a trick of technique, for it has its origin in the very nature of the poet's genius. In its simpler and more direct expression, it seems to spring out of the fearful joy which this type of mind experiences in contact with the strange and weird. Again, as in "The Witch," it may take the form of a bit of pure fantasy, transmitting the fascination which has already seized the poet with a lurking smile at its own absurdity. The opening stanzas tell of a tired old witch who sits down to rest by a churchyard wall ; and who, in jerking off her pack of charms, breaks the cord and spills them all out on the ground :

> And out the dead came stumbling,
> From every rift and crack,
> Silent as moss, and plundered
> The gaping pack.
>
> They wish them, three times over,
> Away they skip full soon :
> Bat and Mole and Leveret,
> Under the rising moon.
>
> Owl and Newt and Nightjar :
> They take their shapes and creep,
> Silent as churchyard lichen,
> While she squats asleep.

． ● ＇ ● ●

Names may be writ ; and mounds rise ;
Purporting, Here be bones :
But empty is that churchyard
Of all save stones.

Owl and Newt and Nightjar,
Leveret, Bat and Mole
Haunt and call in the twilight,
Where she slept, poor soul.

But in its subtler forms the supernatural element of this poetry is more complex and more potent. And it would seem to have a definite relation to the poet's philosophy. Not that it is possible to trace an outline of systematic thought in work like this, where every constituent is milled and sifted to delicate fineness and fused to perfect unity. But if we follow up a hint here and there, and correlate them with the author's prose fiction, we shall not be able to escape the suggestion of a mystical basis to the elusive witchery of so many of his poems. We shall see that it is apparently rooted in an extreme sensitiveness to psychic influences : a sensitiveness through which he becomes, at one end of the scale, acutely aware of the presence of a surrounding spirit world ; and at the other, deeply sympathetic and tender to subhuman creatures.

No crude claim is made on behalf of any mystical

Walter De La Mare

creed ; and still less would one violate the fragile and mysterious charm of a poem like " The Listeners " by so-called interpretation. But placed beside " The Witch," it is clearly seen to treat the supernatural on a higher plane : it is, indeed, a piece of rare and delicate symbolism. There is no recourse to the ready appeal of the grotesque and the marvellous ; and although we find here all the ' machinery ' of a supernatural poem in the older romantic manner— the great empty house standing lonely in the forest, moonlight and silence, and a traveller knocking unheeded at the door—it is a very subtle blending of those elements which has gone to produce the peculiar effect of this piece. Twice the traveller knocks, crying : " Is there anybody there ? " but no answer comes :

> . . . only a host of phantom listeners
>   That dwelt in the lone house then
> Stood listening in the quiet of the moonlight
>   To that voice from the world of men :
> Stood thronging the faint moonbeams on the dark stair,
>   That goes down to the empty hall,
> Hearkening in an air stirred and shaken
>   By the lonely Traveller's call.
> And he felt in his heart their strangeness,
>   Their stillness answering his cry,
> While his horse moved, cropping the dark turf,
>   'Neath the starred and leafy sky ;

For he suddenly smote on the door, even
    Louder, and lifted his head :—
    ' Tell them I came, and no one answered,
      That I kept my word,' he said.

Running through the piece—and more clearly perceived when the whole poem is read—is the thread of melancholy which is inseparably woven into all the poet's work of this kind. And it, too, was a gift of his fairy-godmother when he was born, light in texture as a gossamer and spun out of the softest silk. Melancholy is almost too big a word to fit the thing it is, for there is no gloom in it. It is like the silvery, transparent cloud of thoughtfulness which passes for a moment over a happy face ; and it has something of the youthful trick of playing with the idea of sadness. Hence come the early studies of " Imogen " and " Ophelia," where the poet is so much in love with mournfulness that he revels in making perfect phrases about it.

    Can death haunt silence with a silver sound ?
    Can death, that hushes all music to a close,
    Pluck one sweet wire scarce-audible that trembles,
    As if a little child, called Purity,
    Sang heedlessly on of his dear Imogen ?

But even when this verse approaches a degree nearer to the reality of pain it is still, as it were, a reflected emotion ; and there is no poignance in

it. It is a winning echo of sorrowfulness, caught
by one who has the habit of turning back to listen
and look. Thus the studies of old age which
we sometimes find here are drawn in the true
romantic manner, with a sunset halo about them,
and lightly shadowed by wistfulness and faint regret.
And the thought of death, when it is allowed to
enter, comes as caressingly as sleep. The little poem
called " All That's Past," where the poet is thinking of how far down the roots of all things go, is
only one example of many where melancholy is
toned to the faintest strain of pensive sweetness :

> Very old are the woods ;
>   And the buds that break
> Out of the briar's boughs,
>   When March winds wake,
> So old with their beauty are—
>   Oh, no man knows
> Through what wild centuries
>   Roves back the rose.
>
> .   .   .   .
>
> Very old are we men ;
>   Our dreams are tales
> Told in dim Eden
>   By Eve's nightingales ;
> We walk and whisper awhile,
>   But, the day gone by,
> Silence and sleep like fields
>   Of amaranth lie.

So we might continue to cull passages which represent one aspect or another of the specific quality of Mr de la Mare's poetry. The choice is rich, for there is a remarkably high level of inspiration and workmanship here. But there is a danger in the process, especially with work of so fine a grain ; and one feels bound to repeat the warning that it is impossible to dissect its ultimate essence in this way. We can only come back to our comparison, and recalling the magical music of poems like " Arabia," " Queen Djenira," or " Voices "— in which all the characteristics noted are so intimately blended that it is impossible to disengage them—reiterate the fact that they possess the same inexplicable charm as the romantic work of Coleridge.

But that reminds us of the difference, and all that it implies. For, after all, this poet is a romanticist of the twentieth century, and not of the late eighteenth. It is true that his genius has surprisingly kept its youth (even more, that is to say, than the poet usually does) ; but it is a nonage which is clearly of this time and no other. The signs of this are clear enough. First and foremost, there is his humanity—in which perhaps all the others are included, and with which are certainly associated the simplicity and sincerity of his diction. It is as though the two famous principles on which

Walter De La Mare

the *Lyrical Ballads* were planned had in the fulness
of time become united in the creative impulse of a
single mind. That is not to charge Mr de la Mare
with the combined weight of those two earlier
giants, of course, but simply to observe the truth
which Rupert Brooke expressed so finely when he
said that the poetic spirit was coming back " to its
wider home, the human heart." So that even a
born romanticist like this cannot escape ; and into
the chilly enchantment of an older manner warm
sunlight streams and fresh airs blow.

Obvious links with the life-movement of his time
are not lacking, though as mere external evidence
they are relatively unimportant. Of such are
the synthesis of poetry and science in " The Happy
Encounter"; and the detachment suggested in "Keep
Innocency," where the poet reveals a full consciousness of the gulf between romance and reality. But
the influence goes deeper than that. It is because
he is a child of his age that he has observed children
so lovingly, and has wrought child-psychology into
his verse with such wonderful accuracy. That also
is why he calls so gently out of ' thin-strewn memory
such a homely figure as the shy old maid in her
old-fashioned parlour ; and thence, too, comes the
sympathy with toiling folk—considering them
characteristically in the serene mood when their

work is done—which underlies such pieces as "Old Susan" and "Old Ben":

> Sad is old Ben Thistlewaite,
>   Now his day is done,
> And all his children
>   Far away are gone.
>
> He sits beneath his jasmined porch,
>   His stick between his knees,
> His eyes fixed vacant
>   On his moss-grown trees.
>
>   .   .   .   .   .
>
> But as in pale high autumn skies
>   The swallows float and play,
> His restless thoughts pass to and fro,
>   But nowhere stay.
>
> Soft, on the morrow, they are gone ;
>   His garden then will be
> Denser and shadier and greener,
>   Greener the moss-grown tree.

From the same humane temper come the poet's kindly feeling for animals and his affectionate understanding of·them. Over and over again its positive aspect finds expression, either quaint, comical or tender. And twice at least the negative side of it appears, coming as near to rage at the wanton destruction of animal life as a mellow and balanced temper would ever get. It is a significant

Walter De La Mare

fact that at such moments he takes refuge. in his humour—a humour by turns playful, indignant, and tender, which, growing from a free and sympathetic contact with life, holds the scale counterpoised to a nicety against the glamorous romantic sense. Thus we have this scrap of verse, lightly throwing off a mood of disgust in whimsical idiom :

> I can't abear a Butcher,
>   I can't abide his meat,
> The ugliest shop of all is, his,
>   The ugliest in the street ;
> Bakers' are warm, cobblers' dark,
>   Chemists' burn watery lights ;
> But oh, the sawdust butcher's shop,
>   That ugliest of sights !

And thus in " Tit for Tat " we find this apostrophe to a certain Tom Noddy, just returning from a day of ' sport ' with his gun over his shoulder :

> Wonder I very much do, Tom Noddy,
>   If ever, when you are a-roam,
> An Ogre from space will stoop a lean face,
>   And lug you home :
>
> Lug you home over his fence, Tom Noddy,
>   Of thorn-stocks nine yards high,
> With your bent knees strung round his old iron gun
>   And your head dan-dangling by :

85

And hang you up stiff on a hook, Tom Noddy,
   From a stone-cold pantry shelf,
Whence your eyes will glare in an empty stare,
   Till you are cooked yourself!

The humour there, corresponding in degree to the anger for which it is a veil, is relatively broad. There are various subtler forms of it, however, and one will be found in a charming piece which is apt to our present point. It is called "Nicholas Nye," and tells about an old donkey in an orchard. He is an unprepossessing creature, lame and worn-out : just a bit of animal jettison, thrown away here to end his days in peace. And the poet had a great friendship with him :

But a wonderful gumption was under his skin,
   And a clear calm light in his eye,
And once in a while : he'd smile :—
   Would Nicholas Nye.

Seem to be smiling at me, he would,
   From his bush in the corner, of may,—
Bony and ownerless, widowed and worn,
   Knobble-kneed, lonely and grey ;
And over the grass would seem to pass
   'Neath the deep dark blue of the sky,
Something much better than words between me
   And Nicholas Nye.

Wilfrid Wilson Gibson

THERE are a dozen books by this author, the work of about a dozen years. They began to appear in 1902 ; and they end, so far as the present survey is concerned, with poems that were published in the first half of 1914. They make a good pile, a considerable achievement in bulk alone ; and when they are read in sequence, they are found to represent a growing period in the poet's mind and art which corresponds to, and epitomises, the transition stage out of which English poetry is just passing. That is to say, in addition to the growth that one would expect—the ripening and development which would seem to be a normal process—there has occurred an unexpected thing : a complete change of ideal, with steady and rapid progress in the new direction. So that if Mr. Gibson's later books were compared directly with the early ones, they would appear to be by an entirely different hand. Place *Urlyn the Harper*—which was first published—beside a late play called *Womenkind* or a still more recent dramatic piece called *Bloodybush Edge* ; and the contrast will be complete. On the one hand there is all the charm of romance, in material and in manner—but very little else. On the other hand there is nothing to which the word charm will strictly apply ; an almost complete artistic austerity : but a profound and powerful study of human nature. On the one hand there is a dainty lyrical form appropriate to the theme : there are songs like this one, about the hopeless love of the minstrel for the young queen who is mated with an old harsh king :

> I sang of lovers, and she praised my song,
> The while the King looked on her with cold eyes,
> And 'twixt them on the throne sat mailèd wrong.
>
> I sang of Launcelot and Guenevere,
> While in her face I saw old sorrows rise,
> And throned between them cowered naked Fear.
>
> I sang of Tristram and La Belle Isoud,
> And how they fled the anger of King Mark
> To live and love, deep sheltered in a wood.
>
> Then bending low, she spake sad voiced and sweet,
> The while grey terror crouched between them stark,
> " Sing now of Aucassin and Nicolete."

The later work cannot be so readily illustrated : it is at once subtler and stronger, and depends more upon the effect of the whole than upon any single part. But for the sake of the contrast we may wrest a short passage out of its setting in *Bloodybush Edge*. A couple of tramps have met at night on

Wilfrid Wilson Gibson

the Scottish border; one is a cockney Londoner,
a bad lot with something sinister about him and
a touch of mystery. He has just stumbled out of
the heather on to the road, cursing the darkness
and the loneliness of the moor. The other, a
Border man to whom night is beautiful and the
wild landscape a familiar friend, protests that
it is not dark, that the sky is 'all alive with
little stars ':

TRAMP.   . . . Stars !
  Give me the lamps along the Old Kent Road ;
  And I'm content to leave the stars to you.
  They're well enough ; but hung a trifle high
  For walking with clean boots. Now a lamp or so . . .
DICK. If it's so fine and brave, the Old Kent Road,
  How is it you came to leave it ?
TRAMP.   . . . I'd my reasons. . . .
  But I was scared : the loneliness and all ;
  The quietness, and the queer creepy noises ;
  And something that I couldn't put a name to,
  A kind of feeling in my marrow-bones,
  As though the great black hills against the sky
  Had come alive about me in the night,
  And they were watching me ; as though I stood
  Naked, in a big room, with blind men sitting,
  Unseen, all round me, in the quiet darkness,
  That was not dark to them. And all the stars
  Were eyeing me ; and whisperings in the heather
  Were like cold water trickling down my spine :

89

Contemporary Poets

Putting an early and a late book side by side in this way, the contrast is astonishing. And it is not an unfair method of comparison, because when the new ideal appears it strikes suddenly into the work, and sharply differentiates it at once from all that had been written before. Like the larger movement which it so aptly illustrates, the change is conscious, deliberate, and full of significance ; and it is the cardinal fact in this author's poetical career. It marks the stage at which he came to grips with reality : when he brought his art into relation with life : when the making of poetic beauty as an end in itself could no longer content him ; and the social conscience, already prompting contemporary thought, quickened in him too.

Humanity was the new ideal : humanity at bay and splendidly fighting. It appeared first in the two volumes of 1907 as dramatic studies from the lives of shepherd-folk. Four books had preceded these, in which the texture of the verse was woven of old romance and legend. Another book was yet to come, *The Web of Life*, in which the prettiness of that kind of romanticism would blossom into absolute beauty. But the new impulse grew from the date of *Stonefolds* ; and when the first part of *Daily Bread* appeared, the impulse had become a reasoned principle. In the poem which prefaces

Wilfrid Wilson Gibson

that volume it comes alive, realizes itself and finds
utterance in terms which express much more than
an individual experience.   I quote it for that reason.
The immediate thought has dignity and the personal
note is engaging.   There is, too, peculiar interest
in the clarity and precision with which it speaks,
albeit unconsciously, for the changing spirit in
English poetry.   But the final measure of the poem
is the touch of universality that is latent within it.
For here we have the expression of not only a law
of development by which the poet must be bound,
and not only a poetical synthesis of the most important intellectual movement of this generation,
but an experience through which every soul must
pass, if and when it claims its birthright in the human
family.

> As one, at midnight, wakened by the call
> Of golden-plovers in their seaward flight,
> Who lies and listens, as the clear notes fall
> Through tingling silence of the frosty night—
> Who lies and listens, till the last note fails,
> And then, in fancy, faring with the flock
> Far over slumbering hills and dreaming dales,
> Soon hears the surges break on reef and rock ;
> And, hearkening, till all sense of self is drowned
> Within the mightier music of the deep,
> No more remembers the sweet piping sound
> That startled him from dull, undreaming sleep :

So I, first waking from oblivion, heard,
With heart that kindled to the call of song,
The voice of young life, fluting like a bird,
And echoed that light lilting ; till, ere long,
Lured onward by that happy, singing-flight,
I caught the stormy summons of the sea,
And dared the restless deeps that, day and night,
Surge with the life-song of humanity.

Being wise after the event, one can discover auguries of that change in the very early work. There. is, for example, a group of little poems called *Faring South*, studied directly from peasant life in the south of France. They indicate that even at that time an awakening sympathy with toiling folk had begun to guide his observation ; and they are in any case a very different record of European travel from that of the mere poetaster. There are studies of a stonebreaker, a thresher, a ploughman ; there is a veracious little picture of a housemother, returning home at the end of market-day laden, tired and dusty ; but happy to be under her own vine-porch once more. And most interesting of all the group, there is a shepherd, the forerunner of robuster shepherds in later books, and evidently a figure which has for this author a special attraction.

With folded arms, against his staff he stands,
Sun-soaking, rapt, within the August blaze

Wilfrid Wilson Gibson

The while his sheep with moving rustle graze
The lean, parched undergrowth of stubble lands.

Indifferent 'neath the low blue-laden sky
He gazes fearless in the eyes of noon ;
And earth, because he craves of her no boon,
Yields him deep-breasted, sun-steeped destiny.

But these characters are not living people, they
are types rather than individuals, and idealized a
little. They are, as it were, seen from a distance,
in passing, and in a golden light. Years were to pass
before knowledge and insight could envisage them
completely and a dramatic sense could endow them
with life. Meantime the more characteristic qualities of this early work were to develop indepen-
dently. The lyrical power of it, in particular, was
to enjoy its flowering time, revelling in the sweet
melancholy of old unhappy love stories, in courts
and rose-gardens, kings and queens, knights and
ladies and lute-players. Perhaps the most charming
examples in this kind are "The Songs of Queen
Averlaine." Here are a couple of stanzas from one
of them, in which the queen is brooding sadly over
the thought of her lost love and lost youth :

Spring comes no more for me : though young March blow
To flame the larches, and from tree to tree

The green fire leap, till all the woodland, glow—
Though every runnel, filled to overflow,
Bear sea-ward, loud and brown with melted snow,
Spring comes no more for me !

.   .   .   .   .

Spring comes no more for me : though May will shake
White flame of hawthorn over all the lea,
Till every thick-set hedge and tangled brake
Puts on fresh flower of beauty for her sake ;
Though all the world from winter-sleep awake,
Spring comes no more for me !

They are graceful songs, and their glamour will
not fail so long as there remain lovers to read them.
The critic is disarmed by their ingenuousness : he
is constrained to take them as they stand, with
their warmth and colour, their sweet music and
the occasional flashes of observed truth (like the
March runnels of this poem) which redeem them
from total unreality.   The reward lies close ahead.
For even on this theme of love, and still in the lyric
mood, sanity soon triumphs.   It heralds its victory
with a laugh, and the air is lightened at once from
the scented gloom of romanticism.   " Sing no more
songs of lovers dead," it cries, sound and strong
enough now to make fun of itself.

We are no lovers, pale with dreams,
Who languish by Lethean streams.

Wilfrid Wilson Gibson

Upon our bodies warm day gleams ;
And love that tingles warm and red
From sole of foot to crown of head
Is lord of all pale lovers dead !

The volume from which that stanza is taken, *The Web of Life*, contains this poet's finest lyrics. From the standpoint of art nothing that he has done—and he is always a scrupulous artist—can surpass it ; and the seeker whose single quest is beauty, need go no further down the list of Mr Gibson's works. There are some perfect things in the book : poems like " Song," " The Mushroom Gatherers " and " The Silence," in which the early grace and felicity survive ; and where the lyric ecstasy is deepened by thought and winged by emotion. In one sense, therefore, although this volume is only midway through the period we are concerned with, it has attained finality. We ought to pause on it. We see that it culminates and closes the ' happy singing-flight ' with which this career began. We realize, too, that it has absolute value, as poetry, by virtue of which many a good judge might rank it higher than its remarkable successors. And, indeed, it is hard to break away from its spell. But when we judge *The Web of Life* relatively, when we place it back in the proper niche amongst its kindred volumes, its importance seems to dwindle suddenly. Beside the later books, it grows almost commonplace; we perceive its charm to be of the conventional kind of the whole order of regular English poetry to which it belongs. That is to say, though there is no sign that the work has been directly modelled upon the poets of an earlier generation, its characteristics relate it directly to them. It is consciously—too consciously—poetical. There are pieces which remind us of Keats or the younger Tennyson. Here is a stanza from the poem called "Beauty" which might have been the inspiration of the whole book:

> With her alone is immortality;
> For still men reverently
> Adore within her shrine:
> The sole immortal time has not cast down,
> She wields a power yet more divine
> Than when of old she rose from out the sea
> Of night, with starry crown.
> Though all things perish, Beauty never dies.

Or there are poems in which passion trembles under a fine restraint, as in "Friends":

> Yet, are we friends: the gods have granted this.
> Withholding wine, they brimmed for us the cup
> With cool, sweet waters, ever welling up,
> That we might drink, and, drinking, dream of bliss.

·   ·   ·   ·   ·

Wilfrid Wilson Gibson

> O gods, in your cold mercy, merciless,
> Heed lest time raze your thrones ; and at the sign,
> The cool, sweet-welling waters turn to wine ;
> The spark to day, and dearth to bounteousness.

And there is the group of classical pieces at the end of the book, in which one regretfully passes over the flexible blank-verse of " Helen in Rhodos " and " The Mariners," to choose a still more characteristic passage from " A Lament for Helen " :

> Helen has fallen : she for whom Troy fell
> Has fallen, even as the fallen towers.
> O wanderers in dim fields of asphodel,
> Who spilt for her the wine of earthly hours,
> With you for evermore
> By Lethe's darkling shore
> Your souls' desire shall dwell.
>
> .   .   .   .   .   .
>
> But we who sojourn yet in earthly ways ;
> How shall we sing, now Helen lieth dead ?
> Break every lyre and burn the withered bays,
> For song's sweet solace is with Helen fled.
> Let sorrow's silence be
> The only threnody
> O'er beauty's fallen head.

But this book, which is so good an example of poetic art in the older English manner, is not Mr Gibson's distinguishing achievement. That came

97

immediately afterwards, and was the outcome of the changed ideal which we have already noted. *The Web of Life* may be said to belong to a definite school—though to be sure its relation to that school is not discipular. The books which follow have no such relation : they stand alone and refuse to be classified, either in subject or in form. And while the earlier work would seem to claim its author for the nineteenth century, in *Daily Bread* he is newborn a twentieth-century poet of full stature.

The most striking evidence of the change is in the subject-matter. *Daily Bread*, like *Fires*, is in three parts, and each of them contains six or seven pieces. There is thus a total of about forty poems, every one of which is created out of an episode from the lives of the working poor. Thus we find a young countryman, workless and destitute in a London garret, joined by his village sweetheart who refuses to leave him to starve alone. A farm labourer and his wife are rising wearily in the cold dawn to earn bread for the six sleeping children. There are miners and quarrymen in some of the many dangers of their calling, and their womenfolk enduring privation, suspense and bereavement with tireless courage. There is a stoker, dying from burns that he has sustained at the furnace, whose young wife

retorts with passionate bitterness to a hint of
compensation :

> Money . . . woman . . . money !
> I want naught with their money.
> I want my husband,
> And my children's father.
> Let them pitch all their money in the furnace
> Where he . . .
> I wouldn't touch a penny ;
> 'Twould burn my fingers.
> Money . . .
> For him !

There are fishermen in peril of the sea ; the printer,
the watchman, the stonebreaker, the lighthouse-
keeper, the riveter, the sailor, the shopkeeper ; there
are school-children and factory girls ; outcasts,
tramps and gipsies ; and a splendid company of
women—mothers in childbirth and child-death,
sisters, wives and sweethearts—more heroic in their
obscure suffering and toil than the noblest figure
of ancient tragedy. With deliberate intention,
therefore, the poet has set himself to represent
contemporary industrial life : the strata at the base
of our civilization. He has, as it were, won free at
a leap from illusion, from Romanticism, and the
jealous, tyrannical instinct for Art as Art. Life is
the inspiration now, and truth the objective. The
facts of the workers' lives are carefully observed,

realized in all their significance and faithfully recorded. Sympathy and penetration go hand in hand. Personal faults and follies, superstitions and vices, play their part in these little dramas, no less than the social wrongs under which the people labour. And the conception, in its balance and comprehensiveness, is really great ; for while on the one hand there is an humiliating indictment of our civilization (implicit, of course, but none the less complete) on the other hand there is a proud vindication of the invincible human spirit.

Viewed steadily thus, by a poetic genius which has subdued the conventions of its art, such themes are shown to possess a latent but inalienable power to exalt the mind. They are therefore of the genuine stuff of art, needing only the formative touch of the poet to evoke beauty. And thus we find that although the normal process seems to have been reversed here : although the poet has sought truth first—in event, in character and in environment—beauty has been nevertheless attained ; and of a type more vital and complete than that evoked by the statelier themes of tradition.

As might have been expected the new material and method have directly influenced form ; and hence arises another distinction of these later works. The three parts of *Daily Bread* and the play called

Wilfrid Wilson Gibson

Womenkind are the extreme example ; and their verse is probably unique in English poetry. It has been evolved out of the actual substance on which the poet is working ; directly moulded by the nature of the life that he has chosen to present. The poems here are dramatic ; and whether the element of dialogue or of narrative prevail, the language is always the living idiom of the persons who are speaking. It is nervous, supple, incisive : not, of course, with much variety or colour, since the vocabulary of such people could not be large and its colour might often be too crude for an artist's use. Selection has played its part, in words as in incidents ; but although anything in the nature of dialect has been avoided, we are convinced as we read that this is indeed the speech of labouring folk. We can even recognize, in a light touch such as an occasional vocative, that they are the sturdy folk of the North country. There is a dialogue called " On the Road " which illustrates that, as well as more important things. Just under the surface of it lies the problem of unemployment : a young couple forced to go on tramp, with their infant child, because the husband has lost his job. That, however, inheres in the episode : it is not emphasized, nor even formulated, as a problem. The appeal of the poem is in its fine delineation of character, the interplay of emotion, the rapid and telling dialogue—the pervasive humanitarian spirit; and, once again, an exact and full perception of the woman's point of view. Mr Gibson is a poet of his time in this as well—in his large comprehension and generous acknowledgment of the feminine part in the scheme of things. I do not quote to illustrate that, because it is an almost constant factor in his work. But I give a passage in which the Northern flavour is distinctly perceptible, in addition to qualities which are limited to no locality—the kindliness of the poor to each other and their native courtesy. An old stone-breaker has just passed the starving couple by the roadside and, divining the extremity they are at, he turns back to them :

Fine morning, mate and mistress !
Might you be looking for a job, my lad ?
Well . . . there's a heap of stones to break, down yonder.
I was just on my way . . .
But I am old ;
And, maybe, a bit idle ;
And you look young,
And not afraid of work,
Or I'm an ill judge of a workman's hands.
And when the job's done, lad,
There'll be a shilling.

. . . . .

Wilfrid Wilson Gibson

Nay, but there's naught to thank me for.
I'm old ;
And I've no wife and children,
And so, don't need the shilling.

.   .   .   .   .

Well, the heap's down yonder—
There, at the turning.
Ah, the bonnie babe !
We had no children, mistress.
And what can any old man do with shillings,
With no one but himself to spend them on—
An idle, good-for-nothing, lone old man ?

The curious structure of the verse is apparent
at a glance—the irregular pattern, the extreme
variation in the length of the line, the absence of
rhyme and the strange metrical effects. It is a
new poetical instrument, having little outward
resemblance to the grace and dignity of regular
forms. Its unfamiliarity may displease the eye and
the ear at first, but it is not long before we perceive
the design which controls its apparent waywardness,
and recognize its fitness to express the life that the
poet has chosen to depict. For it suggests, as no
rhyme or regular measure could, the ruggedness
of this existence and the characteristic utterance of
its people. No symmetrical verse, with its sense
of something complete, precise and clear, could
convey such an impression as this—of speech

103

struggling against natural reticence to express the
turmoil of thought and emotion in an untrained
mind.   Mr Gibson has invented a metrical form
which admirably produces that effect, without
condescending to a crude realism.   He has made
the worker articulate, supplying just the coherence
and lucidity which art demands, but preserving,
in this irregular outline, in the plain diction and
simple phrasing, an acute sense of reality.   Here is a
fragment of conversation, one of many similar, in
which this verse is found to be a perfect medium
of the idea.   A wife has been struck by her husband
in a fit of passion : she has been trying to hide from
her mother the cause of the blow, but she is still
weak from the effects of it and has not lied skilfully.
Her mother gently protests that she is trying to
screen her husband :

> Nay ! There's naught to screen.
> 'Twas I that . . . Nay !
> And, if he's hot, at times,
> You know he's much to try him ;
> The racket that he works in, all day long,
> Would wear the best of tempers.
> Why, mother, who should know as well as you
> How soon a riveter is done ?
> The hammers break a man, before his time ;
> And father was a shattered man at forty ;
> And Philip's thirty-five ;

Wilfrid Wilson Gibson

And if he's failed a bit . . .
And, sometimes, over-hasty
Well, I am hasty, too ;
You know my temper ; no one knows it better.

Occasionally, it is true, the principle on which
the verse is built is too strictly applied : the phrase-
ology is abrupt beyond the required effect ; and
the lines, instead of following a rule which seems
to measure their length by a natural pause, are
broken arbitrarily. Speaking broadly, however, it
is fitted to such themes as those of *Daily Bread*—
though one is not so sure about it in a poem like
" Akra the Slave." This is a delightful narrative,
akin in subject to the earlier work, and belonging
to that period much more than to the date at
which it was published, 1910. One cannot linger
upon it, nor even upon the more important work
which followed, and is happily still continuing—
more important because it indicates development
and marked progress along the new lines. The
three parts of *Fires* carry forward the inspiration of
Daily Bread, but now in narrative style, permitting
therefore a relaxation of the austere dramatic truth
of the dialogue form. The verse is modified
accordingly, as will be seen in this passage from
" The Shop " : A workman has entered his favourite
shop—the little general-store of a poor neighbour-

hood—to buy his evening paper. But he is not attended to immediately; and a sickly little girl who has come for a fraction of a loaf and a screw of tea, is also waiting. The shopkeeper is engrossed with a parcel from the country—from a little convalescent son who has gone for the first time to his father's native place:

Next night, as I went in, I caught
A strange, fresh smell. The postman had just brought
A precious box from Cornwall, and the shop
Was lit with primroses, that lay atop
A Cornish pasty, and a pot of cream :
And as, with gentle hands, the father lifted
The flowers his little son had plucked for him,
He stood a moment in a far-off dream,
As though in glad remembrances he drifted
On Western seas : and, as his eyes grew dim,
He stooped, and buried them in deep, sweet bloom :
Till, hearing, once again, the poor child's cough,
He served her hurriedly, and sent her off,
Quite happily, with thin hands filled with flowers.
And, as I followed to the street, the gloom
Was starred with primroses ; and many hours
The strange, shy flickering surprise
Of that child's keen, enchanted eyes
Lit up my heart, and brightened my dull room.

Music has come in again, in frequent and sometimes intricate rhyme ; in metrical lightness and variety ; in a fuller and more harmonious language.

Wilfrid Wilson Gibson

The spirit of this later work remains humanitarian, but it is not centred now solely upon the tragic aspects of the workers' lives. A wider range is taken, and comedy enters, with an accession of urbanity from which the poems gain a mellower note. The world of nature, too, banished for a time in the exclusive study of humanity, returns to enrich this later poetry with a store of loving observation, an intimate knowledge of wild creatures, and the refreshing sense of a healthful open-air life in which, over a deep consciousness of sterner things, plays a jolly comradeship with wind and weather.

Ralph Hodgson

THE format of Mr Hodgson's published work is almost as interesting as the poetry itself—and that is saying a good deal. For all of his poetry that matters (there is an earlier, experimental volume which is not notable) was issued during the two or three years preceding the War in the form of chapbook and broadside.

It was a new publishing venture, quietly launched *At the Sign of Flying Fame,* and piloted now through the rapids of a larger success by the Poetry Bookshop. In a sense, of course, it is not a new thing at all, but a revival of the means by which ballad and romance were conveyed into the hands of the people a couple of centuries ago. Yet it is no imitation of a quaint style for the sake of its picturesqueness, nor the haphazard choice of a vehicle for the author to his public, irrespective of its suitability to either ; nor was it a mere bid for popular favour.

The peculiar interest of the revival lies in the fact that it is part of the larger movement, the renascent spirit of poetry which has been visibly stirring the face of the waters in these past few years. The reappearance of the chapbook synchronized with that, and is closely related with it. For it is found to be as well fitted to the form

108

Ralph Hodgson

and the content of the newest poetry as it is suited
to the need of the newest audience. On the one
hand it brings to the freshly awakened public a
book which is cheap enough to acquire and small
enough readily to become a familiar possession of
the mind. On the other hand, it is suited perfectly
to the simple themes and metrical effects of the
work hitherto published in this form; and is
designed only to include small poems of unques-
tioned excellence. Here may be perceived the
more important factors which go to the formation
of literary taste; and while one would estimate
that the educational value of these little books is
therefore high, meeting aptly the need of the
novice in poetry, it is clear that the discriminating
mind also is likely to find them satisfying.

Mr Hodgson's work, then, will be found in four
or five chapbooks and a thin sheaf of broadsides.
The chapbooks are small and slim, and could all
be picked up between the thumb and finger of
one hand. They are wrapped in cheery yellow
and decorated with impressionistic sketches which,
nine times out of ten, really help the illusion
that the poet is creating. The broadsides—there
are about a dozen of them—are long loose sheets,
each containing a single poem similarly decorated.

Contemporary Poets

The sum of the work is thus quite small. Perhaps there are not more than five-and-twenty pieces altogether, none very long, and amongst them an occasional miniature of a single stanza. Probably the format in which the author has chosen to appear has had an effect in restricting his production. That would be a possible result of the vigorous selection exercised and the limits imposed in space and style. But there are signs that he would not have been in any case a ready writer— the sense these lyrics convey of having waited on inspiration until the veritable moment shone, finding thought and feeling, imagination and technique, ripe to express it. And it was by those signs that watchers knew and acclaimed this author for a poet, despite the slender bulk of his accomplishment, before the Royal Society of Literature had awarded to his work the *Polignac* prize.

The two poems which gained the prize are "The Bull" and "The Song of Honour." Each occupies a whole chapbook to itself, and therefore must be accounted, for this poet, of considerable length. They are, indeed, the most important of his poems. And if one does not immediately add that they are also the most beautiful and the most charming, the reason is something more than an aversion from

110

Ralph Hodgson

dogma and the superlative mood. For the artistic
level of all this work is high, and it would be
difficult, on a critical method, to single out the
finest piece. The decision would be susceptible,
even more than poetical judgments usually are, to
mood and individual bias. One person, inclining
to the smaller, gem-like forms of verse, will find
pieces by Mr Hodgson to flatter his fancy. This
poet has, indeed, a gift of concentrated expression,
before which one is compelled to pause. There
are tiny lyrics here which comprise immensities.
The facile imp that lurks round every corner for the
poor trader in words whispers ' epigram ' as we read
" Stupidity Street " or "The Mystery " or " Reason
has Moons." But is the specific quality of these
delicate creations really epigrammatic ? No, it
would appear to be something more gracious and
more subtly blent with emotion ; having implications that lead beyond the region of stark thought,
and an impulse far other than to sharpen a point.
" Stupidity Street " is an example :

> I saw with open eyes
> Singing birds sweet
> Sold in the shops
> For the people to eat,
> Sold in the shops of
> Stupidity Street.

III

> I saw in vision
> The worm in the wheat,
> And in the shops nothing
> For people to eat ;
> Nothing for sale in
> Stupidity Street.

Analysis of that will discover an anatomy complete enough to those who enjoy that kind of dissection. There are bones of logic and organic heat sufficient of themselves for wonder how the thing can be done in so small a compass. And the strong simple words, which articulate the idea so exactly, confirm the impression of something rounded and complete ; as though final expression had been reached and nothing remained behind. But as a fact there is much behind. One sees this perhaps a little more clearly in " The Mystery " :

> He came and took me by the hand
> Up to a red rose tree,
> He kept His meaning to Himself
> But gave a rose to me.
>
> I did not pray Him to lay bare
> The mystery to me,
> Enough the rose was Heaven to smell,
> And His own face to see.

Again the idea has been crystallized so cleanly out of the poetic matrix that one sees at first only its sharp, bright outline. Perhaps to the analyst it would yield nothing more. But the simpler mind will surely feel, no matter how dimly, the presence of all the imaginings out of which it sprang, a small synthesis of the universe.

Here we touch the main feature of this poet's gift—his power to visualize, to make almost tangible, a poetic conception. So consummate is this power that it dominates other qualities and might almost cheat us into thinking that they did not exist. Thus we might not suspect this transparent verse of reflective depths; and of course, it is not intellectual poetry, specifically so-called. Yet reflection is implied everywhere; and occasionally it is a pure abstraction which gets itself embodied. The poem called "Time" illustrates this. In its opening line— "Time, you old Gipsy-man"—the idea swings into life in a figure which gains energy with every line. One positively sees this restless old man who has driven his caravan from end to end of the world and who cannot be persuaded to stay for bribe or entreaty. And it would be possible quite to forget the underlying thought did not the gravity of it peep between the incisive strokes of the third stanza.

> Last week in Babylon,
> Last night in Rome,
> Morning, and in the crush
> Under Paul's dome;

Contemporary Poets

Under Paul's dial
You tighten your rein—
Only a moment,
And off once again ;
Off to some city
Now blind in the womb,
Off to another
Ere that's in the tomb.

So it is too with this poet's imagination. It deals perpetually with concrete imagery—as for instance when it pictures Eve :

Picking a dish of sweet
Berries and plums to eat,

or presents her, when the serpent is softly calling her name, as

Wondering, listening,
Listening, wondering,
Eve with a berry
Half-way to her lips.

Moreover, the poet does not in the least mind winging his fancy in a homely phrase. He is not afraid of an idiomatic touch, nor of pithy, vigorous words. His conception is vivid enough to bear rigorous treatment; and in the same poem, " Eve," the serpent is found plotting the fall of humanity in these terms :

114

Ralph Hodgson

> Now to get even and
> Humble proud heaven and
> Now was the moment or
> Never at all.

And when his wiles have been successful, Eve's feathered comrades, Titmouse and Jenny Wren, make an indignant ' clatter ' :

> How the birds rated him,
> How they all hated him !
> How they all pitied
> Poor motherless Eve !

That is the nearest approach to fantasy which will be found in this poetry. There is nothing subtle or whimsical here : no half-lights or neutral tones or hints of meaning. This genius cannot fulfil itself in an ' airy nothing.' The imaginative power is too firmly controlled by a sense of fact to admit the bizarre and incredible ; yet there can be no doubt of its creative force when one turns for a moment to either of the prize poems, and particularly to " The Bull." It would be hard to name a finer specimen of verse in which imagination, high and sustained, is seen to be operating through a purely sensuous medium. That is to say, moving in a region of fact, accurately observing and recording the phenomena of a real world, there is yet achieved an imaginative creation of great power—

a bit of all-but-perfect art. Quotation will not serve to illustrate this, since the poem is an organic whole and a principal element of its perfection is its unity. One could, however, demonstrate over again from almost any line the poet's instinct for reality : as for example in the truth, quiet but unflinching, of his presentment of the cruelty inherent in his theme. The passages are almost too painful taken out of their context ; and there may be some for whom they will rob the poem of complete beauty. But the same instinct may be observed visualizing, in strong light and rich colour and incisive movement, the teeming tropical world in which the old bull stands, sick, unkinged and left to die.

> Cranes and gaudy parrots go
> Up and down the burning sky ;
> Tree-top cats purr drowsily
> In the dim-day green below ;
> And troops of monkeys, nutting, some,
> All disputing, go and come ;
>
> .   .   .   .   .
>
> And a dotted serpent curled
> Round and round and round a tree,
> Yellowing its greenery,
> Keeps a watch on all the world,
> All the world and this old bull
> In the forest beautiful.

Ralph Hodgson

This poem is indeed very illustrative of its author's method. One perceives the thought behind (apart, of course, from the mental process of actual composition) ; and one realizes the magnitude of it. But again it is implicit only, and reflection on ' the flesh that dies,' on greatness fallen and worth contemned, hardly wins a couple of lines of direct expression.

In " The Song of Honour " it would seem for the moment as if all that were reversed. This poem is the re-creation of a spiritual experience, a hymn of adoration. It is entirely subjective in conception, and is completely different therefore from the cool objectivity of " The Bull " or " Eve " or " Time." In them the poet is working so detachedly that there is even room for the play of gentle humour now and then. He is working with delight, indeed, and emotion warm enough, but with a joy that is wholly artistic, caring much more for the thing that he is making than for any single element of it. But in " The Song of Honour " it is evident that he cares immensely for his theme ; and hence arise an ardour and intensity which are not present in the other poems. Moreover, the work is the interpretation of a vision, which would seem to imply a mystical quality only latent hitherto ; and there is a rapture of utterance which is not found elsewhere.

The apparent contrast has no reality however. It is possible to catch, though in subtle inflexions it is true, an undertone which runs below even the simplest and clearest of these lyrics. No doubt it is as quiet, as subdued, as it well could be—this soft, complex harmony flowing beneath the ringing measure. But one can distinguish a note here and a phrase there which point directly to the dominant theme of "The Song of Honour." There is a hint of it, for example, in "The Mystery," where the soul is imagined as standing, reverent but without fear, within the closed circle of the unknown, and joyfully content to accept as the pledge and symbol of that which it is unable to comprehend, the beauty of the material world. One may see in that a familiar attitude of the modern mind; the perception that there *is* a mystery, which somehow perpetually eludes the creeds and philosophies, but which seems to be attaining to gradual revelation and fulfilment in actual existence. A vision of the unity of that existence was the inspiration of this greater poem : a realization, momentary but dazzling, of the magnificence of being : of its joy, of its continuity, of the progression of life through countless forms of that which we call matter to an ultimate goal of supreme glory.

I do not say that any thesis, in those or kindred

Ralph Hodgson

terms, was the origin of this Song. I feel quite
sure that it had no basis so abstract. It was born
in a mood of exaltation, kindled perhaps by such
an instant of flaming super-consciousness as may
be observed in the spiritual experience of other
contemporary poets. The moment of its inception
is recorded in the opening of the poem :

> I climbed a hill as light fell short,
> And rooks came home in scramble sort,
> And filled the trees and flapped and fought
> And sang themselves to sleep ;

Silence fell upon the landscape as darkness came
and the stars shone out.

> I heard no more of bird or bell,
> The mastiff in a slumber fell,
> I stared into the sky,
> As wondering men have always done
> Since beauty and the stars were one,
> Though none so hard as I.

> It seemed, so still the valleys were,
> As if the whole world knelt at prayer,
> Save me and me alone ;

So true is the poet to his impulse towards clarity
and the concrete, so unerringly does he select the
strong, familiar word with all its meaning clear
on the face of it, that it is possible to regard the

Song simply as a religious poem—a hymn of adoration to a Supreme Being :

> I heard the universal choir,
> The Sons of Light exalt their Sire
> With universal song,
> Earth's lowliest and loudest notes,
> Her million times ten million throats
> Exalt Him loud and long,

Pure religion the poem is, but its implications are broader than any creed. And, define it as we may, it remains suggestive of the most vital current of modern thought. For it takes its stand upon the solid earth, embraces reality and perceives in the material world itself that which is urging joyfully toward some manifestation of spiritual splendour. Thus the poet hears the Song rising from the very stocks and stones :

> The everlasting pipe and flute
> Of wind and sea and bird and brute,
> And lips deaf men imagine mute
> In wood and stone and clay,

The pæan is audible to him, too, from lowly creatures in whom life has not yet grown conscious, from the tiniest forms of being, from the most transient of physical phenomena.

> The music of a lion strong
> That shakes a hill a whole night long,

Ralph Hodgson

A hill as loud as he,
The twitter of a mouse among
Melodious greenery,
The ruby's and the rainbow's song,
The nightingale's—all three,
The song of life that wells and flows
From every leopard, lark and rose
And everything that gleams or goes
Lack-lustre in the sea.

But it is in humanity that the Song attains its fullest
and noblest harmony. Out of the stuff of actual
human life the spiritual essence is distilled, making
the wraiths of a mystical imagination poor and pale
by comparison.

I heard the hymn of being sound
From every well of honour found
In human sense and soul :
The song of poets when they write
The testament of Beautysprite
Upon a flying scroll,
The song of painters when they take
A burning brush for Beauty's sake
And limn her features whole—

.   .   .   .

The song of beggars when they throw
The crust of pity all men owe
To hungry sparrows in the snow,
Old beggars hungry too—
The song of kings of kingdoms when
They rise above their fortune men,
And crown themselves anew,—

Ford Madox Hueffer

THERE is a collected edition of Mr Hueffer's poetry published in that year of dreadful memory nineteen hundred and fourteen. It is a valuable possession. Its verse-content may not—of course it cannot—appeal in the same degree to all lovers of poetry. For reasons that we shall see, it is more liable than most poetic art to certain objections from those whose taste is already formed and who therefore, wittingly or unwittingly, have adopted a pet convention. They may boggle at a word or a phrase in terminology which is avowedly idiomatic. They may wince occasionally at a free rhyme or grow a little restive at the irregularities of a rhyme-scheme, or resent an abrupt change of rhythm in the middle of a stanza just as they believed they had begun to scan it correctly. If they are the least bit sentimental (and it is not many who have cast out, root and branch, the Anglo-Saxon vice) they will be chilled here and there by an ironic touch, repelled by an apparent levity, or irritated at the contiguity of subjects and ideas which seem inept and unrelated. The classicist will grumble that the unities are broken; the idealist will shudder at a bit of actuality; the formalist will eye certain new patterns with disfavour; and even the realist, with so much after his own heart, will be graceless enough to be impatient at recurrent signs of a romantic temperament.

So, in half a dozen different ways, the literary person of as many different types may find that he is just hindered from complete enjoyment of what he nevertheless perceives to be good work. If he be honest, however, and master of his moods, he will be willing to admit that it *is* good; and that none of these objections invalidate the essential poetry of the book. That has its own winning and haunting qualities, quite strong enough to justify the claim that the volume is a valuable possession. That is to say, there is refreshing beauty in it, considered simply as a work of art and judged only from the point of view of the conventional lover of poetry. There are other values, however, immediate or potential. There is, for example, to the believer in Mr Hueffer's theory, promise of the power which his method would have upon all the kind, jolly, intelligent, but unliterary people, could they be induced to read poetry at all. As a mere corollary from the literary quibbles already named, one would expect such people to find this volume delightful—an expectation by no means daunted by the declared fate of earlier productions. One sees that the evident sincerity of the work, the attitude of that particular personality to life, the free hand and the right instinct in the selection of incident, and the use of language that is homely and picturesque, ought to be potent attractions to the reader who finds conventional poetic poetry stilted and artificial.

Moreover, so successful has the author's method been in many cases that even the *littérateur* must pause and think. He will observe how well the new artistry suits the new material; he will note the exhilaration of the final effect; and when, returning to his beloved poets of the last generation, he finds that some of their virtue seems to have fled meantime, he will ask himself whether the life of our time may not *demand* poetic presentation in such forms as the younger poets are making. Which is to say that he will be a convert to Mr Hueffer's impressionism.

That point is debatable, of course; but what will hardly be questioned, apart from the joy we frequently experience here in seeing a thing consummately done, is the importance of this work as an experiment. That is obviously another kind of value, with a touch of scientific interest added to the æsthetics. And the importance of the experiment is enhanced, or at any rate we realize

it more fully, from the fact that the poet has been
generous enough to elaborate his theory in a preface.
That is no euphemism, as other prefaces and theories
of exasperating memory might seem to suggest.
It is real generosity to give away the fundamentals
of your art, to show as clearly as is done here the
principles upon which you work and the exact
means which are taken to give effect to them. It
is courageous too, particularly when confessions
are made which supply a key to personality. For
the hostile critic is thus doubly armed. But the
' gentle reader ' is armed too ; and Mr Hueffer
would seem to have been wise, even from the point
of view of mere prudence, to take the risk.

The reader of this book then will find the poems
doubly interesting in the light that the preface
throws upon them. He may, of course, read and
enjoy them without reference to it—that is the
measure of their poetic value. Or, on the other
hand, he may read the preface, brim full of stimulating ideas, without reference to the poetry.
But the complete significance of either can only be
appreciated when they are taken in conjunction.
For instance, we light upon this phrase indicating
the material of the poet's art : " Modern life, so
extraordinary, so hazy, so tenuous, with still such
definite and concrete spots in it." It is a charming

phrase, and from its own suggestiveness gently constrains one to think. But if we turn at once to the most considerable poem of the collection, "To All the Dead," we shall see our poet in the very act of recording the life that he visualizes in this way; and we shall see how remarkably the texture of the poem fits the description in the passage just quoted: "life hazy and tenuous, with such definite and concrete spots."

To tell the truth, haze is the first thing we see when observing the effect of this poem. It is pervasive too, and for a time nothing more is visible save two or three islets of concrete experience, projecting above it and appearing to float about in it, unstable and unrelated. This first effect is rather like that of a landscape in a light autumn ground-mist, which floats along the valley-meadows leaving tree-tops and hillsides clear. Or it is like trying to recollect what happened to you on a certain memorable day. The mood comes back readily enough, golden or sombre; but the events which induced it, or held it in check, or gave it so sudden a reverse only return reluctantly, one by one, and not even in their proper order; so that we have to puzzle them out and rearrange and fit them together before the right sequence appears.

Such is the main impression of "To All the Dead."

Ford Madox Hueffer

But the artist has been at work here selecting his incidents with a keen eye and sensitive touch, brooding over them with a temperament of complex charm, and for all their apparent disjunction, relating and unifying them, as in life, with the subtlest and frailest of links. As a consequence, at a second glance the haze begins to lift, while at a third the whole landscape is visible, a prospect very rich and fair despite the ugly spots which the artist has not deigned to eliminate, and which, as a fact, he has deliberately retained.

But there is no doubt the first glance is puzzling. If one were not caught by the interest of those concrete spots it might even be tiresome, and one would probably not trouble to take the second glance. But they are so curious in themselves, and sketched so boldly, that we are arrested; and the next moment the general design emerges. First the picture of the ancient Chinese queen— a Mongolian Helen—

> With slanting eyes you would say were blind—
> In a dead white face.

That, with its quaint strange setting and its suggestion of a guilty love story, is a thing to linger over for its own sake, apart from its apparent isolation. Nor do we realize fully until later (although something subtler than intelligence has already perceived it), that in this opening passage the theme has been stated, and that the key-note was struck in the line

She should have been dead nine thousand year. . . .

But we pass abruptly, in the second movement, to our own time and to the heart of our own civilization. We are paying a call on a garrulous friend in the rue de la Paix. He is an American and therefore a philosopher ; but as he descants on the 'nature of things,' doubtless in the beautiful English of the gentle American, we let our attention wander to things that touch us more sharply, to sights and sounds outside the window, each vividly perceived and clearly picked out, but all resolving themselves into a symbol, vaguely impressive, of the complicated whirl of life. And this passage again, with its satiric flavour and dexterity of execution, we are content to enjoy in its apparent detachment, until we glimpse the link which unites it to the larger interest of the whole.

The link with that ancient queen is in a flash of contrast—a couple of Chinese chiropodists, grinning from their lofty window at a *mannequin* on the opposite side of the street. And as the theme is developed, episodes which seem

128

Ford Madox Hueffer

irrelevant at first, are soon found to have their relation with the thought—of death and tragic passion—
on which the poet is brooding. At a chance word
dropped by the American host the confused and per-
plexing sights and sounds of the outer world vanish ;
and the philosophical lecture, droning hitherto just on
the edge of consciousness, fades even out of hearing—

> . . . I lost them
> At the word " Sandusky." A landscape crossed them ;
> A scene no more nor less than a vision,
> All clear and grey in the rue de la Paix.

He is seven years back in time and many hundreds
of miles away, pushing up a North American river
in a screaming, smoky steamer, between high banks
crowned with forests of fir :

> And suddenly we saw a beach—
>
> A grey old beach and some old grey mounds
> That seemed to silence the steamer's sounds ;
> So still and old and grey and ragged.
> For there they lay, the tumuli, barrows,
> The Indian graves. . . .

So, rather obliquely perhaps as to method, but with
certainty of effect, we are prepared for the culmination in the third movement. The poet has
fled from civilization and ' Modern Movements '
to the upland heather of a high old mound above the
town of Trèves. And here, on a late autumn

129

evening, he lingers to think. He remembers that it is the eve of All Souls' Day; and remembers too that the mound on which he is seated is an old burying-place of great antiquity. In the cold and dark of his eerie perch, certain impressions of the last few days return to him, just those which have been subtly galling a secret wound and impelling him to flee—the tragedy of the Chinese queen, the vision of the old tumuli at Sandusky Bay, the unheeded platitudes of his friend—

> . . . *" From good to good,*
> *And good to better you say we go."*
> (There's an owl overhead.)   *" You say that's so ? "*
> My American friend of the rue de la Paix ?
> *" Grow better and better from day to day."*
> Well, well I had a friend that's not a friend to-day;
> Well, well, I had a love who's resting in the clay
> Of a suburban cemetery.

One has felt all through that something weird is impending; but I am sure that no ghost-scene so curiously impressive as that which follows has ever been written before. It could not have been done, waiting as it was for the conjuncture of time and temperament and circumstance. But here it is, a thing essentially of our day; with its ironic mood, its new lore, its air of detachment, its glint of grim humour now and then, and its intense passion, both of love and of despair, which the

130

fugitive show of nonchalance does but serve to accentuate. Passion is the dominant note as the myriad wraiths of long-dead lovers crowd past the brooding figure in the darkness.

> And so beside the woodland in the sheen
> And shimmer of the dewlight, crescent moon
> And dew wet leaves I heard the cry " Your lips !
> Your lips ! Your lips." It shook me where I sat,
> It shook me like a trembling, fearful reed,
> The call of the dead. A multitudinous
> And shadowy host glimmered and gleamed,
> Face to face, eye to eye, heads thrown back, and lips
> Drinking, drinking from lips, drinking from bosoms
> The coldness of the dew—and all a gleam
> Translucent, moonstruck as of moving glasses,
> Gleams on dead hair, gleams on the white dead shoulders
> Upon the backgrounds of black purple woods. . . .

That poem naturally comes first in a little study, because it is the most considerable in the collection, and again because it is the most characteristic. It is very convenient, too, for illustrating those theories of the preface, as for example, that the business of the poet is " the right appreciation of such facets of our own day as God will let us perceive . . . the putting of certain realities in certain aspects . . . the juxtaposition of varied and contrasting things . . . the genuine love and the faithful rendering of the received impression." But on æsthetic grounds one is not so sure of " To All the Dead " for the first place. Perhaps it tries to include too many facets of life—or death ; perhaps we get a slight impression as regards technique that the poet is *consciously* experimenting ; and there is a shade of morbidity haunting it. In many of the shorter pieces there is a nearer approach to perfection. " The Portrait," for instance, a symbolical picture of life, has only one flaw ; a slight excess of a trick of repetition which is a weakness of our author. It is mere carping, however, to find fault with a piece which is so noble in idea and gracious in expression ; and it seems a crime to spoil the lovely thing by mutilating it. But with a resemblance of theme, the poem is so strongly contrasted in manner with " To All the Dead " that one cannot resist quoting from it at this point. The theme here is relatively simple : Life, symbolized in the figure of a woman, seated upon a tomb in a sequestered graveyard. The mood is one of serene melancholy, not rising to passion or dropping to satire ; and the gentle unity of thought and feeling leaves the mind free to receive the impression of beauty.

> She sits upon a tombstone in the shade ;
>
> .   .   .   .   .
>
> Being life amid piled up remembrances
> Of the tranquil dead.

Ford Madox Hueffer

. . . So she sits and waits.
And she rejoices us who pass her by,
And she rejoices those who here lie still,
And she makes glad the little wandering airs,
And doth make glad the shaken beams of light
That fall upon her forehead : all the world
Moves round her, sitting on forgotten tombs
And lighting in to-morrow.

That was written earlier than " To All the Dead,"
but, like the two songs which come immediately
after it in this volume, and like the " Suabian
Legend," it is amongst Mr Hueffer's best things.
One notes the pervasive temperament in all this
work. Indeed, its artistic significance seems to lie
in having expressed strikingly a vivid personality.
It is a very individual temper, rooted in acute
sensibility ; but reflective power is visibly present,
with a vein of irony running through it, touched
now and then to bitterness. In one aspect after
another this individuality is revealed, and the
changing moods, gentle or tender or wrathful,
are matched by changing forms. It follows that
there are many varied measures here ; and
most of them have some new feature. A few
are very irregular, and all are, of course, modelled
to suit the author's impressionistic theory. And
the fact that these forms are in the main so well
adapted to their themes : that they do succeed

in conveying a vivid impression, is as much as to say that the poet has evolved a technique which exactly fits his own genius. It may or it may not carry much further than that; and the extent to which the new instrument would respond to other hands may be problematical. One would suppose that some of its qualities at least would be a permanent gain, particularly the larger range which brings within its compass so many fresh aspects of life on the one hand and on the other a richer idiom. But whether or no these are qualities which will pass into the substance of future poetry, there can be no question that the method has achieved here an intense presentment of life.

Thus we have the fulmination of "Süssmund's Address to an Unknown God"; violent, bitter, and unreasoned, the mere rage of weary mind and body against the goads of modern existence. Thus, in the "Canzone à la Sonata" as in "The Portrait" a single serious thought is rendered in grave unrhymed stanzas which have all the dignity of blank verse with something more than its usual vivacity; and thus, too, in "From Inland," one of the exquisite pieces of the volume, the whole of a tragedy is suggested by the rapid sketching of two or three brief scenes. Again the verse is perfectly fitted to

Ford Madox Hueffer

the theme; the sober rhythm matching the quietness of retrospect; memory tenderly grieving in
simple rhymes which vary their occurrence as
emotion rises and falls.

> . . . We two," I said,
> " Have still the best to come."   But you
> Bowed down your brooding, silent head,
> Patient and sad and still. . . .
> . . . Dear !
> What would I give to climb our down,
> Where the wind hisses in each stalk
> And, from the high brown crest to see,
> Beyond the ancient, sea-grey town,
> The sky-line of our foam-flecked sea ;
> And, looking out to sea, to hear,
> Ah !   Dear, once more your pleasant talk ;
> And to go home as twilight falls
> Along the old sea-walls !
> The best to come !   The best !   The best !
> One says the wildest things at times,
> Merely for comfort.   But—*The best !*

Again, in " Grey Matter " and "Thanks Whilst
Unharnessing," the colloquial touch is right and
sure.   In the latter poem, the almost halting time
of the opening lines clearly suggests the tired horse
as he draws to a standstill in the early darkness of
a winter evening : there is a quicker movement as
the robin's note rings out ; the farmer's song is

broken at intervals as he moves about the business
of unharnessing, and when he stands at the open
stable door, peering through the darkness at the
robin on the thorn, the impression of relief from
toil, of gratitude for home and rest, of simple
kindliness and humanity, is complete—

> Small brother, flit in here, since all around
> The frost hath gripped the ground ;
> And oh ! I would not like to have you die.
> We's help each other,
> Little Brother Beady-eye.

One might continue to cite examples : the rapid
unrhymed dialogue of " Grey Matter," which continues so long as there is a touch of controversy in
the talk of husband and wife, and changes to a lyric
measure as emotion rises ; the real childlikeness of
the " Children's Song " ; or the mingled pain and
sweetness of " To Christina at Nightfall," epito-
mising life in its philosophy and reflecting it in its
art. But it is unnecessary to go further ; and this
last little poem (I will not do it violence by extracting
any part of it) is perhaps the most complete vindication of our poet's theories : its vivid impressions
conveyed with a touch at once firm and tender ;
intense thought and feeling rendered with gracious
homeliness.

An Irish Group

THE spirit of poetry is native to Ireland. It awakened there in the early dawn, and has hardly slumbered in two thousand years. Probably before the Christian era it had become vocal ; and as long as twelve hundred years ago it had woven for the garment of its thought an intricate and subtle prosody. You would think it had grown old in so great a time. You would almost expect to find, in these latter days, a pale and mournful wraith of poetry in the green isle. You would look for the symbol of it in the figure of some poor old woman, like the legendary Kathleen ni Houlihan, who is supposed to incarnate the spirit of the country. But even while you are looking it will happen with you as it happened before the eyes of the lad in the play by Mr Yeats. The bent form will straighten and the old limbs become lithe and free, the eyes will sparkle and the cheeks flush and the head be proudly lifted. And when you are asked, " Did you see an old woman ? " you will answer with the boy in the play :

> I did not ; but I saw a young girl, and she had
> the walk of a queen.

So it is with the later poetry of Ireland. One

would not guess, in the more recent lyrics, that
these singers are the heirs of a great antiquity.
Their songs are as fresh as a blade of grass : they
are as new as a spring morning, as young and sweet
as field flowers in May. They partake of youth in
their essence ; and they would seem to proceed
from that strain in the Irish nature which has
always adored the young and beautiful, and which
dreamed, many centuries ago, a pagan paradise of
immortal youth which has never lost its glamour :

> Where nobody gets old and godly and grave,
> Where nobody gets old and crafty and wise,
> Where nobody gets old and bitter of tongue.

Doubtless we owe this air of newness largely to
the rebirth of literature in the Isle. When we say
that poetry has never slumbered there, we get as
near to the truth as is possible ; it seems always to
have been quick, eager and spontaneous, and never
to have drowsed or faded. But there was a black
age when it was smitten so hard by external mis-
fortune that it nearly died. It was early in the nineteenth century when, as Dr Hyde tells, " The old
literary life of Ireland may be said to come to a close
amidst the horrors of famine, fever and emigration."
All that W. B. Yeats, Dr Hyde, and Lady Gregory
have done to build the new literary life of their

land cannot be fully realized yet. But out of their labours has surely sprung the movement which we call the Irish Literary Renaissance—a movement in which, disregarding cross currents, the detached observer would include the whole revival, whether popular or æsthetic. By fostering the Gaelic they have awakened in the people themselves a sense of the dignity of their own language and literature. By the translation of saga and romance, the patient gathering of folk-tale and fairy-lore, the search for and interpretation of old manuscripts, they have given to native poets a mass of material which is peculiarly suited to their genius. And since approximately the year 1890 they have seen their reward in the work of a band of brilliant writers. Romance is re-born in the novel; the poetry of the old saga blooms again in the lyric; and a vital new development has given to Ireland what she never before possessed—a native drama.

Now it is true that the larger figures of the movement have receded a little; the one in whom the flame of genius burned most fiercely has passed into silence. And Synge being gone, there is no hand like his, cunning to modulate upon every string of the harp. There is no voice of so full a compass, booming out of tragic depths or shrilling satiric laughter or sweet with heroic romance;

breathing essential poetry and yet rich with the
comedy of life. It is a fact to make us grieve the
more for that untimely end, but it is not a cause
for despair. For there are many legatees of the
genius of Synge. They are slighter figures—naturally so, at this stage of their career—but they
belong, as he did, to the new birth of the nation's
genius and they draw their inspiration directly
from their own land.

Here we touch a constant feature of Irish poetry.
Dr. Hyde tells that from the earliest times the
bards were imbued with the spirit of nationality :
that their themes were always of native gods and
heroes, and that they were, in a sense, the guardians
of national existence. The singers of a later day
curiously resemble them in this. Sometimes it is a
matter of outward likeness only, the new poets
having drawn directly upon the stories which have
been placed in their hands from the old saga. But
much more often it is a rooted affinity—a thing of
blood and nerve and mental fibre. Then, although
the gods may bear another name and the heroes
be of a newer breed and the national ideal may be
enlarged, it is still with these things that the poets
are preoccupied.

This has become to the scoffer a matter of jest,
and to the grumbler a cause of complaint—that the

An Irish Group

Irish poet is obsessed by race. They say that they can guess beforehand what will be the mood, the manner and the subject of nine Irish poems out of ten. They are very clever people, so they probably could get somewhere near the mark. And they would naturally find themselves cramped in these narrow bounds. Religion and history and national ideals would give them no scope. But when they maintain that this is a radical defect, I am not at all convinced. I remember that many of the world's great books proceeded from an intense national self-consciousness ; and I ask myself whether it may not be a law in the literary evolution of a people, as well as in their political development, that they proceed by way of a strong, free and proud spirit of nationality to something wider. The reply may be that that is a relatively early stage through which, in a normal literary progress, Ireland should have passed long since. True, but normal growth and advance have never been possible to her ; and recalling the events of her history, it is something of a marvel that the literary genius should have survived at all.

In contrast with modern English poetry, impatient as it is to escape from tradition, these traits which mark a line of descent so clearly are the more striking. One may even smile a little at them—

whimsically, as we do when we see a youth or a young girl reproducing the very looks and tones and gestures of an older generation. There is something comical in the unconscious exactitude of it. But the laugh comes out of the deeper sources of comedy. There lies below it, subconsciously perhaps, a profound sense of those things in life which are most precious and most enduring.

One of the gayer features of this family likeness is the persistence of a certain kind of satire. We know from Dr Hyde's *Literary History of Ireland* that an important function of the ancient bards was to satirize the rivals and enemies of their chieftain. They had, of course, to sing his victories, to inspire and encourage his warriors and to weave into verse the hundreds of romances which had come down to them from times older still. But their equipment was not complete unless it included a good stinging power of ridicule; and the *ollamh*, or chief bard, was commonly required to castigate in this way the king of some other province who happened to have given offence. But it is not to be supposed that the rival *ollamh* would remain silent under the punishment inflicted on his lord; and one can imagine the battle of wits which would follow. Or, if we need any assurance as to the caustic power of the bard, it may be found in one quaint

An Irish Group

incident. The hero Cuchulain was ranged against Queen Maeve of Connacht in her famous raid into Ulster about the year 100 B.C. Maeve was astute as well as warlike, and when she had failed several times to induce Cuchulain to engage singly with one of her warriors, she sent to him a threat that her bards " would criticize, satirize and blemish him so that they would raise three blisters on his face " . . . and Cuchulain instantly consented to her wish.

I cannot guess how many blisters have been raised by Irish satirists since that date, but I know the art has not died out. There are modern practitioners of it. Synge made the national susceptibility smart ; and yet his satire, to the mere onlooker, would seem sympathetic enough. So, too, with Miss Susan Mitchell. She pokes fun at her compatriots with perfect good humour and we cannot believe that they would be annoyed by it. But you never can tell. Perhaps the witty philosophy of " The Second Battle of the Boyne " would not appeal to an Ulster Volunteer ; and it is conceivable that even a Nationalist might resent the sly shaft at the national pugnacity. The opening stanza tells about an old man, whose name of portent is Edward Carson MacIntyre. His little grandchild runs in to him from the field carrying a dark round thing

that she has found, and she trundles it along the
floor to the old man's feet.

> Now Edward Carson MacIntyre
>   Was old, his eyes were dim,
> But when he heard the crackling sound,
>   New life returned to him.
> " Some tax-collector's skull," he swore,
> " We used to crack them by the score."
>
> " Why did you crack them, grandpapa ? "
>   Said wee Victoria May ;
> " It surely was a wicked thing
>   These hapless men to slay."
> " The cause I have forgot," said Mac.
> " All I remember is the crack."
>
>   .   .   .   .   .
>
> " And some men said the Government
>   Were very much to blame ;
>   And I myself," says MacIntyre,
> " Got my own share of fame.
> I don't know why we fought," says he,
> " But 'twas the devil of a spree."

Again it is possible (though hardly probable one
would think) that Mr George Moore does not really
enjoy the fun so cleverly poked at him in the stanzas,
" George Moore Comes to Ireland."   Safe in our
own detachment, the criticism seems delicious,
brightly hitting off the personality which has grown
so familiar in M Moore's work, and especially in
144

An Irish Group

"Hail and Farewell": the delightful garrulity, the disconcerting candour, the intimacy and naïve egoism, and the perfectly transparent what-a-terror-I-was-in-my-youth air. The speaker in the poem is, of course, Mr Moore himself; and it will be seen how cunningly the author has caught his attitude, particularly to the work of Mr W. B. Yeats—

> I haven't tried potato cake or Irish stew as yet;
> I've lived on eggs and bacon, and striven to forget
> A naughty past of ortolan and frothy omelette.
>
> .   .   .   .   .
>
> But W. B. was the boy for me—he of the dim, wan clothes;
> And—don't let on I said it—not above a bit of pose;
> And they call his writing literature, as everybody knows.
>
> If you like a stir, or want a stage, or would admirèd be,
> Prepare with care a naughty past, and then repent like me.
> My past, alas! was blameless, but this the world won't see.

When Miss Mitchell's satire is engaged on personalities in this way, it has a piquancy which may obscure the subtler flavour of it. But the truth is that it is often literary in a double sense, both in subject and in treatment. So we may find a theme of considerable general interest in the world of

145

literature, treated in the allusive literary manner
which has so much charm for the booklover. And
to that is added a racy and vigorous satirical touch.
Thus, for instance, is the question of Synge's *Playboy*
handled. Ridicule is thrown on the stupid rage
with which it was received, and on the folly which
generalized so hotly from the play to the nation,
deducing wild nonsense against a whole people
and its literature because the man who killed his
father in the story is befriended by peasants. Here
is a snatch of it :

> I can't love Plato any more
> Because a man called Sophocles,
>   Who lived in distant Attica,
> Wrote a great drama *Œdipus*,
>   About a Greek who killed his da.
> I know now Plato was a sham,
>   And Socrates I brush aside,
> For Phidias I don't care a damn,
>   For every Greek's a parricide.

So, too, comes the burlesque touch in the " Ode
to the British Empire " :

> God of the Irish Protestant,
>   Lord of our proud Ascendancy,
> Soon there'll be none of us extant,
>   We want a few plain words with thee.
>   Thou know'st our hearts are always set
>   On what we get, on what we get.

An Irish Group

The genial temper of this work pervades even the political pieces. Miss Mitchell is no respecter of persons or institutions : she finds food for derision in friend as well as foe. But her laughter is not bitter—unless, perhaps, a tinge comes in when she touches that old source of bitterness, the gulf between the Saxon and the Celt—

We are a pleasant people, the laugh upon our lip
Gives answer back to your laugh in gay good fellowship ;
We dance unto your piping, we weep when you want
    tears ;
Wear a clown's dress to please you, and to your friendly
    jeers
Turn up a broad fool's face and wave a flag of green—
But the naked heart of Ireland, who, who has ever seen ?

There is, however, a more important strain of heredity in the new Irish poetry ; and it comes directly through the renaissance of which we have already spoken. There are two lines of development which begin in that rebirth ; but they proceed almost at right angles from each other. One, the clearer and more direct, is towards work of a specifically literary order. The other is tending to a simple and direct rendering of life. On the one hand we find poetry which is romantic in manner and heroic in theme. This is largely of narrative form, and seems to hold within it the promise of epic growth. On the other hand, there is a lyric form of less pretension and wilder grace ; music so fresh and apparently artless as to mock the idea of derivation. Yet it, too, owes its vitality to the same impulse, and is, perhaps, its healthiest blossoming.

The treasury of Irish romance has been eagerly drawn upon by the literary poet ; and splendid stories they are for his purpose. Every one by this time knows the incomparable Deirdre legend, in one or other of the fine versions by Mr Yeats, Mr Trench or Synge. Deirdre, as a heroine of the ancient world, positively shines beside a Helen or a Cleopatra. In her is crystallized the Celtic conception of womanhood, with her free, clean, brave, generous soul ; magnificently choosing her true mate rather than wed the High King Conchubar ; and with her lover magnificently paying the penalty of death.

We have become almost as familiar, too, with the Hosting of Maeve, the prowess of Cuchulain, and the mythological figures of Dagda and Dana, who are the Zeus and Hera of early Irish religion. Here is a fragment of a poem by Mr James Cousins called "The Marriage. of Lir and Niav." The personages of the story belong to very early myth. To find Lir you must go back past the heroes and the demigods : further still, past the gods themselves, to their ancestors. For Lir was the father

An Irish Group

of Mananan the sea-god; and he was the Lord of
the Seven Isles. Niav (or Niamh) is described as
the Aphrodite of Irish myth; which probably
accounts for the symbolism in the passage where
Lir first sees her—

> But, as upon the breathless hour of eve,
> The gentle moon, smiling amid the wreck
> And splendid remnant of the flaming feast
> Wherewith Day's lord had sated half the world,
> Sets a cool hand on the tumultuous waves,
> And soothes them into peace, and takes the throne,
> And beams white love that wakens soft desire
> In waiting hearts; so in that throbbing pause
> Came Niav, daughter of the King whose name
> May not be named till First and Last are one.
>   . . . And He who stood
> Unseen, apart, marked how about Her form,
> Clothed white as foam, Her sea-green girdle hung
> Like mermaid weed, and how within her wake
> There came the sound and odour of the sea,
> The swift and silent stroke of unseen wings,
> And little happy cries of mating birds;

This poem appeared in one of Mr Cousins
earlier books, *The Quest*, published in 1904; and it
is interesting to observe in it the little signs which
indicate the nearness of the poet at that time to
the source of his inspiration. The stories from the
three great national cycles of romance had been
made accessible in the years just preceding; and the

poetic imagination seems to have been charmed by their quaint manner as well as stimulated by their vigour. Hence we find in this poem one or two familiar epic devices which have apparently been adopted as a means to catch the tone of the old story, and to convey a sense of its antiquity. There is, for instance, the trick of repetition that we know so well, a whole phrase recurring, either word for word or varied very slightly, at certain intervals through the poem. Thus we have the phrase which appears in the passage quoted above, and which is several times repeated in other places—

> —the King whose name
> May not be named till First and Last are one.

Thus, too, we find the frequent use of simile of an involved and elaborate order. Mr Cousins reveals himself as poet and artist in this device alone. Imagination and mastery of technique are alike implied in fancies so beautifully wrought. The opening lines of the passage we have given supply an example, and another may be taken from " Etain the Beloved." It is simpler than most, but it illustrates very aptly the grace of idea and expression which is characteristic of this poet. The scene is an assembly of the people before King Eochaidh ; and the chief bard is presenting their urgent petition to him—

An Irish Group

He ceased, and all the faces of the crowd
Shone with the light that kindles when the boon
Of speech has eased the heart ; as when a cloud
Falls from the labouring shoulder of the moon,
And all the world stands smiling silver-browed.

In the same poem of Etain we may note the free
use of description and the rich colour and profuse
detail which mark romantic work of this kind. The
story of Etain has a mythological association. She
was the beloved wife of Mider, one of the ancient
gods ; but she seems to have been driven out of
the hierarchy and to have become incarnate in
the form of a young girl of great beauty. King
Eochiadh, not knowing of her divine origin, wooed
her and made her queen. But Mider followed her
to earth and won her back from her human lover.
There is an exquisite stanza in which the King
sends to seek for his bride, and tells how they will
find her—

" She shall be found in some most quiet place
   Where Beauty sits all day beside her knee
   And looks with happy envy on her face ;
   Where Virtue blushes, her own guilt to see,
   And Grace learns new, sweet meanings from her grace ;
   Where all that ever was or will be wise
   Pales at the burning wisdom of her eyes."

News is brought to the King that Etain is found,
and he goes to the remote and lonely place that

151

his messengers have told him of. He comes upon
her unaware—

> There by the sea, Etain his destined bride
> Sat unabashed, unwitting of the sight
> Of him who gazed upon her gleaming side,
> Fair as the snowfall of a single night ;
> Her arms like foam upon the flowing tide ;
> Her curd-white limbs in all their beauty bare,
> Straight as the rule of Dagda's carpenter.

There is, too, in this poetry of Mr Cousins, a
very tender feeling for Nature. Perhaps it does not
quite accord with the spirit of the wild time out of
which the stories came ; but that opens up a larger
question into which we are not bound to enter.
For if we are going to quarrel with the treatment
of epic material in any but the vigorous, ' primitive '
manner, we shall make ourselves the poorer by
rejecting much beautiful poetry. We may even
find ourselves robbed of Virgilian sweetness. But
most of us will be wise enough to take good things
wherever we find them ; and may, therefore, rejoice in stanzas like these, which describe the
stirring of wild creatures at dawn :

> Somewhere the snipe now taps his tiny drum ;
> The moth goes fluttering upward from the heath ;
> And where no lightest foot unmarked may come,
> The rabbit, tiptoe, plies his shiny teeth
> On luscious herbage ; and with strident hum

An Irish Group

The yellow bees, blustering from flower to flower,
Scatter from dew-filled cups a sparkling shower.

The meadowsweet shakes out its feathery mass ;
And rumorous winds, that stir the silent eaves,
Bearing abroad faint perfumes as they pass,
Thrill with some wondrous tale the fluttering leaves,
And whisper secretly along the grass
Where gossamers, for day's triumphal march,
Hang out from blade to blade their diamond arch.

There is, however, a very different manner in which these early legends are being treated by some of the Irish poets. One may call it 'Celtic,' in the hope of conveying some impression of it in a single word. But if you would get nearer than that, you may take one or two fragments from Mr Yeats' *The Celtic Twilight*—such as " the voice of Celtic sadness and of Celtic longing for infinite things . . . the vast and vague extravagance that lies at the bottom of the Celtic heart." And to phrases like that, which adumbrate the spirit of the work, you must add a style which is allusive, mystic, and symbolical : in fact, a mode of expression rather like Mr Yeats' own early poetry. But the crux of the matter lies there. For the production of really good work of this kind demands just the equipment which Mr Yeats happens to possess : the right temperament and the right degree (a high one) of poetic craftsmanship. It is a

rare combination—unique, of course, in so far as
the element of individuality enters. And attempts
which have been made to gain the same effects
with a different natural endowment have failed in
proportion as temperament was unsuited or 'the
capacity for taking pains' was less. Hence 'Celtic'
poetry, in the specific sense, has fallen into some
disfavour. Yet when mood and material and craft
'have met and kissed each other,' it is clear that
authentic beauty is created; and that of a kind
which cannot be made in any other way. Thus we
might choose, from the romantic work of Miss Eva
Gore Booth, passages where all the desirable qualities
seem to meet. There is, for instance, the poem
which prefaces her *Triumph of Maeve*, from which
I take the last two stanzas. Here is finely caught
that unrest of soul which we have been taught to
believe essentially Celtic; though it probably haunts
every imaginative mind, of whatever race.

> There is no rest for the soul that has seen the wild eyes
>   of Maeve;
> No rest for the heart once caught in the net of her
>   yellow hair—
> No quiet for the fallen wind, no peace for the broken wave;
> Rising and falling, falling and rising with soft sounds
>   everywhere,
> There is no rest for the soul that has seen the wild eyes
>   of Maeve.

An Irish Group

I have seen Maeve of the Battles wandering over the
    hill
And I know that the deed that is in my heart is her
    deed ;
And my soul is blown about by the wild winds of her
    will,
For always the living must follow whither the dead
    would lead—
I have seen Maeve of the Battles wandering over the
    hill.

From the same romance we may select a speech
by Fionavar, Queen Maeve's beautiful young
daughter. The sense of the supernatural enters
here, for the occasion is Samhain, the pagan All
Souls' Eve. It is a night when gods and fairies are
abroad, and Fionavar has seen things strange and
awesome :

As I came down the valley after dark,
The little golden dagger at my breast
Flashed into fire lit by a sudden spark ;
I saw the lights flame on the haunted hill,
My soul was blown about by a strange wind.
Though the green fir trees rose up stark and still
Against the sky, yet in my haunted mind
They bent and swayed before a magic storm :
A wave of darkness thundered through the sky,
And drowned the world. . . .

In *Nera's Song*, again, as in the whole romance,

we find the element of dreams which is supposed to be an indubitable sign of the Celtic temperament. Nera, who is the Queen's bard, has just returned after an absence of one whole year in the Land of Faëry ; and though it is autumn, his arms are full of primroses, the fairies' magical flower :

> I bring you all my dreams, O golden Maeve,
> There are no dreams in all the world like these
> The dreams of Spring, the golden fronds that wave
> In faery land beneath dark forest-trees,—
> I bring you all my dreams.
>
> I bring you all my dreams, Fionavar,
> From that dim land where every dream is sweet,
> I have brought you a little shining star,
> I strew my primroses beneath your feet,
> I bring you all my dreams.

There is yet another style in which the heroic tales are occasionally treated, and it is directly contrasted with either of those which we have just considered. Examples of it may be found in Miss Alice Milligan's book of *Hero Lays*, where it will be seen that the poet's chief concern is with the story itself, rather than with the manner of telling. In such a piece as " Brian of Banba," for instance, the action is clear and moves rapidly. There is a sense of morning air and light in the poem which is very

An Irish Group

refreshing after the atmosphere of golden afternoon, or evening twilight, in which we have been wandering. It comes partly from the blithe swing of the rhythm : partly from the vigour and clear strength of diction. And a true dramatic sense imparts the life and movement of quickly changing emotion.

Banba is one of the many beautiful old names for Ireland ; and Brian was perhaps her greatest king. He lived about the time of our English Alfred and, like him, Brian fought continually against the invading Dane. He, too, when a young man, lived for a long time the life of an outlaw—outcast even from his own clan because he would not suffer the Danish yoke. The poem relates an incident of Brian's appearance at the palace of his brother, King Mahon, after a long absence. He strides into the gay assembly alone, his body worn thin by privation and his garments ragged.

" Brian, my brother," said the King, in a tone of scornful wonder,
" Why dost thou come in beggar-guise our palace portals under ?
Where hast thou wandered since yester year, on what venture of love hast thou tarried ?
Tell us the count of thy prey of deer, and what cattleherds thou hast harried.

· · · · ·

"I have hunted no deer since yester year, I have
harried no neighbour's cattle,
I have wooed no love, I have joined no game, save
the kingly game of battle;
The Danes were my prey by night and day, in their
forts of hill and hollow,
And I come from the desert-lands alone, since none
are alive to follow.
Some were slain on the plundered plain, and some in
the midnight marching;
Some were lost in the winter floods, and some by the
fever parching;
Some have perished by wounds of spears, and some
by the shafts of bowmen;
And some by hunger and some by thirst, and all are
dead; but they slaughtered first
　　　Their tenfold more of their foemen."

The King impulsively offers him gifts for a reward,
but Brian declines them :

"I want no cattle from out your herds, no share of
your shining treasure;
But grant me now"—and he turned to look on the
listening warriors' faces—
"A hundred more of the clan Dal Cas, to follow me
over plain and pass :
To die, as fitteth the brave Dal Cas, at war with
the Outland races."

It must not be supposed, however, that these
poets are working solely upon romantic themes,

more or less in the epic manner. On the contrary,
direct treatment of the saga is declining, even with
the poets who, like those we have named, were
formerly preoccupied with it. Mr Cousins' volume
of 1915 is sharply symptomatic of the change.
Subjects of more social and more immediate interest
are engaging attention, and legendary material is
passing into a phase of allusion and symbol. Con-
currently, there is a development of the pure lyric
which gives great promise, being sound and
sweet and vigorous. It has all the signs of
vitality, drawing its inspiration directly from
life, keeping close to the earth, as it were, and
often dealing with the large and simple things of
existence.

One may not make too precise a claim here for
affiliation with the literary revival ; but observing
the movement broadly, it would appear that this
is its more popular manifestation, springing out
of the devotion to the old language of the country,
its folklore and the life of its people. That
current of the stream would touch actual
existence much more closely than æsthetic or
academic study ; and while one might regard Lady
Gregory and Mr Yeats as the pioneers of the
movement on the specifically literary side, on the
other hand there are Dr Hyde, A. E., and others,

whose influence must have counted largely in these new lyrics of life.

There are about half a dozen poets who are making these sweet, fresh songs. They have not published very much, but that follows from the nature of the medium in which they are working. Lyrical rapture is brief, and the form of its expression correspondingly small. Very seldom can it be sustained so long and so keenly as, for example, in Mr Stephens' " Prelude and a Song," for the wise poet accepts the natural limits of inspiration and technique. But this little group does not, of course, include all the Irish lyrists. The poets whom we may describe as literary—who have, at any rate, the more obvious connexion with the revival— have made beautiful lyrics too. But they are sharply contrasted in subject or style, or both, with those others. Thus we may take a " Spring Rondel " by Mr Cousins, which is supposed to be sung by a starling :

> I clink my castanet,
>   And beat my little drum ;
>   For spring at last has come,
> And on my parapet
> Of chestnut, gummy-wet,
>   Where bees begin to hum,
> I clink my castanet,
>   And beat my little drum.

An Irish Group

" Spring goes," you say, " suns set."
　　　So be it ! Why be glum ?
　　　Enough, the spring has come ;
　　And without fear or fret
　　I clink my castanet,
　　　And beat my little drum.

The lyrical virtues of that need no emphasis :
the quick, true reflection of a mood : the lightness
of touch and grace of expression. It is, however,
mainly by qualities of form that one is delighted
here—the art's the thing. To make a rondel at all
seems an achievement ; and to make it so daintily,
with playful fancy and feeling caught to the nicest
shade, almost compels wonder. But that is characteristic of the kind of verse of which I am
speaking, another aspect of which may be seen in
a captivating fragment which has been translated
by this poet from the Irish of some period before
the tenth century. It is called " The Student " ; and
to find the like of it, with its combined love of
nature and of learning, one must seek a certain
' Clerk of Oxenford ' and endow him with the
spirit of his own springtime poet—

　　　High on my hedge of bush and tree
　　　A blackbird sings his song to me,
　　　And far above my linèd book
　　　I hear the voice of wren and rook.

Contemporary Poets

From the bush-top, in garb of grey,
The cuckoo calls the hours of day.
Right well do I—God send me good !—
Set down my thoughts within the wood.

It is not often that these poets are occupied
with " Modern Movements," wherein they differ
from their English contemporaries. For that
reason, it is the more significant that one public
question has moved them deeply. Thus we find
Miss Mitchell writing of womanhood :

Oh, what to us your little slights and scorns,
You who dethrone us with a careless breath.
God made us awful queens of birth and death,
And set upon our brows His crown of thorns.

And Miss Gore-Booth, thinking of the sheltered
ignorance of many of the women who opposed the
suffrage for their sex, makes a little parable :

The princess in her world-old tower pined
A prisoner, brazen-caged, without a gleam
Of sunlight, or a windowful of wind ;
She lived but in a long lamp-lighted dream.

They brought her forth at last when she was old ;
The sunlight on her blanchèd hair was shed
Too late to turn its silver into gold.
" Ah, shield me from this brazen glare ! " she said.

An Irish Group

Mr Cousins, too, has several noble sonnets on the theme, from which we may select part of the one called " To the Suffragettes " :

> Who sets her shoulder to the Cross of Christ,
> Lo ! she shall wear sharp scorn upon her brow
> And she whose hand is put to Freedom's plough
> May not with sleek Expediency make tryst :
>
> .   .   .   .   .
>
> O fateful heralds, charged with Time's decree,
> Whose feet with doom have compassed Error's wall ;
> Whose lips have blown the trump of Destiny
> Till ancient thrones are shaking toward their fall ;
> Shout ! for the Lord hath given to you the free
> New age that comes with great new hope to all.

The main point of contrast, in turning to the more ' popular ' lyrics, is their simplicity. It is a difference of manner as well as of material. You will not find in this verse either an elaborate metrical form, or the treatment of questions such as that which we have just noted. Those things belong to a more complex condition, both of life and of letters, than that which is reflected here. And if such a contrast always implied separation in time, we could believe ourselves to be in a different epoch—a younger and more ingenuous age. But that, of course, by no means follows. Even if we regard it as figured by a kind of separation in space, with town and university on the one hand and the broad land and toiling people on the other, it is still too arbitrary and, moreover, it is incomplete. No room is found for the wanderers in neutral territory.

The contrast is rather like that between the newer English poetry and the old. It is indicative of a current of thought which is running throughout Europe, and which may be observed in England, stimulating the more vital work of contemporary poets. That, crudely stated, is a perception of the value of life—of the whole of life, sense and spirit, heart and brain and soul. As the poet is seized by it, he is carried into a larger and more vivid world, one of manifold significance and beauty which he had never before perceived. He grasps eagerly at *all* the stuff of existence, persistently seeks his inspiration in life instead of in literature, and having rejected the artifice of ·conventional terminology, begins to create a new kind of poetry.

Now that undercurrent is not visible in a superficial glance at this Irish poetry. Even native critics seem to have missed it, or tend to refer it to anything rather than to the whole movement of the national mind towards reality. But that is not surprising, indeed. For the limpidity of these lyrics is quite untroubled; they are innocent of

164

An Irish Group

ulterior purpose, and free from the least chill of philosophical questioning into origins or ends. The impulse out of which they came is instinctive : their very art, at least in the selection of themes, is spontaneous. An excellent example is the whole volume by Mr Joseph Campbell called *The Mountainy Singer*. He has another, *Irishry*, but although that is very interesting in its studies of Irish life, it is not so good as poetry, nor is it so apt to our present purpose, because a tinge of self-consciousness has crept into it. Let us take, however, the piece which gives its name to the first of these two books :

> I am the mountainy singer—
> The voice of the peasant's dream,
> The cry of the wind on the wooded hill,
> The leap of the fish in the stream.
>
> Quiet and love I sing—
> The carn on the mountain crest,
> The cailin in her lover's arms,
> The child at its mother's breast.
>
> . . . . .
>
> Sorrow and death I sing—
> The canker come on the corn,
> The fisher lost in the mountain loch,
> The cry at the mouth of morn.

Contemporary Poets

> No other life I sing,
> For I am sprung of the stock
> That broke the hilly land for bread,
> And built the nest in the rock !

That comes directly out of life, and the confidence and sincerity of it are a result. Thus the Irish poet also follows the impulse towards familiar human experience which is prompting his English contemporary. And partly because of his loyalty to himself ; partly because this poet happens to be in touch with the land—quite literally the oldest and commonest thing of all, except the sea —there comes into his poetry a sense of natural dignity and strength. His themes are simple and touched with universal significance. Thus there is the song of ploughing :

> I will go with my father a-ploughing
> To the green field by the sea,
> And the rooks and the crows and the seagulls
> Will come flocking after me.
> I will sing to the patient horses
> With the lark in the white of the air,
> And my father will sing the plough-song
> That blesses the cleaving share.

One finds, too, a song of reaping, and one of winter, and one of night.

There is a love-song, pretty and tender, and

An Irish Group

fresh with the suggestion of breezes and blue skies,
which begins like this :

> My little dark love is a wineberry,
> As swarth and as sweet, I hold ;
> But as the dew on the wineberry
> Her heart is a-cold.

There is a piece, in *Irishry*, which tells of the
wonder of childhood, and another in the same book
which reverently touches the thought of motherhood and old age :

> As a white candle
> In a holy place,
> So is the beauty
> Of an aged face.

> As the spent radiance
> Of the winter sun,
> So is a woman
> When her travail done.

> Her brood gone from her,
> And her thoughts as still
> As the waters
> Under a ruined mill.

So we might turn from one to another of these
old and ever-new themes : not alone in this poet's
work, but also in that of Mr Padraic Colum, whom
he resembles. We shall notice in their music a

characteristic harmony. It is a blending of three diverse elements : the individual, the national, and the universal. One would expect a discord sometimes ; but the measure of the success of this verse is that it contrives to be, at one and the same time, specifically lyrical (and therefore a reflection of personality), definitely Irish, and completely human. Most of the poems will illustrate this, but for an obvious example take this one by Mr Campbell :

> I met a walking-man ;
> His head was old and grey.
> I gave him what I had
> To crutch him on his way.
> The man was Mary's Son, I'll swear ;
> A glory trembled in his hair !
>
> And since that blessed day
> I've never known the pinch :
> I plough a broad townland,
> And dig a river-inch ;
> And on my hearth the fire is bright
> For all that walk by day or night.

If one found that on a bit of torn paper in the wilds of Africa, one would know it for unquestionable Irish. There are half a dozen signs, but the spirit of the last two lines is enough. The element of personality is there, too ; clearly visible in tone and choice of words to those who know the poet's work a little. But stronger than all is the human note, with all that it implies of man's need of religion, his incorrigible habit of making God in his own image, and the half comical, half pathetic materialism of his faith.

There are, of course, some occasions when the blending is unequal : when one or other of the three elements, usually that of national feeling, weighs down the balance. But, on the other hand, there are many pieces in which it is very intimate and subtle. Then it follows that the poet is at his best, for he has forgotten the immediacy of self and country and the world of men and things in the joy of singing. Of such is this " Cradle Song " by Mr Colum :

> O, men from the fields !
> Come softly within.
> Tread softly, softly,
> O ! men coming in.
>
> Mavourneen is going
> From me and from you,
> To Mary, the Mother,
> Whose mantle is blue !
>
> From reek of the smoke
> And cold of the floor,
> And the peering of things
> Across the half-door.

Contemporary Poets

O, men from the fields !
Soft, softly come thro'.
Mary puts round him
Her mantle of blue.

Such also is Mr Colum's " Ballad Maker," from which I quote the first and last stanzas :

Once I loved a maiden fair,
Over the hills and far away.
Lands she had and lovers to spare,
Over the hills and far away.
And I was stooped and troubled sore,
And my face was pale, and the coat I wore
Was thin as my supper the night before.
Over the hills and far away.

.   .   .   .   .

To-morrow, Mavourneen a sleeveen weds,
Over the hills and far away ;
With corn in haggard and cattle in shed,
Over the hills and far away.
And I who have lost her—the dear, the rare,
Well, I got me this ballad to sing at the fair,
'Twill bring enough money to drown my care,
Over the hills and far away.

It is an arresting fact, however, that the spirit of nationality is strong in the work of these poets. True, one may distinguish between a national sense, keen and directly expressed, and the almost

170

subconscious influence of race. The first is a theme deliberately chosen by the poet and variously treated by him. It is a conscious and direct expression—of aspiration or regret. Racial influence is something deeper and more constant : something, too, which quite confounds the sceptic on this particular subject. Whether from inheritance or environment, it has 'bred true' in these poets ; and it will be found to pervade their work like an atmosphere. It belongs inalienably to themselves : it is of the essence of their genius, and it is revealed everywhere, in little things as in great, in cadency and idiom as well as in an attitude to life and a certain range of ideas.

But though we may make the distinction, it will hardly do to disengage the strands, because they are so closely bound together. We may only note the predominance of one or the other, with an occasional complete and perfect combination. Perhaps the work in which they are least obvious is the slim volume of Miss Ella Young. But, even here, and choosing two poems where the artistic instinct has completely subdued its material, we shall find some of the signs that we are looking for ; and not altogether *because* we are looking for them. Thus a sonnet, called "The Virgin Mother," suggests its origin in its very title and, moreover, it is occupied with a thought of death and a sense of blissful quietude which are familiar in Irish poetry.

> Now Day's worn out, and Dusk has claimed a share
> Of earth and sky and all the things that be,
> I lay my tired head against your knee,
> And feel your fingers smooth my tangled hair.
> I loved you once, when I had heart to dare,
> And sought you over many a land and sea ;
> Yet all the while you waited here for me
> In a sweet stillness shut away from care.
> I have no longing now, no dreams of bliss.
> But drowsed in peace through the soft gloom I wait
> Until the stars be kindled by God's breath ;
> For then you'll bend above me with the kiss
> Earth's children long for when the hour grows late,
> Mother of Consolation, Sovereign Death.

In the blank-verse piece called "Twilight" it is again the title which conveys the direct sign of affinity, but it will also be found to lurk in every line :

> The sky is silver-pale with just one star,
> One lonely wanderer from the shining host
> Of Night's companions. Through the drowsy woods
> The shadows creep and touch with quietness
> The curling fern-heads and the ancient trees.
> The sea is all a-glimmer with faint lights
> That change and move as if the unseen prow
> Of Niamh's galley cleft its waveless floor,

An Irish Group

And Niamh stood there with the magic token,
The apple-branch with silver singing leaves.
The wind has stolen away as though it feared
To stir the fringes of her faery mantle
Dream-woven in the Land of Heart's Desire,
And all the world is hushed as though she called
Ossian again, and no one answered her.

Now that, in inspiration and imagery, is very
clearly derived from native legendary sources. But
no one would expect to find in such work a direct
expression of national feeling. The backward-
looking poet, the one who is drawn instinctively
to old themes and times, has not usually the temper
for politics, even on the higher plane. Or if he
have, he will make a rigid separation in style and
treatment between his poetry in the two kinds.
Thus Miss Milligan sharply differentiates her lays
on heroic subjects from her lyrics. The lays try
to catch the spirit of the age out of which the
stories came. The lyrics, as lyrics should, reflect
no other spirit than the poet's own. The lays are
somewhat strict in form : they are in a brisk narrative style, with a swinging rhythm and plenty of
vigour. The songs, depending on varying sense
impressions and fluctuating emotion, are more
irregular as to form and, at the same time, stronger
in their appeal to human sympathy. It is in them

that the poet is able to express the passionate love
of country which, superimposed on a deep sense of
Ireland's melancholy history and an intense longing
for freedom, is the birthright of so many Irish poets.
One would like to quote entire the lovely " Song of
Freedom," in which the poet hears in wind and wave
and brook a joyous prophecy.   But here is the last
stanza :

> To Ara of Connacht's isles,
> As I went sailing o'er the sea,
> The wind's word, the brook's word,
> The wave's word, was plain to me—
> " *As we are, though she is not*
> *As we are, shall Banba be—*
> *There is no King can rule the wind*
> *There is no fetter for the sea.*"

More beautiful and significant, perhaps, is a
fragment from " There Were Trees in Tir-Conal " :

> Fallen in Erin are all those leafy forests ;
> The oaks lie buried under bogland mould ;
> Only in legends dim are they remembered,
> Only in ancient books their fame is told.
> But seers, who dream of times to come, have promised
> Forests shall rise again where perished these ;
> And of this desolate land it shall be spoken,
> " In Tir-Conal of the territories there are trees."

The prophetic figure there, of course, is symbolical ;
but thinking of the basis it has in fact—of the schemes

which are afoot in the Isle for afforestation—one cannot help wondering whether it was consciously suggested by them. Not that there need be the slightest relation, of course. The poetical soul will often take a leap in the dark and reach a shining summit long before the careful people who travel by daylight along beaten tracks are half way up the hill. Still, there is proof that this group of writers is keenly interested in the question of the land and the organized effort to reclaim it. It is the more practical form of their patriotism, and the sign by which one knows it for something more than a sentiment. It is a deeply rooted and reasoned sense that the well-being of a nation, and therefore its strength and greatness, come ultimately from the soil and depend upon the close and faithful relation of the people to it. That surely is the conviction which underlies the work of a poet like Mr Padraic Colum, and particularly such a piece as his " Plougher " :

Sunset and silence ! A man : around him earth savage,
    earth broken ;
Beside him two horses—a plough !

Earth savage, earth broken, the brutes, the dawn-man
    there in the sunset,
And the Plough that is twin to the Sword, that is
    founder of cities !

.   .   .   .   .

Slowly the darkness falls, the broken lands blend with
the savage ;
The brute-tamer stands by the brutes, a head's breadth
only above them.

A head's breadth? Ay, but therein is hell's depth, and
the height up to heaven,
And the thrones of the gods and their halls, their
chariots, purples and splendours.

In closing this study we must take a glance at
two recent volumes, one containing the poetry of
Mr Seumas O'Sullivan and the other Mr Cousins'
latest work. Mr O'Sullivan's book is curiously
interesting, inasmuch as it unites certain contrasted
qualities which are found separately in the other
poets we have been considering. Thus, this poet
is ' literary ' in the sense of knowing and loving
good books, in his familiarity with the old literature
of his country, and in the fact that those things
have had a palpable influence upon him. Tem-
peramentally he is an artist, with the artistic
instinct to subordinate everything to the beauty of
his work. But he is also like the more ' popular '
poets in his lyrical gift and in the range and depth
of his sympathies ; so that his collected poems of
1912 may be regarded in some degree as an epitome
of modern Irish poetry. There you will find work
which indicates that its author might have lived
very happily in a visionary world of æsthetic delight.

176

An Irish Group

He might have chosen always to sing about gods
and heroes and fair ladies with " white hands,
foam-frail." But, just as clearly, you will see that
he has been aroused from dreams. Vanishing rem-
nants of them are perceptible in such a piece as
" The Twilight People "; and when they are gone,
in that serene moment before complete awakening,
when the light is growing and the birds call and a
fresh air blows, you get a piece like " Praise ":

> Dear, they are praising your beauty,
> The grass and the sky :
> The sky in a silence of wonder,
> The grass in a sigh.
>
> I too would sing for your praising,
> Dearest, had I
> Speech as the whispering grass,
> Or the silent sky.
>
> These have an art for the praising
> Beauty so high.
> Sweet, you are praised in a silence,
> Sung in a sigh.

Then comes the awakening, sudden and sharp,
with an impulse to spring out and away from those
old dreams of myth and romance :

> Bundle the gods away :
> Richer than Danaan gold,
> The whisper of leaves in the rain,
> The secrets the wet hills hold.

Contemporary Poets

A spiritual adventure seems to be implied in the poem from which this fragment is taken, similar to that which Mr Cousins has recorded in " Straight and Crooked." It is the call of reality : the impulse which is drawing the poetic spirit closer and closer to life, and bidding it seek inspiration in common human experience. Thus when we find Mr O'Sullivan invoking the vision of earth we soon discover that ' earth ' means something more to him than ' countryside '—the beauty of Nature and of pastoral existence. It comprises also towns and crowded streets and busy people ; and it seems to mean ultimately any aspect of human existence which has the power to induce poetic ecstasy. An infinitely wider range is thus open to the poet, and though this little volume does not pretend to cover any large part of it, there are pieces which suggest its almost boundless possibility. Let us put two of them together. The first, " A Piper," describes a little street scene :

> A Piper in the streets to-day
> Set up, and tuned, and started to play,
> And away, away, away on the tide
> Of his music we started ; on every side
> Doors and windows were opened wide,
> And men left down their work and came,
> And women with petticoats coloured like flame

An Irish Group

And little bare feet that were blue with cold,
Went dancing back to the age of gold,
And all the world went gay, went gay,
For half an hour in the street to-day.

That expresses the rapture which is evoked
directly by the touch of the actual. The next
piece, a fragment from " A Madonna," is equally
characteristic; but its inspiration came through
another art, a picture by Beatrice Elvery :

Draw nigh, O foolish worshippers who mock
With pious woe of sainted imagery
The kingly-human presence of your God.
Draw near, and with new reverence gaze on her.
See you, these hands have toiled, these feet have trod
In all a woman's business ; bend the knee.
For this of very certainty is she
Ordained of heavenly hierarchies to rock
The cradle of the infant carpenter.

Under the diverse sources from which such poems
immediately spring, there flows the current which
is fertilizing, in greater or less degree, much modern
poetry. It has been running strongly in England
for some years, but hitherto Irish poets have hardly
seemed conscious of it, though it was visibly moving
them. Its presence there was mainly felt in the
silence of Mr Yeats, whose lovely romanticism
fell dumb at its touch. But, significantly, the

179

latest poetic utterance of Ireland is a cry of complete realization. It has remained for Mr Cousins to hear the call of his age more consciously than his compatriots ; and it is left to him, in grace and courage, to declare it :

> . . . From a sleep I emerge. I am clothed again
>   with this woven vesture of laws ;
> But I am not, and never again shall be the man that
>   I was.
> At the zenith of life I am born again, I begin.
> Know ye, I am awake, outside and within.
> I have heard, I have seen, I have known ; I feel the
>   bite of this shackle of place and name,
> And nothing can be the same.
>
> .   .   .   .   .
>
> I have sent three shouts of freedom along the wind.
> I have struck one hand of kinship in the hands of
>   Gods, and one in the hands of women and men.
> I am awake.   I shall never sleep again.

Rose Macaulay

THERE is one small volume of poems by Miss Macaulay, called *The Two Blind Countries*. It is curiously interesting, since it may be regarded as the testament of mysticism for the year of its appearance, nineteen hundred and fourteen. That is, indeed, the most important fact about it ; though no one need begin to fear that he is to be fobbed off with inferior poetry on that account. For the truth is that the artistic value of this work is almost, if not quite, equal to the exceptional power of abstraction that it evinces. Poetry has really been achieved here, extremely individual in manner and in matter, and of a high order of beauty.

One is compelled, however, though one may a little regret the compulsion, to start from the fact of the poet's mystical tendency. Not that she would mind, presumably ; the title of her book is an avowal, clear enough at a second glance, of its point of view. But the reader has an instinct, in which the mere interpreter but follows him, to accept a poem first as art rather than thought ; and if he examine it at all, to begin with what may be called its concrete beauty. I will not say that the order is reversed in the case of Miss

Macaulay's poetry, since that would·be to accuse
her of an artistic crime of which she is emphatically
not guilty. But it is significant that the greater
number of pieces in this book impress the mind
with the idea they convey, simultaneously with the
sounds in which it is expressed. And as the idea
is generally adventurous, and sometimes fantastic,
it is that which arrests the reader and on which he
lingers, at any rate long enough to discover its
originality.

But though the mystical element of the work is
suggested in its very title, one discovers almost as
early that it is mysticism of a new kind. It belongs
inalienably to this poet and is unmistakably of this
age. The world of matter, this jolly place of light
and air and colour and human faces, is vividly
apprehended; but it is seen by the poet to be ringed
round by another realm which, though unsub-
stantial, is no less real. Indeed, so strong is her
consciousness of that other realm, and its presence
so insistently felt, that sometimes she is not sure
to which of the two she really belongs. In the
first poem of· the book, using the fictive 'he' as
its subject, she indicates her attitude to that region
beyond sense. In the physical world, this 'blind
land' of 'shadows and droll shapes,' the soul is
an alien wanderer. Constantly it hears a 'clamorous

Rose Macaulay

whisper ' from the other side of the door of sense, coming from the

> . . . muffled speech
>> Of a world of folk.

But no cry can reach those others : no clear sight can be had of them, and no intelligible word of theirs can come back.

> Only through a crack in the door's blind face
>> He would reach a thieving hand,
> To draw some clue to his own strange place
>> From the other land.

> But his closed hand came back emptily,
>> As a dream drops from him who wakes ;
> And naught might he know but how a muffled sea
>> In whispers breaks.

> .   .   .   .   .

> On either side of a gray barrier
>> The two blind countries lie ;
> But he knew not which held him prisoner,
>> Nor yet know I.

This poem may be said to state the theme of the whole book. It would appear, however, that in the difficult feat of giving form to thought so intangible, the poet has attained here a detachment which is almost cold. But it would be unfair to judge her manner of expression from one poem ; and it happens that there is another piece, built

183

upon a similar theme, which is much more characteristic. It is called "Foregrounds," and here again the two countries are conceived as bordering upon each other, inter-penetrating, but sharply contrasted as night from day. The contrast favours a more vivid setting, and the subjective treatment, admitting deeper emotion, infuses a warmth that "The Alien" lacked. Moreover, the psychic region is here called simply the *dream-country*; and, presented in the delicate suggestion of a moonlit night, it hints only at the lure of the mystery, and nothing of its terror. Throughout the poem, too, runs exuberant joy in common earthly things, in the beauty of nature and in human feeling; and this is followed, in the closing lines of each stanza, by an afterthought and a touch of melancholy: reflection coming, in the most natural way, close upon the heels of emotion. Thus the first lines revel in the glory of spring; and then, almost audibly, the tone drops to the lower level of one who perceives that glory as the veil of something beyond it.

> The pleasant ditch is a milky way,
>   So alight with stars it is,
> And over it breaks, like pale sea-spray,
> The laughing cataract of the may
>   In luminous harmonies.

Rose Macaulay

(Cloak with a flower-wrought veil
The face of the dream-country.
The fields of the moon are kind, are pale,
And quiet is she.)

Thus, too, in the third stanza, the recurrent idea of an alien spirit is caught into imagery which glows with light and colour : imagery so simple and sensuous as almost to mock abstraction and quite to disguise it ; but bearing at its heart the essence of a philosophy. Again the soul is imagined as standing at the barrier of the two countries, when reality has melted to an apparition and the sense of that other realm has grown acute. Bereft of the comfortable earth, but powerless still to enter the dream-country : standing lonely and fearful at the cold verge of the mystic region, the spirit will seek to draw about it the garment of appearance :

I will weave, of the clear clean shapes of things,
    A curtain to shelter me ;
I will paint it with kingcups and sunrisings,
And glints of blue for the swallow's wings,
    And green for the apple-tree.
        (Oh, a whisper has pierced the veil
        Out of the dream-country,
As a wind moans in the straining sail
        Of a ship lost at sea.)

In reading this poem, and in others too, one is

Contemporary Poets

struck by the hold which the real world has upon
our poet. It is a surprising fact in one of so speculative a turn, and is the clearest sign by which we
recognize her work as of our time and no other.
Her thought may be projected very far, but her
feet are generally upon solid ground. Perhaps I
ought rather to say that they are always there ;
for it is more than probable that bed-rock may
exist in two or three poems where I have been
unable to get down to it. It is in any case safe to
say that a sense of reality—shown in human sympathy and tenderness for lowly creatures, in love
of nature and perception of beauty, in truth to
fact, in a touch of shrewd insight and a sense of
humour bred of the habit of detachment—is very
strong. I do not suggest that these qualities are
everywhere apparent. By their nature they are
such as could not often enter into the framework
of poems so subtly wrought. But they are woven
into the texture of the poet's mentality, and have
even directed its method. So that, remote as may
be the idea upon which she is working, it is generally
brought within the range of sight ; and, intangible
though it may seem, it is given definite and charming
shape. And if there were not one obvious proof
of this steady anchorage, we might have happy
assurance of it in the clarity and precision of her

186

thought. But fortunately there *is* obvious proof. There is, for instance, this delicious passage in the poem from which I have just quoted, surely proving a kinship with our own 'blind country' as close as with that other and something dearer :

> The jolly donkeys that love me well
>   Nuzzle with thistly lips ;
> The harebell is song made visible,
> The dandelion's lamp a miracle,
>   When the day's lamp dips and dips.

There are, too, a sonnet called " Cards " and the very beautiful longer poem, " Summons," in which the glow of human love makes of the supernatural a mere shadow. In " Cards " the scene is a ' dim lily-illumined garden,' and four people are playing there by candle light. But out of the darkness which rings the circle of flickering light sinister things creep, menacing the frail life of one of the players.

> But, like swords clashing, my love on their hate
> Struck sharp, and drove, and pushed. . . . Grimly
>   round you
> Fought we that fight, they pressing passionate
> Into the lit circle which called and drew
> Shadows and moths of night. . . . I held the gate.
> You said, " Our game," more truly than you knew.

Again we perceive this sense of reality in the

187

humour of a poem like " St Mark's Day " or
" Three." It is a quality hearty and cheery in the
way of one who knows all the facts, but has reckoned
with them and can afford to laugh. It has a depth
of tone unexpected in an artist whose natural
impulse seems to be towards delicate line and
neutral tint ; and there is a tang of salt in it which
one suspects of having been added of intent—as a
quite superfluous preservative against sentimentality.
" St Mark's Day " is very illuminating in this
respect, and in the bracing sanity under which
mere superstition wilts. The village girl, teased
by neighbours into believing that her spectre was
seen the night before and that therefore she must
die within the year, is a genuine bit of rustic
humanity. No pòrtrait of her is given ; but in two
or three strong touches she stands before us,
plump, rosy and rather stupid ; hale enough to
live her fourscore years, but sobbing in foolish
fright as her sturdy arms peg the wet linen upon
the line.

> I laughed at her over the sticky larch fence,
>   And said, " Who's down-hearted, Dolly ? "
>
> And Dolly sobbed at me, " They saw you, too ! "
>   (And so the liars said they had,
> Though I've not wasted paper nor rhymes telling you),
>   And, " Well," said I, " *I'm* not sad."

Rose Macaulay

" But since you and me must die within the year,
    What if we went together
To make cowslip balls in the fields, and hear
    The blackbirds whistling to the weather ? "

So in the water-fields till blue mists rose
    We loitered, Dolly and I,
And pulled wet kingcups where the cold brook
    goes,
    And when we've done living, we'll die.

The realism of that goes deeper than its technique, and is a notable weapon in the hands of such an idealist.   But in " Three," another humorous poem, something more surprising has been accomplished.   " St Mark's Day " is a bit of pure comedy, and might have been written by a poet for whom *one* ' blind country ' was the beginning and end of all experience.   That is to say, it is interesting as proof of a healthy grasp on the real world.   But in " Three," though reality is no less strong, with art matching it in bold and vigorous strokes, there is achieved an uncanny sense of the supernatural.   Thus, despite certain comic touches, and a sunny noonday scene, the consciousness grows first of a ghostly presence (in the accepted sense of the spirit of one dead) ; and then of an obscure but disturbing awareness of a hidden life close at hand which most people have experienced at some time or other. The poet has sketched these two of her "Three" with an equally light hand, smiling amusedly, as it were, at her own fantasy; but she has differentiated them quite clearly. For the true ghost, conjured out of the stuff of memory, association and the influence of locality, is a creature of pure imagination. He is not so much described as suggested, and only dimly felt. There is a stanza devoted to the Cambridge landscape in the hot noon, and then—

> In the long grass and tall nettles
>   I lay abed,
> With hawthorn and bryony
>   Tangled o'erhead.
> And I was alone with Hobson,
>   Two centuries dead.

> Hidden by sprawling brambles
>   The Nine Waters were;
> From a chalky bed they bubbled up,
>   Clean, green, and fair.
> And I was alone with Hobson,
>   Whose ghost walks there.

But it seems that the poet is not alone with the pleasant ghost of the old university carrier. There

Rose Macaulay

is a third presence near, hidden and silent, but malign; and the stanzas in which this secret presence grows to realization are remarkably done. They illustrate this poet's ability to create illusion out of mere scraps of material, and those of a commonplace kind; and they rely for their verbal effect upon the homeliest words. Yet the impression of an intangible something is so strong, that when the very real head of the tramp appears the contrast provokes a sudden laugh at its absurdity.

> And something yawned, and from the
> > grass
> > A head upreared;
> And I was not alone with Hobson,
> > For at me leered
> A great, gaunt, greasy tramp
> > With a golden beard.
>
> He had a beard like a dandelion,
> > And I had none;
> He had tea in a beer-bottle,
> > Warm with the sun;
> He had pie in a paper bag,
> > Not yet begun.

The vigorous handling of that passage, and its comical actuality, make an excellent foil to the subtler method of presenting the two spirits, living and dead. And the poem as a whole may be said to reflect the two chief elements in this work. It is true that in a more characteristic piece the ideal will prevail over the real. And consequently, imagination will there be found to weave finer strands, while thought goes much further afield. Thus, in " Crying for the Moon," and in " The Thief," one may follow the idea very far ; and in both poems we move in the pale light and dim shadow where mystery is evoked at a hint. Never, I think, was there such an eerie dawn as that in " The Thief " ; yet never was orchard-joy more keenly realized—

> He stood at the world's secret heart
>   In the haze-wrapt mystery ;
> And fat pears, mellow on the lip,
>   He supped like a honey-bee ;
> But the apples he crunched with sharp
>   white teeth
>   Were pungent, like the sea.

Probably it is in work like this, where both blind countries find expression, that Miss Macaulay is most successful. But when she gives imagination licence to wander alone in the ideal region, it occasionally seems to go out of sight and sound

Rose Macaulay

of the good earth. That happens in " Completion,"
a poem which is frankly mystical in theme, symbolism and terminology. There is not a touch of
reality in it; and neither its fine strange music,
nor glowing colour, nor certain perfect phrases,
nor the language, at once rich and tender and
strong, can make it more than the opalescent
wraith of a poem. But perhaps that is just what
the author intended it to be!

In any case " Completion " does correspond to,
and daintily express, the mystical strain which is
dominant in this work. It is, however, the extreme
example of it. It stands at the opposite pole from
" St Mark's Day," and antithetical to that, it might
have been written by a mystic for whom the material
world was virtually nothing. Moreover, it might
belong to almost any time, or not to time at all;
whereas the mysticism of the book as a whole is
peculiarly that of its own author and its own day.
It is individual—a thing of this poet's personality
and no other—in the evidence of a finely sensitive
spirit, of an acute gift of vision, imaginative power
which ranges far and a fine capacity for abstract
thought. But all these qualities are sweetly controlled by a humane temper that has been nurtured
on realities.

Hence comes a duality in which it is, perhaps,

193

Contemporary Poets

not too fanciful to see a feature of contemporary thought—intensely interested in the region of ideas, but frankly claiming the material world as the basis and starting-point of all its speculation. One might put it colloquially (though without the implied reproach) as making the best of both worlds: humanity recognizing an honourable kinship with matter, but reaching out continually after the larger existence which it confidently believes to be latent in the physical world itself.

A voice may be raised to protest that that is too vaguely generalized; and if so, the protestant may turn for more precise evidence to such poems as "Trinity Sunday" and "The Devourers." There he will perceive, after a moment's reflection, the store of modern knowledge—of actual data—which has been assimilated to the mystical element here. Let him consider, for example, the first two stanzas of "The Devourers," and other similar passages:

> Cambridge town is a beleaguered city;
>   For south and north, like a sea,
> There beat on its gates, without haste or pity,
>   The downs and the fen country.
>
> Cambridge towers, so old, so wise,
>   They were builded but yesterday,
> Watched by sleepy gray secret eyes
>   That smiled as at children's play.

Rose Macaulay

It is clear that the knowledge really has been assimilated—it is not a fragmentary or external thing. It is absorbed into the essence of the work and will not be found to mar its poetic values. But by a hint, a word, a turn of expression or a mental gesture, one can see that learning both scientific and humane (a significant union) has gone into the poetic crucible. There are signs which point to a whole system of philosophy : there is an historical sense, imaginatively handling the data of cosmic history ; and there are traces which lead down to a basis in geology and anthropology. Yet these elements are, as I said, perfectly fused : it would be difficult to disengage them. And inimical as they may seem to the very nature of mysticism, they are constrained by this poet to contribute to her vision of a world beyond sense.

From this point of view "Trinity Sunday" is the most important poem in the book. It records an experience which the mystic of another age would have called a revelation, and which he would have apprehended through the medium of religious emotion. But this poet attains to her ultimate vision through the phenomena of the real world, apprehended in terms of the ideal. The warm breath of Spring, rich with scent and sound of the teeming earth, stirs it to awakening. But though

195

she is walking in familiar Cambridge with, characteristically, the scene and time exactly placed : though friendly faces pass and cordial voices give a greeting, all that suddenly shrivels at the touch of the wild earth spirit. Space and time curl away in fold after fold ; and with them pass successive forms of strange life immensely remote. But even while reality thus terribly unfolds, it is perceived to be the *stuff of the world's live brain ;* to have existence only in idea.

> And the fens were not.   (For fens are dreams
>   Dreamt by a race long dead ;
> And the earth is naught, and the sun but seems :
>   And so those who know have said.)

Thus the facts of science have gone to the making of this poem, as well as the theories of an idealist philosophy.   It is through them both that imagination takes the forward leap.   But neither the one nor the other can avail to utter the revelation ; and even the poet's remarkable gift of expression can only suffice to suggest the awfulness of it.

> So veil beyond veil illimitably lifted :
>   And I saw the world's naked face,
> Before, reeling and baffled and blind, I drifted
>   Back within the bounds of space.

John Masefield

THERE is one sense at least in which Mr Masefield is the most important figure amongst contemporary poets. For he has won the popular ear, he has cast the poetic spell further than any of his compeers, and it has been given to him to lure the multitudinous reader of magazines—that wary host which is usually stampeded by the sight of a page of verse.

Now I know that there are cultured persons to whom this fact of uncritical appreciation is an offence, and to them a writer bent upon purely scientific criticism would be compelled to yield certain points. But they would be mainly on finicking questions, as an occasional lapse from fineness in thought or form, an incidental banality of word or phrase ; or a lack of delicate effects of rhyme and metre. And the whole business would amount in the end to little more than a petulant complaint ; an impertinent grumble that Mr Masefield happens to be himself and not, let us say, Mr Robert Bridges ; that his individual genius has carved its own channels and that, in effect, the music of the sea or the mountain torrent does not happen to be the same thing as the plash of a fountain in a valley.

But having no quarrel with this offending popularity: rejoicing in it rather, and the new army of poetry-readers which it has created; and believing it to be an authentic sign of the poetic spirit of our day, one is tempted to seek for the cause of it. Luckily, there is a poem called " Biography " which gives a clue and something more. It is a pæan of zest for life, of the intense joy in actual living which seems to be the dynamic of Mr Masefield's genius. There is, most conspicuous and significant, delight in beauty; a swift, keen, accurate response of sense to the external world, to sea and sky and hill, to field and flower. But there is fierce delight, too, in toil and danger, in strenuous action, in desperate struggle with wind and wave, in the supreme effort of physical power, in health and strength and skill and freedom and jollity; and above all, first, last and always, in ships. But there is delight no less in communion with humanity, in comradeship, in happy memories of kindred, in still happier mental kinships and intellectual affinities, in books, in ' glittering moments ' of spiritual perception, in the brooding sense of man's long history.

These are the ' golden instants and bright days ' which correctly spell his life, as this poet is careful to emphasize; and we perceive that the rapture which they inspire in him, the ardour with which he takes this sea of life, is of the essence of his poetry.

John Masefield

It is seen most clearly in the lyrics; and that is natural, since these are amongst his early work, and youth is the heyday of joy. It is found in nearly all of them, of course in varying degree, colouring substance and shaping form, evoking often a strong rhythm like a hearty voice that sings as it goes.

> So hey for the road, the west road, by mill and forge and fold,
> Scent of the fern and song of the lark by brook, and field, and wold;

Or again, in " Tewkesbury Road,"

> O, to feel the beat of the rain, and the homely smell of the earth,
> Is a tune for the blood to jig to, a joy past power of words;
> And the blessed green comely meadows are all a-ripple with mirth
> At the noise of the lambs at play and the dear wild cry of the birds.

And it rings in many songs of the sea, telling of its beauty or terror, its magic and mystery and hardship, its stately ships and tough sailormen and strange harbourages, its breath of romance sharply tingling with reality, its lure from which there is no escape—

> I must go down to the seas again, for the call of the running tide
> Is a wild call and a clear call that may not be denied;

And all I ask is a windy day with the white clouds
flying,
And the flung spray and the blown spume, and the
sea-gulls crying.

Under the wistfulness of that throbs the same zest
as that which finds expression in " Laugh and be
Merry " ; but the mood has become more buoyant—

Laugh and be merry, remember, better the world with
a song,
Better the world with a blow in the teeth of a wrong.
Laugh, for the time is brief, a thread the length of
a span.
Laugh and be proud to belong to the old proud
pageant of man.

Sometimes a minor key is struck, as in " Prayer ; "
but even here the joy is present, revealing itself
in sharp regret for the beloved things of earth. It
manifests itself in many ways, subtler or more
obvious ; but mainly I think in a questing, venturous
spirit which must always be daring and seeking
something beyond. Whether in the material world
or the spiritual, it is always the same—whether
it be sea-longing, or hunger for the City of God, or
a vague faring to an unknown bourne, or the eternal
quest for beauty. The poem called " The Seekers "
is beautifully apt in this regard. Simply, clearly,
directly, it expresses the alpha and omega of this
genius : the zest which is its driving force and the

aspiration, the tireless and ceaseless pursuit of an ideal, which is its objective.

> Not for us are content, and quiet, and peace of mind,
> For we go seeking a city that we shall never find.

> There is no solace on earth for us—for such as we—
> Who search for a hidden city that we shall never see.

There is the spirit of adventure, the eternal allure of romance, as old and as potent as poetry itself. And surely nothing is more engaging, nothing quicker and stronger and more universal in its appeal, than zest for life finding expression in this way. In these early lyrics its spontaneous and simple utterance is very winning ; but in the later narrative poems it is none the less present because, having grown a little older, it is a little more complex and not so obvious in its manifestation. Under these longer poems too runs the stream of joy, somewhat quieter now, perhaps, subdued by contemplation, brought to the test of actuality, shaping a different form through the conflict of human will, but still deep and strong, and, as in the earlier work, expressing its ultimate meaning through the spirit of high adventure.

Thus " The Widow in the Bye Street," which was the first written of these four narrative poems, is the adventure of motherhood. " Oh ! " will protest some member of the dainty legion which lives in terror of appearances, "it is a story of lust and murder!" But no; fundamentally, triumphantly, it is a tale of mother-love, venturing all for the child. Only superficially is it a tragedy of ungoverned desire and rage, made out of the incidence of character which we call destiny. The mother's spirit prevails over all that, and remains unconquerable. In " Daffodil Fields " there is the adventure of romantic passion. The " Everlasting Mercy," so obviously as hardly to need the comment, is the high adventure of the soul; and " Dauber," less clearly perhaps, though quite as certainly, is that too. But while in the first of these two poems the spirit's spark is struck into ' absolute human clay,' in " Dauber " it is burning already in the brain of an artist. Saul Kane, when his soul comes to birth at the touch of religion, puts off bestiality and rises to a joyful perception of the meaning of life. The Dauber, with that precious knowledge already shining within him, but twinned with another, the supreme and immortal glory of art, with his last breath cries holy defiance to the elements that snatch his life—*It will go on.*

But there is another reason for the popularity of this poet's work; and it also is deducible from the poem called " Biography." I mean the complete and robust humanity which is evinced there. One sees, of course, that this has a close relation with the zest that we have already noted; that it is indeed the root of that fine flower. But the balance of this personality—with power of action and of thought about equally poised, with the mystic and the humanitarian meeting half-way, with the ideal and the real twining and intertwining constantly, with sensuous and spiritual perception almost matched—determines the quality by which Mr Masefield's poems make so wide and direct an appeal. If reflectiveness were predominant, if the subjective element outran the keen dramatic sense, if the ideal were capable of easy victory over the material (it does conquer, but of that later), this would be poetry of a very different type. Whether it would be of a finer type it is idle to speculate, the point for the moment being that it would not command so large an audience. By just so far as specialization operated, the range would be made narrower.

It is this sense of humanity which wins; not only explicit, as, for example, in the deliberate choice of subject avowed once for all in the early poem called " Consecration "—

> The men of the tattered battalion which fights till
>   it dies,
> Dazed with the dust of the battle, the din and the cries,

·   ·   ·   ·   ·

Contemporary Poets

The sailor, the stoker of steamers, the man with
   the clout,
The chantyman bent at the halliards putting a tune
   to the shout,

.   .   .   .   .

Of the maimed, of the halt and the blind in the
   rain and the cold—
Of these shall my songs be fashioned, my tales be told.

There the poet is responding consciously to the
time-spirit : the awakening social sense which,
moving pitifully amongst bitter and ugly experience,
was to evoke the outer realism of his art. That, of
course, being passionately sincere, is a powerful influence. But stronger still is the unconscious force
of personality, this completeness of nature which in
" Biography " is seen as a rare union of powers that
are nevertheless the common heritage of humanity ;
and which is implicit everywhere in his work,
imbuing it with the compelling attraction of large
human sympathy.

Out of this arise the curiously contrasted elements
of Mr Masefield's poetry. For, as in life itself, and
particularly in life that is full and sound, there is
here a perpetual conflict between opposing forces.
It is, perhaps, the most prominent characteristic of
this work. It pervades it throughout, belongs to
its very essence and has moulded its form. It is, of

204

John Masefield

course, most readily apparent in the poet's art.
Here the battling forces of his genius, transferred to
the creatures whom he has created, have made these
narrative poems largely dramatic in form. Here,
too, we come upon a clash of realism with romance
and idyllic sweetness. That bald external realism
has found much disfavour with those who do not
or will not see its relation to the underlying reality.
And one observes that the critic who professes most
to dislike it hastens to quote the gaudiest example,
practically ignoring the many serene and gracious
passages.

But, putting aside the prejudice which has been
fostered by a conventional poetic language, this
realistic method does seem to conflict with certain
other characteristics of the work—with the essential
romance of the spirit of adventure, for instance.
There does at first glance appear to be a disturbing
lack of unity between that ardent, wistful and elusive
spirit, and the grim actuality here, of incident and
diction ; or, on the other hand, between the raw
material of this verse and its elaborate metrical form,
or its frequent passages of rare and delicate beauty.
But is it more than an appearance ? I think not.
I believe that the incongruity exists only in a canon
of poetical taste which is false to the extent that it
is based too narrowly. That canon has appro-

Contemporary Poets

priated romance to a certain order of themes and,
almost as exclusively, to a certain manner of expression. Most of our contemporary poets have cheer-
fully repudiated the convention so far as it governed
language ; building up, each for himself, a fresh,
rich, expressive idiom in which the magic of romance
is often vividly recreated. Some of them, and Mr
Masefield pre-eminently, have gone further. They
have perceived the potential romance of all life, and
have broken down the old limit which prescribed to
the poet only graceful figures and pseudo-heroic
themes. They have set themselves to express the
wonder and mystery, the ecstasy and exaltation
which inhere, however obscurely, in the lowliest
human existence.

Thus we have Saul Kane, the village wastrel of
"The Everlasting Mercy," glimpsing his heritage,
for a moment, in a lucid interval of a drunken orgy.
Suddenly, for a marvellous instant, he is made aware
of beauty, smitten into consciousness of himself
and a fugitive apprehension of reality.

> I opened window wide and leaned
> Out of that pigstye of the fiend
> And felt a cool wind go like grace
> About the sleeping market-place.
> The clock struck three, and sweetly, slow
> The bells chimed Holy, Holy, Holy ;
> .   .   .   .   .

206

John Masefield

And summat made me think of things.
How long those ticking clocks had gone
From church and chapel, on and on,
Ticking the time out, ticking slow
To men and girls who'd come and go,

.   .   .   .   .

And how a change had come.   And then
I thought, " You tick to different men."
What with the fight and what with drinking
And being awake alone there thinking,
My mind began to carp and tetter,
" If this life's all, the beasts are better."

The elements of that passage, and cumulatively
to its end, are genuinely romantic : the heightened
mood, the night setting of darkness and solemnity,
the wondering and regretful gaze into the past, and
the sense of eternal mystery.   So, too, though from
a very different aspect, is the amazing power of the
mad scene in this poem.   The fierce zest of it
courses along a flaming pathway and is as exhilarating
in its speed and vigour as any romantic masterpiece
in the older manner.   It is difficult to quote, in
justice to the author, from so closely woven a texture;
but there is a short passage which illustrates over
again the physical development that we have
already noted balancing mental and spiritual qualities in this genius.   It is the exultation of Kane in

his swiftness, as he rages through the streets with
a crowd toiling after him.

> The men who don't know to the root
> The joy of being swift of foot,
> Have never known divine and fresh
> The glory of the gift of flesh,
> Nor felt the feet exult, nor gone
> Along a dim road, on and on,
> Knowing again the bursting glows,
> The mating hare in April knows,
> Who tingles to the pads with mirth
> At being the swiftest thing on earth.
> O, if you want to know delight,
> Run naked in an autumn night,
> And laugh, as I laughed then. . . .

The sensuous ecstasy of that is as strongly contrasted with the pensiveness of the previous scene
at the window as it is with the gentle rhapsody
which follows the drunkard's conversion. Of that
rhapsody what can one say ? It is a piece about
which words seem inadequate, or totally futile.
Perhaps one comment may be made, however.
Reading it for the twentieth time, and marvelling
once more at the religious emotion which, in its naïve
sweetness and intensity is so strange an apparition
in our day, my mind flew, with a sudden sense of
enlightenment, back to Chaucer. At first, reflection
made the transition seem abrupt to absurdity ; but

the connexion had no doubt been helped sub-consciously by the apt fragment from Lydgate on the fly-leaf of this poem. Thence it was but a step to the large humanity, the sympathy and tolerance and generosity, the wide understanding bred of practical knowledge of men and affairs, of the father of poets. An actual likeness gleamed which was at the same time piquant and satisfying. For, first, it stimulated curiosity regarding the use by this poet of the Chaucerian rhyme-royal in three of these long poems. That evinces a leaning on traditional form rather curious in so independent an artist. And then it teased the mind with suggestions that led out of range—about mental affinities, and the different manifestations of the same type of genius, born into ages so far apart.

It is not, of course, a question of exact or direct comparison between, let us say, the *Canterbury Tales* and these narrative poems of the twentieth century. It is rather a matter of the spirit of the whole work, of the personality and its reaction to life, which satisfy one individual at least of a resemblance. Of course it is not easily susceptible of proof ; but there are passages from the two poets which in thought, feeling, and even manner of expression, will almost form a parallel. Consider this stanza from a minor poem of Chaucer,

a prayer to the Virgin in the quaint form of an
" A. B. C."

> Xristus, thy sone, that in this world alighte,
> Up-on the cros to suffre his passioun,
> And eek, that Longius his herte pighte,
> And made his herte blood to renne adoun ;
> And al was this for my salvacioun ;
> And I to him am fals and eek unkinde,
> And yit he wol not my dampnacioun—
> This thanke I you, socour of al mankinde.

The childlike faith of that, the quiet rapture
of adoration, the abandon and simple confidence,
are curiously matched by the following passage
from " The Everlasting Mercy." Saul Kane has
found his soul in the mystical re-birth of Christi-
anity, and dawn coming across the fields lightens
all his world with new significance.

> O Christ who holds the open gate,
> O Christ who drives the furrow straight,
> O Christ, the plough, O Christ, the laughter
> Of holy white birds flying after,
> Lo, all my heart's field red and torn,
> And Thou wilt bring the young green corn,
> The young green corn divinely springing,
> The young green corn for ever singing ;
> And when the field is fresh and fair
> Thy blessèd feet shall glitter there.
> And we will walk the weeded field,
> And tell the golden harvest's yield,

John Masefield

The corn that makes the holy bread
By which the soul of man is fed,
The holy bread, the food unpriced,
Thy everlasting mercy, Christ.

So one might go on to contrast the several characteristics of this poetry, and to trace them back to the combination of qualities in the author's genius. This elemental religious emotion, dramatically fitted as it is to the character, could only have found such expression by a mind which deeply felt the primary human need of religion, and which was relatively untroubled by abstract philosophy. But set over against that is the almost pagan joy in the senses, the vigour and love of action which make so strong a physical basis to this work; whilst, on the other hand, there stands the astonishing contrast between the lyrical intensity of the idyllic passages of these poems; and the dramatic power (at once identified with humanity and detached from it) which has created characters of ardent vitality.

There is, of course, a corresponding technical contrast; but the fact that it does 'correspond' is an answer to the critics who object to the violence of certain scenes or to a literal rendering here and there of thought or word. Granted that this poet is not much concerned to polish or refine his verse, it remains true that the same sense of fitness which closes three of these tragedies in exquisite serenity, governs elsewhere an occasional crudity of expression or a touch of banality. It is largely—though not always—a question of dramatic truth. The medium is related to the material of this poetry and ruled by its moods. Hence its realism is not an external or arbitrary thing. It is something more than a trick of style or the adoption of a literary mode, being indeed a living form evolved by the reality which the poet has designed to express.

The root of the matter lies in a stanza of "Dauber." The young artist-seaman, who is the protagonist here, has for long been patiently toiling at his art at the prompting of instinct—the æsthetic impulse to capture and make permanent the beauty of the material world. But the pressure of reality upon him, the unimaginable hardships of a sailor's existence, have threatened to crush his spirit. A crisis of physical fear and depression has supervened ; terror of the storms that the ship must soon encounter, of the frightful peril of his work aloft, and of the brutality of his shipmates, has shaken him to the soul. For a moment, even his art is obscured, shrouded and almost lost in the whirl of these overmastering realities. But when it emerges from the chaos it brings revelation to the painter of its own inviolable relation with those same realities.

John Masefield

        . . . a thought occurred
Within the painter's brain like a bright bird :

That this, and so much like it, of man's toil,
Compassed by naked manhood in strange places,
Was all heroic, but outside the coil
Within which modern art gleams or grimaces ;
That if he drew that line of sailors' faces
Sweating the sail, their passionate play and change,
It would be new, and wonderful, and strange.

That that was what his work meant ; it would be
A training in new vision. . . .

One might almost accept that as Mr Masefield's
own confession of artistic faith ; it only needs the
substitution of the word ' poet ' for the word
' painter ' in the second line. But it is not quite
complete as it stands ; and an important article
of it will be discovered by reading this poem
through and noting the triumph of the ideal over
the real, which is the essential meaning of the work.
It is not the most obvious interpretation, perhaps.
The idealist broken by the elements, wasted and
thrown aside, is hardly a victorious figure on the
face of things. But, in spite of that, the poem is a
song of victory—of spirit over matter, of the ideal
over reality, of art over life.

The fact is all the more remarkable when we turn
for a moment to note the poet's grip on facts. We

have just seen that profound sense of reality lying at the base of his technical realism; and it has been won, through a comprehensive experience, by virtue of the balance of his equipment. There is no bias here, of mind or spirit, which would have changed the clear humanity of the poet into the philosopher or the mystic. The naïveté and simple concrete imagery in the expression of religious feeling are far removed from mysticism. And, on the other hand, one cannot conceive of Mr Masefield formally ranged with the abstractions of either the materialist or the idealist school. Yet it is true that " Dauber " raises the practical issue between the two ; and because the poet has realized life profoundly and dares to tell the truth about it, the triumph of the ideal is the more complete. He shows his hero scourged by the elements until all sense is lost but that of physical torture—

>   . . . below
> He caught one giddy glimpsing of the deck
> Filled with white water, as though heaped with snow.
>   . . . all was an icy blast.
>
> Roaring from nether hell and filled with ice,
> Roaring and crashing on the jerking stage,
> An utter bridle given to utter vice,
> Limitless power mad with endless rage
> Withering the soul ;

John Masefield

With greater daring still we are shown the spirit itself, cowering in temporary defeat before material force—

> "This is the end," he muttered, "come at last!
> I've got to go aloft, facing this cold.
> I can't. I can't. I'll never keep my hold.
>   . . . I'm a failure. All
> My life has been a failure. They were right.
>
> .   .   .   .   .
>
> I'll never paint. Best let it end to-night.
> I'll slip over the side. I've tried and failed."

And then, finally, the poet does not shrink from the last and grimmest reality. He seems to say— Let material force do its utmost against this man. Admit the most dreadful possibility; shatter the life, with its fine promise, its aspiration and toil and precious perception of beauty, and fling it to the elements which claim it. Nevertheless the spirit will conquer, as it has won in the long fight hitherto and will continue to win. When the Dauber had been goaded almost beyond endurance by the cruelty of his shipmates, and when their taunts had availed at last to conjure in him a sickening doubt of his vocation, the poet represents him as turning instinctively to his easel, and healed in a moment of all the abasement and derision—

215

> He dipped his brush and tried to fix a line,
> And then came peace, and gentle beauty came,
> Turning his spirit's water into wine,
> Lightening his darkness with a touch of flame :

So, too, when the horror of the storm and the immense danger of his work aloft had shaken his manhood for a moment : when he saw his life as one ' long defeat of doing nothing well ' and death seemed an easy escape from it, a rallying cry from the spirit sent him to face his duty :

> And then he bit his lips, clenching his mind,
> And staggered out to muster, beating back
> The coward frozen self of him that whined.

And in the last extremity, when he lay upon the deck broken by his fall and rapidly slipping back into the eternal silence, the ideal gleamed before him still. *It will go on!* he cried ; and the four small words, considered in their setting, with the weight of the story behind them, have deep significance. For they bring a challenge to reality from a poet who has very clearly apprehended it ; and in their triumphant idealism they put the corner-stone upon his philosophy and his art.

Harold Monro

THE poetry of Mr Monro—that which counts most, the later work—is of fine texture and subtle perfume. It is, moreover, individual in its thought and form; and the unusual elements in it, which are yet not sufficiently bizarre to snatch attention, offer a new kind of charm to the poetry lover. But that person, as we know, still prefers to take his poetry in the traditional manner; and hence the audience for work like this, delicately sensitive and quietly thoughtful, is likely to be small. It will be fully appreciative, however, gladly exchanging stormy raptures for a quiet and satisfying beauty; and it will be of a temper which will delight to trace in this work, subdued almost to a murmur, the same influences which are urging some of his contemporaries to louder, more emphatic, and more copious expression.

A particular interest of this poetry is precisely the way in which those influences have been subdued. It is that which gives the individual stamp to its art; but, curiously, it is also that which marks its heredity, and defines its place in the succession of English poetry. There is independence here, but not isolation; nor is there violent conflict with

an older poetic ideal. On the contrary, a recon-
ciliation has been made ; balance has been attained ;
and revolutionary principles, whether in the region
of technique or ideas, have been harnessed and
controlled. So that this work, while fairly representing the new poetry, is clearly related in the
direct line to the old. A little " Impression," one
of a group at the end of the volume called *Before
Dawn*, will illustrate this :

> She was young and blithe and fair,
> Firm of purpose, sweet and strong,
> Perfect was her crown of hair,
> Perfect most of all her song.
>
> Yesterday beneath an oak,
> She was chanting in the wood :
> Wandering harmonies awoke ;
> Sleeping echoes understood.
>
> To-day without a song, without a word,
> She seems to drag one piteous fallen wing
> Along the ground, and, like a wounded bird,
> Move silent, having lost the heart to sing.
>
> She was young and blithe and fair,
> Firm of purpose, sweet and strong,
> Perfect was her crown of hair,
> Perfect most of all her song.

One may cite a piece like that, breaking away, in
the third stanza, to a rhythm better fitted to express the tragic change of mood, as an example of

normal development in English prosody. And that is, perhaps, the final significance of Mr Monro's work. With less temptation to waywardness than a more exuberant genius, he has achieved a completer harmony. But it was not so easy a task as the quiet manner would cheat one into supposing ; and, of course, it has not always been so successfully done. There are many pieces—beautiful nevertheless—where external influences have not been completely subdued. From them one may measure the strength with which contemporary thought claims this poet. For it appears that he, too, cannot be at ease in Zion ; that he is troubled and ashamed by reason of a social conscience ; that he is haunted by an unappeasable questioning spirit; that he is perpetually seeking after the spiritual element in existence. Indeed, so clear and persistent is this last motive, that if one were aiming epithets it would be possible to fit the word ' religious ' to the essential nature of Mr Monro's poetry. Of course, no poet, be he great or small, can be packed into the compass of a single word. His work will mean much more, and sometimes greatly different from that. And the word religious in this connexion is more than usually hazardous, for almost all the connotations are against it. It is true that the common meaning, bandied on the lips of happy irresponsibles, has no

application here. On the contrary, it seems sometimes completely reversed; and the good un-
thinking folk would find themselves nonplussed by
such a piece as that called " The Poets are Waiting,"
in the chapbook which Mr Munro published at the
end of 1914. Yet it is of the essence of religion ;
and it most faithfully presents the spiritual crisis
which was precipitated by the Great War for many
who had clung to a last vague hope of some intelligent providence—

> To what God
> Shall we chant
> Our songs of Battle ?
>
> Hefty barbarians,
> Roaring for war,
> Are breaking upon us ;
> Clouds of their cavalry,
> Waves of their infantry,
> Mountains of guns.
> Winged they are coming,
> Plated and mailed,
> Snorting their jargon.
> Oh to whom shall a song of battle be chanted ?
>
> Not to our lord of the hosts on his ancient throne,
> Drowsing the ages out in Heaven alone.
> The celestial choirs are mute, the angels have fled :
> Word is gone forth abroad that our lord is dead.

Harold Monro

To what God
Shall we chant
Our songs of Battle ?

I do not wish to stress unduly the spiritual element in this work, but it compels attention for two reasons. It is a dominant impulse, supplying themes which occur early and late and often; and the manner of its expression reveals a link with the past generation which is analogous to the technical connexion that we have already noted.

The signs of descent from the Victorians are naturally to be found in the early poems. There is, for example, the inevitable classic theme treated in the (also inevitable) romantic manner, and making a charming combination, despite the grumblings of the realist and the pedant. That, however, is a very obvious and external mark of descent. A more interesting sign is in the spirit of " A Song at Dawn," a wail to the Power of Powers which the author probably wishes to forget. So I will not quote it. The point about it is the celerity with which it sends thought flying back to Matthew Arnold and " Dover Beach." Yet there is an important difference. For whilst the Victorian muses upon the decay of faith with exquisite mournfulness, the ' Georgian ' takes an attitude of greater detachment. Instead of grieving for a dead or dying

221

system of theology, he seeks to question the reality which lies behind it.

In the volume of 1911, called *Before Dawn*, there are several poems which pursue the same quest. Sometimes the method is one of provocative directness, as in the dramatic piece called " God " ; and at other times it is by way of symbol or suggestion, as in " Moon-worshippers " or " Two Visions." From the nature of things, however, the pieces in which the argumentative attitude is taken are the less satisfying, as poetry. Thus the colloquy in " God " just fails, from the polemical theme, of being truly dramatic ; while, on the other hand, its form prevents it from rising into such lovely lyrism as that of " The Last Abbot." In the former poem we are to imagine all sorts and conditions of people coming in and out of an old English tavern on market day ; and all of them ready and willing to enlighten a travel-stained pilgrim there as to " Who and what is God ? " One sees the allegory, of course ; but, somehow, that is less convincing than the touches of satirical portraiture which we find in passing, and which point to this poet's gift of objectivity. The judge and the priest, the soldier and sailor and farmer, the beggar, thief and merchant, are presented mainly as types : that, of course, being demanded by the allegory. And when a poet arrives to solve the problem, he also speaks 'in character'—though we recognize the voice for one more modern than his reputed age.

> . . . God is a spirit, not a creed;
> He is an inner outward-moving power:
>
> .   .   .   .
>
> He is that one Desire, that life, that breath,
> That Soul which, with infinity of pain,
> Passes through revelation and through death
> Onward and upward to itself again.
>
> Out of the lives of heroes and their deeds,
> Out of the miracle of human thought,
> Out of the songs of singers, God proceeds;
> And of the soul of them his Soul is wrought.

There follows a quick clatter of disputation, broken by the entrance of the philosopher; and the pilgrim's question being put to him, he replies—

> God? God! There is no GOD.

Thus 'the spirit that denies' abruptly shatters the poetic vision; and the artistic effect is, correspondingly, to break the music of the previous stanzas with a sudden discord. The design of the work required that the philosopher should be heard, and dramatic fitness suggested that his most effective entrance would be here, rending the fair new synthesis with denial. And the resulting dissonance is inherent in the very scheme of the poem.

That defect does not appear in "The Last Abbot," which is also engaged upon the thought of the universal soul. Here an old monk, knowing that he is drawing near the end of life, quietly talks to the brethren of his order about life and death and after-death. There is no argument, no discussion even. No other voice is raised to interrupt the meditative flow of the old man's message, which is, in fact, a recantation. And, as a consequence, the poem has a unity of serene reflectiveness, rising at times to lyrical ecstasy. He is thinking of his approaching death—

> Oh, I, with light and airy change,
> Across the azure sky shall range,
> When I am dead.
>
> . . . . .
>
> I shall be one
> Of all the misty, fresh and healing powers.
> Dew I shall be, and fragrance of the morn,
> And quietly shall lie dreaming all the noon,
> Or oft shall sparkle underneath the moon,
> A million times shall die and be reborn,
> Because the sun again and yet again
> Shall snatch me softly from the earth away:
> I shall be rain;
> I shall be spray;

Harold Monro

At night shall oft among the misty shades
Pass dreamily across the open lea ;
And I shall live in the loud cascades,
Pouring their waters into the sea.
. . . Nought can die :
All belongs to the living Soul,
Makes, and partakes, and is the whole,
All—and therefore, I.

So much then for the poet's cosmic theory, presented more or less directly. This explicit treatment may, as we see, give individual passages where
thought and feeling are completely fused, and the
idea gets itself born into a shape sufficiently concrete for the breath of poetry to live in it. But
the final effect of such poems is apt to be dimmed
by the shadow of controversy. A subtler method
is used, however, justified in a finer type of art.
In " Don Juan in Hell," for instance, there is a
symbolical presentment of the theme : a conception
of life which is a corollary from the poet's theory
of the universe. Don Juan is here an incarnation
of the vital forces of the world, of the positive
value and power of life which is in eternal conflict with a religion of negation. And, a new-
comer among the shades in Hell, he turns his
scorn upon them for the lascivious passion which
found it necessary to invent sin.

225

Light, light your fires,
That they may purify your own desires !
They will not injure me.
This fire of mine
Was kindled from the torch that will outshine
Eternity.

. . . . .

Proud, you disclaim
That fair desire from which all came ;
Unworthy of your lofty human birth,
Despise the earth.
O crowd funereal,
Lifting your anxious brows because of sin,
There is no Heaven such as you would win,
Nor any other Paradise at all,
Save in fulfilling some superb desire
With all the spirit's fire.

The same idea is woven into " Moon-worshippers,"
with delicate grace. It constitutes a precise charge,
in the poem " To Tolstoi," that the great idealist
has forsworn the ' holy way of life ' ; and, recurring
in many forms more or less explicit, culminates in
the charming allegory called " Children of Love."
This is a later poem, mature in thought and masterly
in form. The theme is by this time a familiar one
to the poet : he has considered it deeply and often.
And having gone through the crucible so many
times, it is now of a fineness and plasticity to be

handled with ease. It runs into the symbolism
here so lightly as hardly to awaken an echo of afterthought, and shapes to an allegory much too winning
to provoke controversy. The first two stanzas of
the poem imagine the boy Jesus walking dreamily
under the olives in the cool of the evening :

> Suddenly came
> Running along to him naked, with curly hair,
> That rogue of the lovely world,
> That other beautiful child whom the virgin Venus bare.
>
> The holy boy
> Gazed with those sad blue eyes that all men know.
> Impudent Cupid stood
> Panting, holding an arrow and pointing his bow.
>
> (Will you not play ?
> Jesus, run to him, run to him, swift for our joy.
> Is he not holy, like you ?
> Are you afraid of his arrows, O beautiful dreaming boy?)
>
> .   .   .   .   .
>
> Marvellous dream !
> Cupid has offered his arrows for Jesus to try ;
> He has offered his bow for the game.
> But Jesus went weeping away, and left him there
>   wondering why.

That may be taken as Mr Monro's most representative poem. On our theory, therefore (of this

Contemporary Poets

work as a link with the older school), the piece might serve to indicate the point which contemporary poetry has reached, advancing in technique and in thought straight from the previous generation. Not that it is the most ' advanced ' piece (in the specific sense of the word) which one could cite from modern poets. Many and strange have been the theories evolved on independent lines, just as numerous weird technical effects have been gained by breaking altogether with the tradition of native prosody. But Mr Monro's poetry continues the tradition ; and whether it be in content or in form, it has pushed forward, in the normal manner of healthy growth, from the stage immediately preceding.

The new technical features are clear enough, and all owe their origin to a determination to gain the greatest possible freedom within the laws of English versification. Rhyme is no longer a merely decorative figure, gorgeous but tyrannical. It is an instrument of potential range and power, to be used with restraint by an austere artist. In " Children of Love " it occurs just often enough to convey the gentle sadness of the emotional atmosphere. But very beautiful effects are gained without it, as, for instance, in another of these later poems, called " Great City "—

228

Harold Monro

When I returned at sunset,
The serving-maid was singing softly
Under the dark stairs, and in the house
Twilight had entered like a moonray.
Time was so dead I could not understand
The meaning of midday or of midnight,
But like falling waters, falling, hissing, falling,
Silence seemed an everlasting sound.

The verse is not now commonly marked by an exact number of syllables or feet, nor the stanza divided into a regular number of verses, except where the subject requires precision of effect. An order of recurrence does exist, however, giving the definite form essential to poetry. But it is determined by factors which make for greater naturalness and flexibility than the hard-and-fast division into ten- or eight-foot lines and stanzas of a precise pattern. The ruling influences now are various— the thought which is to be expressed, and the phases through which it passes: the nature and strength of the emotion, the ebb and flow of the poetic impulse.

Thus, while metrical rhythm is retained, it has been freed from its former monotonous regularity, and has become almost infinitely varied. The dissyllable, dominant hitherto, has taken a much humbler place. Every metre into which English words will run is now adopted, and fresh combinations are constantly being made ; while upon the poetic rhythm itself is super-imposed the natural rhythm of speech. In most of these devices Mr Monro, and others, are presumably following the precept and example of the Laureate ; but in any case there can be no doubt of the richness, suppleness, and variety of the metrical effects attained. Most of the pieces in this little chapbook illustrate at some point the influence of untrammelled speech-rhythm ; and in one, called " Hearthstone," it is rather accentuated. I quote from the poem for that reason : the slight excess will enable the device to be observed more readily, but will not obscure other characteristic qualities which are clearly marked here—of tenderness, quiet tone, and delicate colouring.

I want nothing but your fireside now.

. . . . .

Your book has dropped unnoticed : you have read
So long,you cannot send your brain to bed.
The low quiet room and all its things are caught
And linger in the meshes of your thought.
(Some people think they know time cannot pause.)
Your eyes are closing now though not because
Of sleep. You are searching something with your
        brain ;
You have let the old dog's paw drop down again . . .

Harold Monro

Now suddenly you hum a little catch,
And pick up the book. The wind rattles the latch ;
There's a patter of light cool rain and the curtain
    shakes ;
The silly dog growls, moves, and almost wakes.
The kettle near the fire one moment hums.
Then a long peace upon the whole room comes.
So the sweet evening will draw to its bedtime end.
I want nothing now but your fireside, friend.

Thus the technique of modern poetry would seem
to be moving towards a more exact rendering of the
music and the meaning of our language. That is
to say, there is, in prosody itself, an impulse towards
truth of expression, which may be found to correspond to the heightened sense of external fact in
contemporary poetic genius, as well as to its closer
hold upon reality. Thence comes the realism of
much good poetry now being written : triune, as
all genuine realism must be, since it proceeds out
of a spiritual conviction, a mental process and actual
craftsmanship. That Mr Monro's work is also
trending in this direction, almost every piece in
his last little book will testify. And if it seem a
surprising fact, that is only because one has found
it necessary to quote from the more subjective of
his early lyrics. It would have been possible, out of
the narrative called " Judas," or the " Impressions "
at the end of *Before Dawn,* to indicate this poet's

objective power. He has a gift of detachment; of cool and exact observation; and to this is joined a dexterity of satiric touch which serves indignation well. Hence the portraits of the epicure at the Carlton and the city swindler in the rôle of county gentleman. Hence, too, poems like "The Virgin" or "A Suicide": though here it is unfortunate that imagination has been allowed to play upon abnormal subjects. The result may be an acute psychological study; and interesting on that account. But if it is to be a choice between two extremes, most people will prefer work in which fantasy has gone off to a region in the opposite direction. There is one poem in which this bizarre sprite has taken holiday; and thence comes the piece of glimmering unreality called "Overheard on a Saltmarsh."

> Nymph, nymph, what are your beads?
> Green glass, goblin. Why do you stare at them?
> Give them me.
>   No.
> Give them me. Give them me.
>   No.
> Then I will howl all night in the reeds,
> Lie in the mud and howl for them.
>
> Goblin, why do you love them so?

Harold Monro

They are better than stars or water,
Better than voices of winds that sing,
Better than any man's fair daughter,
Your green glass beads on a silver ring.

Hush I stole them out of the moon.

Give me your beads, I desire them.
                                        No.
I will howl in a deep lagoon
For your green glass beads, I love them so.
Give them me.   Give them.
                        No.

But in his more representative work, the intellectual realism which comes from an acute sense of
fact is clearly operative.   We have seen, too, from
the earliest published verse of this poet, the continual
struggle of what one may call a religion of reality—
belief in the sanctity and beauty and value of the
real world—for spiritual mastery.   In the later
poems the two elements become deepened and are
more closely combined : they are, too, seeking expression through a technique which is directed to the
same realistic purpose.   And as a result we get such
a piece of quiet fidelity as " London Interior " ;
or a tragedy like " Carrion," in which the logic of
life and death, controlling emotion with beautiful
gravity, is suddenly broken by a sob.   It is the
last of four war-poems ; a series representing the

233

call of battle to the soldier, his departure, a fighting retreat, and finally, in " Carrion," his death—

It is plain now what you are.   Your head has dropped
Into a furrow.   And the lovely curve
Of your strong leg has wasted and is propped
Against a ridge of the ploughed land's watery swerve.

.   .   .   .   .

You are fuel for a coming spring if they leave you here ;
The crop. that will rise from your bones is healthy
    bread.
You died—we know you—without a word of fear,
And as they loved you living I love you dead.

No girl would kiss you.   But then
No girls would ever kiss the earth
In the manner they hug the lips of men :
You are not known to them in this, your second birth.

.   .   .   .   .

Hush, I hear the guns.   Are you still asleep ?
Surely I saw you a little heave to reply.
I can hardly think you will not turn over and creep
Along the furrows trenchward as if to die.

Sarojini Naidu

MRS NAIDU is one of the two Indian poets who within the last few years have produced remarkable English poetry. The second of the two is, of course, Rabindranath Tagore, whose work came to us a little later, who has published more, and whose recent visits to this country have brought him more closely under the public eye. Mrs Naidu is not so well known; but she deserves to be, for although the bulk of her work is not so large, its quality, so far as it can be compared with that of her compatriot, will easily bear the test. It is, however, so different in kind, and reveals a genius so contrasting, that one is piqued by an apparent problem. How is it that two children of what we are pleased to call the changeless East, under conditions nearly identical, should have produced results which are so different?

Both of these poets are lyrists born; both come of an old and distinguished Bengali ancestry; in both the culture of East and West are happily met; and both are working in the same artistic medium. Yet the poetry of Rabindranath Tagore is mystical, philosophic, and contemplative, remaining oriental therefore to that degree; and permitting a doubt of the *Quarterly* reviewer's dictum that " Gitanjali "

235

is a synthesis of western and oriental elements. The complete synthesis would seem to rest with Mrs Naidu, whose poetry, though truly native to her motherland, is more sensuous than mystical, human and passionate rather than spiritual, and reveals a mentality more active than contemplative. Her affiliation with the Occident is so much the more complete ; but her Eastern origin is never in doubt.

The themes of her verse and their setting are derived from her own country. But her thought, with something of the energy of the strenuous West and something of its ' divine discontent,' plays upon the surface of an older and deeper calm which is her birthright. So, in her " Salutation to the Eternal Peace," she sings

> What care I for the world's loud weariness,
> Who dream in twilight granaries Thou dost bless
> With delicate sheaves of mellow silences ?

Two distinguished poet-friends of Mrs Naidu— Mr Edmund Gosse and Mr Arthur Symons—have introduced her two principal volumes of verse with interesting biographical notes. The facts thus put in our possession convey a picture to the mind which is instantly recognizable in the poems. A gracious and glowing personality appears, quick and warm with human feeling, exquisitely sensitive to beauty and

Sarojini Naidu

receptive of ideas, wearing its culture, old and new, scientific and humane, with simplicity ; but, as Mr Symons says, " a spirit of too much fire in too frail a body," and one moreover who has suffered and fought to the limit of human endurance.

We hear of birth and childhood in Hyderabad ; of early scientific training by a father whose great learning was matched by his public spirit : of a first poem at the age of eleven, written in an impulse of reaction when a sum in algebra ' *would not* come right ' : of coming to England at the age of sixteen with a scholarship from the Nizam college ; and of three years spent here, studying at King's College, London, and at Girton, with glorious intervals of holiday in Italy.

We hear, too, of a love-story that would make an idyll ; of passion so strong and a will so resolute as almost to be incredible in such a delicate creature ; of a marriage in defiance of caste ; of wedded happiness and of children. And all through, as a dark background to the adventurous romance of her life, there is the shadow of weakness and ill-health. That shadow creeps into her poems, impressively, now and then. Indeed, if it were lacking, the bright oriental colouring would be almost too vivid. So, apart from its psychological and human interest, we may be thankful for such a

poem as " To the God of Pain." It softens and
deepens the final impression of the work.

> For thy dark altars, balm nor milk nor rice,
> But mine own soul thou'st ta'en for sacrifice.

The poem is purely subjective, of course, as is the
still more moving piece, " The Poet to Death," in
the same volume.

> Tarry a while, till I am satisfied
> Of love and grief, of earth and altering sky ;
> Till all my human hungers are fulfilled,
> O Death, I cannot die !

We know that that is a cry out of actual and repeated
experience ; and from that point of view alone it has
poignant interest.   But what are we to say about
the spirit of it—the philosophy which is implicit
in it ?   Here is an added value of a higher kind,
evidence of a mind which has taken its own stand
upon reality, and which has no easy consolations
when confronting the facts of existence.   For this
mind, neither the religions of East nor West are
allowed to veil the truth ; neither the hope of Nir-
vana nor the promise of Paradise may drug her sense
of the value of life nor darken her perception of the
beauty of phenomena.   Resignation and renunciation are alike impossible to this ardent being who
loves the earth so passionately ; but the ' sternly

scientific ' nature of that early training—the description is her own—has made futile regret impossible, too. She has entered into full possession of the thought of our time ; and strongly individual as she is, she has evolved for herself, to use her own words, a " subtle philosophy of living from moment to moment." That is no shallow epicureanism, however, for as she sings in a poem contrasting our changeful life with the immutable peace of the Buddha on his lotus-throne—

> Nought shall conquer or control
> The heavenward hunger of our soul.

It is as though, realizing that the present is the only moment of which we are certain, she had determined to crowd that moment to the utmost limit of living.

From such a philosophy, materialism of a nobler kind, one would expect a love of the concrete and tangible, a delight in sense impressions, and quick and strong emotion. Those are, in fact, the characteristics of much of the poetry in these two volumes, *The Golden Threshold* and *The Bird of Time*. The beauty of the material world, of line and especially of colour, is caught and recorded joyously. Life is regarded mainly from the outside, in action, or as a pageant ; as an interesting event or a picturesque group. It is not often brooded over, and reflection is generally evident in but the lightest touches. The proportion of strictly subjective verse is small, and is not, on the whole, the finest work technically.

The introspective note seems unfavourable to Mrs Naidu's art : naturally so, one would conclude, from the buoyant temperament that is revealed. The love-songs are perhaps an exception, for one or two, which (as we may suppose) treat fragments of the poet's own story, are fine in idea and in technique alike. There is, for example, " An Indian Love Song," in the first stanza of which the lover begs for his lady's love. But she reminds him of the barriers of caste between them ; she is afraid to profane the laws of her father's creed ; and her lover's kinsmen, in times past, have broken the altars of her people and slaughtered their sacred kine. The lover replies :

> What are the sins of my race, Beloved, what are my people to thee ?
> And what are thy shrine, and kine and kindred, what are thy gods to me ?
> Love recks not of feuds and bitter follies, of stranger, comrade or kin,
> Alike in his ear sound the temple bells and the cry of the *muezzin.*

There is also in the second volume the " Dirge," in which the poet mourns the widowed state of a friend whose husband has just died; and which almost unconsciously reveals the influence of centuries of Suttee upon the mind of Indian womanhood.

> Shatter her shining bracelets, break the string
> Threading the mystic marriage-beads that cling
> Loth to desert a sobbing throat so sweet,
> Unbind the golden anklets on her feet,
> Divest her of her azure veils and cloud
> Her living beauty in a living shroud.

Even here, however, the effect is gained by colour and movement; by the grouping of images rather than by the development of an idea; and that will be found to be Mrs Naidu's method in the many delightful lyrics of these volumes where she is most successful. The " Folk Songs " of her first book are an example. One assumes that they are early work, partly because they are the first group in the earlier of the two volumes; but more particularly because they adopt so literally the advice which Mr Edmund Gosse gave her at the beginning of her career. When she came as a girl to England and was a student of London University at King's College, she submitted to Mr Gosse a bundle of manuscript poems. He describes them as accurate and careful work, but too derivative; modelled too palpably on the great poets of the

previous generation. His advice, therefore, was
that they should be destroyed, and that the author
should start afresh upon native themes and in her
own manner. The counsel was exactly followed:
the manuscript went into the wastepaper basket,
and the poet set to work on what we cannot doubt
is this first group of songs made out of the lives of
her own people.

There is all the hemisphere between these lyrics
and those of late-Victorian England. Here we find
a " Village Song " of a mother to the little bride
who is still all but a baby; and to whom the fairies
call so insistently that she will not stay " for bridal
songs and bridal cakes and sandal-scented leisure."
In the song of the " Palanquin Bearers " we positively see the lithe and rhythmic movements which
bear some Indian beauty along, lightly " as a pearl
on a string." And there is a song written to one
of the tunes of those native minstrels who wander,
free and wild as the wind, singing of

> The sword of old battles, the crown of old kings,
> And happy and simple and sorrowful things.

The " Harvest Hymn " raises thanksgiving for
strange bounties to gods of unfamiliar names; and
the " Cradle Song " evokes a tropical night, heavy
with scent and drenched with dew—

242

Sarojini Naidu

> Sweet, shut your eyes,
> The wild fire-flies
> Dance through the fairy *neem* ;
> From the poppy-bole,
> For you I stole
> A little, lovely dream.

In its lightness and grace, this poem is one of the exquisite things in our language : one of the little lyric flights, like William Watson's " April," which in their clear sweetness and apparent spontaneity are like some small bird's song. Mrs Naidu has said of herself—" I sing just as the birds do " ; and as regards her loveliest lyrics (there are a fair proportion of them) she speaks a larger truth than she meant. Their simplicity and abandonment to the sheer joy of singing are infinitely refreshing ; and fragile though they seem, one suspects them of great vitality. In the later volume there is another called " Golden Cassia "—the bright blooms that her people call mere ' woodland flowers.' The poet has other fancies about them ; sometimes they seem to her like fragments of a fallen star—

> Or golden lamps for a fairy shrine,
> Or golden pitchers for fairy wine.

> Perchance you are, O frail and sweet !
> Bright anklet-bells from the wild spring's feet,

> Or the gleaming tears that some fair bride shed
> Remembering her lost maidenhead.

Contemporary Poets

The tenderness and delicacy of verse like that
might mislead us. We might suppose that the
qualities of Mrs Naidu's work were only those
which are arbitrarily known as feminine. But this
poet, like Mrs Browning, is faithful to her own
sensuous and passionate temperament. She has not
timidly sheltered behind a convention which, because some women-poets have been austere, pre-
scribes austerity, neutral tones, and a pale light
for the woman-artist in this sphere. And, as a
result, we have all the evidence of a richly-dowered
sensibility responding frankly to the vivid light and
colour, the liberal contours and rich scents and great
spaces of the world she loves ; and responding no
less warmly and freely to human instincts. Occasionally her verse achieves the expression of sheer
sensuous ecstasy. It does that, perhaps, in the two
Dance poems—from the very reason that her art is
so true and free. The theme requires exactly that
treatment ; and in " Indian Dancers " there is
besides a curiously successful union between the
measure that is employed and the subject of the
poem—

Their glittering garments of purple are burning like
  tremulous dawns in the quivering air,
And exquisite, subtle and slow are the tinkle and tread
  of their rhythmical, slumber-soft feet.

Sarojini Naidu

The love-songs, though in many moods, are always the frank expression of emotion that is deep and strong. One that is especially beautiful is the utterance of a young girl who, while her sisters prepare the rites for a religious festival, stands aside with folded hands dreaming of her lover. She is secretly asking herself what need has she to supplicate the gods, being blessed by love ; and again, in the couple of stanzas called " Ecstasy," the rapture has passed, by its very intensity, into pain.

> Shelter my soul, O my love !
>   My soul is bent low with the pain
> And the burden of love, like the grace
>   Of a flower that is smitten with rain :
> O shelter my soul from thy face !

But, when all is said, it is the life of her people which inspires this poet most perfectly. In the lighter lyrics one sees the fineness of her touch ; and in the love-poems the depth of her passion. But, in the folk-songs, all the qualities of her genius have contributed. Grace and tenderness have been reinforced by an observant eye, broad sympathy and a capacity for thought which reveals itself not so much as a systematic process as an atmosphere, suffusing the poems with gentle pensiveness. And always the artistic method is that of picking out the theme in bright sharp lines, and presenting the idea concretely, through the grouping of picturesque facts. There is a poem called " Street Cries " which is a vivid bit of the life of an Eastern city. First we have early morning, when the workers hurry out, fasting, to their toil ; and the cry ' Buy bread, Buy bread' rings down the eager street ; then midday, hot and thirsty, when the cry is ' Buy fruit, Buy fruit ' ; and finally, evening.

> When twinkling twilight o'er the gay bazaars,
> Unfurls a sudden canopy of stars,
> When lutes are strung and fragrant torches lit
> On white roof-terraces where lovers sit
> Drinking together of life's poignant sweet,
> *Buy flowers, buy flowers,* floats down the singing
> street.

Another of these shining pictures will be found in " Nightfall in the City of Hyderabad," Mrs Naidu's own city ; and again in the song called " In a Latticed Balcony." But there are several others in which, added to the suggestion of an old civilization and strange customs, there is a haunting sense of things older and stranger still. Of such is this one, called " Indian Weavers."

> Weavers, weaving at break of day,
> Why do you weave a garment so gay ? . . .

Sarojini Naidu

Blue as the wing of a halcyon wild,
We weave the robes of a new-born child.

.   .   .   .   .   .

Weavers, weaving solemn and still,
Why do you weave in the moonlight chill ? . . .
White as a feather and white as a cloud,
We weave a dead man's funeral shroud.

John Presland

IN coming to the work of John Presland there is a note of personal interest first. The name is a pseudonym; and Mrs Skelton, the lady whose identity it covered hitherto, has yielded at last to importunity and has consented to reveal her authorship. It is an act so much the more gracious by reason of her strong wish to remain anonymous; and the writer of these studies is therefore constrained to offer thanks publicly to Mrs Skelton for her indulgence.

But if one does not at the same time apologize for the importunity, that is because the betrayal of the secret serves the ends of art and thought. One did not probe it out of a vulgar curiosity, nor ask to reveal it from a petty wish to be the first to divulge an interesting literary fact. There were other implications, as, for example, jealousy for the honour of womanhood. Now that may not be, in a simple sense, a motive of the highest order, but it is at least respectable. In its wider reference, which includes the whole influence of women in literature, it is of high importance; while for a study of contemporary poetry which observes in any degree the relation between the poet and his time, the feminine origin of this body of work is of primary interest.

John Presland

Thus the prominent dramatic feature of John Presland's poetry does more than arrest the eye. It excites the mind. One is pricked by all sorts of speculation—on the trend of contemporary poetry towards the dramatic form and the virility which that implies; on the alleged subjectivity of women and the way in which that generalization is proved too arbitrary by the fine drama of the two ladies who called themselves Michael Field, by Margaret Woods, and now by John Presland.

Out of ten volumes of poetry published by this poet, six are fully-wrought plays and one is a tragic love-story told in duologue. That is a larger proportion of actual drama than most of the modern poets give; but the dramatic impulse is strong in the work of nearly all of them. It is the clearest sign of their vitality, testifying as it does to roots which go far down into life. There are very few who are content simply to sing. Indeed, it hardly seems to be a matter of choice, but of an urgency, secret and compelling as a natural instinct, by means of which life is commanding expression in literary art. And in the impulse towards this objective form of art women are seen to be sharing fully.

That is not to suggest that there is not a true lyrical gift to this generation. On the contrary, there are so many singers of lovely songs that one might call it an Age of Minstrels, and predict by analogy the speedy appearance of the supreme poet. So long as poets continue to be born young we shall not lack for songs ; and probably in every age there may be one rare singer like W. H. Davies, for whom destiny has conspired. From the tyranny of life he has escaped into a virtual isolation. Owing allegiance chiefly to Nature, unspoilt by books, and saving his spirit humane and merry and sweet from the petty constraints of civilization, he carols as lightly as a robin or a thrush. But he is almost a solitary exception, and may serve to prove the rule that the pure lyric—some intimate emotion bubbling over into music—cannot say all that demands to be said when the poetic spirit is completely in touch with life.

Now, in all the most vital of this modern verse, poetry has come so close to life as to claim its identity. It has left the twilight of unreality and stepped into clear day. It has broken down the exclusiveness which penned it within a prescribed circle of theme and of language ; and it has taken hold upon the world, real and entire. Moreover, the life upon which it seizes in this way is wider, more complex, more meaningful and varied than ever before. Political and social changes have

John Presland

made humanity a larger thing—whether regarded
in the actual numbers which democracy thus
brings within the poetic ken, or in their manifold
significance. Horizons, both mental and material,
have been extended. Science presses on in quiet
confidence, the dogmatic phase being over ; and
its methods as well as its data pass readily into the
collective mind. Religion, no longer synonymous
with a single creed or form of worship, can find
room within itself for all the spiritual activity of
mankind everywhere ; and in the juster proportion
thus attained, nobler syntheses are shaping. A
constructive social sense replaces the old negative
commands with a positive duty of service. Values
are changing ; new ideals quicken, struggle and
fructify ; fresh aspects of life, and visions of human
destiny, are opened up ; while in every sphere the
spirit of inquiry and the experimental method
generate an energy of conflict which the timid and
the sleepy loathe, but which is nevertheless the
dynamic of progress.

The poetry of to-day is the very spirit of that
multiform life, giving the eternity of art to whatever is finest in it ; and for that reason its manner
of expression is almost infinitely varied, and often
very different from the poetic forms of other ages.
That, indeed, is the witness to its vitality : the fact

that it is a living organism, capable of adaptation, growth and development. Old forms are modified and new ones created to embody the new ideas. All the resources of prosody are drawn upon—when they will serve—and used with the utmost freedom. And when, as frequently happens, they will not serve; when the established rules of English verse seem inadequate to the present task, they are challenged and thrown aside. Thus there arises, in the technique of poetry itself, a corresponding conflict to that in the world of ideas, indicating a similar vigour and equally prophetic of advance.

In all this variety, however, the dramatic element is constant; and it seems to be growing stronger. Leaving out of account for the moment the large body of actual drama produced by Michael Field, Mr Yeats and others, the element is seen to be present in many poems which have not the shape of drama at all. In the narratives of Mr Masefield, for example, it may be found informing astonishingly an elaborate stanza or the rhymed couplet; just as the tragedies of *Daily Bread* are wrought out by Mr Gibson in a quite original unrhymed verse of great austerity. And much of Mr Abercrombie's work is dramatic in essence, apart from his plays in regular form.

But there is one fact to be noted in coming

John Presland

from those poets to the drama of John Presland.
With them the dramatic impulse is often secondary
and subconscious, and it has to fight its way against
a twin impulse towards lyricism. It is strong but
not yet dominant; vital, but not yet aware of
its own potentiality. It throbs below the surface
of alien forms, but it rarely breaks away to an
independent existence. And even when it achieves
consciousness, as it does most completely perhaps
in the work of Mrs Woods, traces of the struggle
cling about it still—in a lyrical *motif*, or a fragment
of song embedded in the structure of a play, or in
a lyric intensity of feeling. With John Presland,
however, the general tendency is reversed. The
dramatic impulse has become a definite and prevailing purpose, with the lyrical element subordinated to it; and, as a consequence, we have
here a drama of full stature, a complete, organic,
and acutely conscious art-form.

This work reveals in its author an endowment of
those qualities which most insistently urge towards
the dramatic form: imagination, both creative
and constructive, and a gift of almost absolute
objectivity. In all the six plays these qualities are
conspicuous. Indeed, they are so strong that they
effectually screen the poet's personality; and, if
she had written nothing but the plays, it is little

that one might hope to discover of the individual mind behind them. That is naturally a very desirable result from the dramatist's point of view, and one test of his art. But it pricks mere human curiosity, and provokes unregenerate glee in the fact that the poet has published lyrics too, four volumes of them; and that they, from their more subjective nature, yield up the outlines of a definite individuality.

But, indeed, one's delight is not sheer mischief. It is partly at least in seeing the artistic virtue of this largesse in the lyric—the spontaneity which is equally a merit with the reticence of drama. One is glad, too, of the light thus thrown upon the poet's own philosophy, her affiliations, outlook, and attitude to life. Judging by the plays alone, we might be cheated into a belief in the complete detachment of our author. The use of historical themes and the rigour of art create an effect of isolation. She would seem to stand outside the stress of her own time and aloof from the influences which commonly shape the artist. The lyrics show that impression to be false and help to correct it. For while they do not relate the poet, in any narrow sense, to what are specifically called ' modern movements,' they prove that she has an eager interest in her world, and that, being in that world and of it,

John Presland

she is yet ' on the side of the angels.' There is, for
example, a splendid fire of reproach in the poem
" To Italy," proving a capacity for noble indignation as well as a close hold upon current affairs.
The poem is dated September 29, 1911, and is a
protest at the action of Italy against Tripoli ; and if
it might have been written yesterday, and addressed
to D'Annunzio for the tragic folly of his occupation
of Fiume, that is not because Italy alone among
nations has moments of madness :

> Hearken to your dead heroes, Italy ;
> Hearken to those who made your history
> A bright and splendid thing . . .
>   . . . What Mazzini said
> Have you so soon forgotten ?   You, who bled
> With Garibaldi, and the thousand more ?
> He spoke, and your young men to battle bore
> His gospel with them, of men's brotherhood,
> Of Justice, that before the tyrant, stood
> Accusing, and of truth and charity.
> His dust to-day lies with you, Italy ;
> Where lie his words ?   That sword is in your hand
> To seize unrighteously another's land—
> Your fleet in foreign waters.   By what right
> Dare you act so, save arrogance of might,
> Such cruel force as ground the Austrian heel
> Upon your Lombard cities, ringed with steel
> Unhappy Naples and despairing Rome,
> That exiled Garibaldi from his home,

That served itself with sycophants and knaves,
That filled the prisons and the nameless graves,
Till, like a sunrise o'er a stormy sea,
Flashed out the spirit of free Italy?

Like all John Presland's work, this poem is closely woven : quotation does not serve it well, but this passage will at least indicate a theme and temper which light up personality. There is, in the same volume, *Songs of Changing Skies*, a bit of spiritual autobiography called " To Robert Browning." It destroys at once any fiction of literary isolation ; although to be sure there are cute critics who will declare that the resemblance to Browning in some of these lyrics is too obvious to need the discipular confession. It may be that these clever people are right. Yes, perhaps one would recognize certain signs in poems like " A Present from Luther " and " An Error of Luther's." But the whole question of influence is nearly always made too much of, especially in its mere outward marks. Granting the love of Browning and the debt to his teaching, which are honourably acknowledged here, some effect upon thought and early style would be inevitable. But a deeper and more potent cause of the resemblance lies in a real affinity of mind, in buoyancy and breadth and tenacious belief in good ; and in a similar poetic equipment. One must not

256

John Presland

launch upon a comparison, but it may be observed that this poet has profited by the master's faults, artistic and philosophical, at least as much a, by his merits. For, probably warned by example, she works with patient care to express her thought simply; and she has attained a style of perfect clearness. While her philosophy, though full of brave hope, has escaped the unreason of that optimism which declares that 'All's well.' True, she makes Joan say, in the last words of " Joan of Arc " :

> . . . . so near eternity
> The evil dwindles, good alone remains,
> And good triumphant—God is merciful.

But that is dramatically appropriate—the logic of Joan's character. And it seems to me that a more intimate and sincere expression is to be found in the chastened mood of a sonnet called " To April " :

> There will be other days as fair as these
> Which I shall never see; for other eyes
> The lyric loveliness of cherry trees
> Shall bloom milk-white against the windy skies
> And I not praise them; where upon the stream
> The faëry tracery of willows lies
> I shall not see the sunlight's flying gleam,
> Nor watch the swallow's sudden dip and rise

257

Contemporary Poets

Most mutable the forms of beauty are,
Yet Beauty most eternal and unchanged,
Perfect for us, and for posterity
Still perfect; yearly is the pageant ranged.
And dare we wish that our poor dust should mar
The wonder of such immortality?

The wistfulness of that wins by its grace where
a more strenuous optimism provokes a challenge;
just as the tentative 'perhaps' in the last line of
" Sophocles' Antigone " softly woos the sceptic:

There are fair flowers that never came to fruit;
Cut by sharp winds, or eaten by late frost,
Barrenly in forgetfulness, they're lost
To little-heedful Nature; so, in suit,
Beneath the footsteps of calamity
Young lives and lovely innocently come
To total up old evil's deadly sum—
Do the gods pity dead Antigone?
We look too close, we look too close on earth
At good and evil; blind are Nature's laws
That kill, or make alive, and so are done.
Not in the circle of this death and birth
May we perceive a justifying cause,
Beyond, perhaps, for God and good are one.

One must not pause to gather up the threads of
personality in these three volumes of lyrics; and,
with the more important work in drama still ahead,
it is only possible just to glance at their specific

John Presland

values. All the pieces are not equally good, of
course, but there is a proportion of exquisite
poetry in each volume. The proportion is probably
greatest in *Songs of Changing Skies*, and of this
best work there are at least three kinds. There is
that which one may call the lyric proper, small in
size, simple in design, light in texture, the free
expression of a single mood. Such is " From a
Window," in which the peculiar charm of the
poet's verse in this kind is well seen. It is not a
showy attractiveness : it does not storm the senses
nor clamour for approval. It enters the mind
quietly, and perhaps with some hesitancy ; but
having entered, it takes absolute possession.

> To-night I hear the soft Spring rain that falls
> Across the gardens, in the falling dusk,
> The Spring dusk, very slow ;
> And that clear, single-noted bird that calls
> Insistently, from somewhere in the gloom
> Of wet Spring leafage, or the scattering bloom
> Of one tall pear-tree.
> On, on, on, they go,
> Those single, sweet, reiterated sounds,
> Having no passion, similarly free
> Of laughter, and of memory, and of tears,
> Poignantly sweet, across the falling rain,
> They fall upon my ears.

The delicate rapture of that will fairly represent

much of the nature poetry in these volumes, as well as the very individual *Poems of London,* published in 1918. It will be seen that there is a close relation between means and end; that the simple language, natural phrasing and controlled freedom of movement, directly subserve the final effect of clear sweetness. A similar adaptation will be found in verse which is written in a sharply contrasted manner. In " Atlantic Rollers," for instance, we have a bigger theme, demanding by its nature a swifter and stronger treatment. And surely the wild energy and sound, the dazzling light and colour of stormy breakers have been almost brought within sight and hearing, in the speed and vigour of this poem. There is the opening rush, with its secret obedience to rhythm; there is a choice of words which are themselves dynamic; the rapid, cumulative pressure of the verse, with epithets only to help the rising movement until the crest is reached, at say the tenth or twelfth line; and then a slight diminution of speed and force, as a richer style describes the breaking wave.

> Do you dare face the wind now? Such a wind,
> Bending the hardy cliff-grass all one way,
> Hurling the breakers in huge battle-play
> On these old rocks, whose age leaves Time behind,
> —The whorls and rockets of the fiery mass

John Presland

Ere earth was earth—shoots over them the spray
In furious beauty, then is twisted, wreathed,
Dispersed, flung inland, beaten in our face,
Until we pant as if we hardly breathed
The common air. See how the billows race
Landward in white-maned squadrons that are shot
With sparks of sunshine.
              Where they leap in sight
First, on the clear horizon, they fleck white
The blue profundity; then, as clouds shift,
Are grey, and umber, and pale amethyst;
Then, great green ramparts in the bay uplift,
Perfect a moment, ere they break and fall
In fierce white smother on the rocky wall.

The third kind of lyric is perhaps the most interesting, for it points directly to the poet's dramatic gift. It appears quite early in this work; and indeed, a striking example of it is the duologue which gives its name to the author's first book, *The Marionettes*, published in 1907. It is described in the sub-title as " A Puppet Show," and a definition of its form would probably be a dramatic lyric. " Outside Canossa," on the other hand, is frankly narrative in form, and has an historical theme. It relates the famous episode of the humiliation of the Emperor Henry IV by Hildebrand, and is necessarily concerned with material that is static in its nature. It must define and describe the scene,

announce the antecedents of the story, and throw
light upon character. In spite of this, however,
the conception of the poem is dramatic; and
certain vivid situations have been created. As
we read we actually live in this snow-clothed,
silent forest world; we stand inside the king's tent
as he returns each evening from his barefoot, bare-
headed penance outside Hildebrand's castle gate;
and we tremble, with the waiting courtiers, at the
outraged pride in his eyes.

> Yesterday,
> Speech leapt from out the King, as leaps
> A sword-blade, dazzling in the sun
> From out its scabbard; as there leaps
> Fire from the mountain, ere it run
> Destruction-dealing, far and wide.
> "Rather as Satan damned, I say,
> Falling through pride, yet keeping pride,
> Than buy salvation at this price. . . ."

To the enraged King the Queen enters softly,
carrying her little son; and though her husband
has threatened death to any who should approach
him, though he sits with his unsheathed dagger
ready to strike, she walks steadily to his side, places
the child upon his knee, and goes slowly out without
a word.

> Through the door
> The King has hurled the dagger, holds

John Presland

His son against his breast, and pain
Contorts him, like a smitten oak;
Then sets the child upon the floor,
And rises, and undoes the clasp
Of his great mantle (like a stain
Of blood it lies about his feet).
Next from his head he takes the crown,
Holds it arm's-length, and drops it down
Suddenly, from his loosened grasp,
And for the third time goes he forth,
Barefooted as a penitent,
Humble, and excommunicate,
To stand all day in falling snow
Outside Canossa's guarded gate,
Till Hildebrand shall mercy show.

The dramatic sense is clearly operative there.
Here is an instinct which perceives the kinetic
values of things; which seizes upon the true stuff
of drama, and, contemplating a character, an event
or a situation, feels it start into life under the touch
and sees it move forward and rush to a crisis before
the eyes. In the lyrics this quality is often merely
latent; but in the plays it has come to full power
and has found expression through its own proper
medium. It is, of course, the originating impulse
of drama as well as the force that shapes it; and if
we would take some measure of this creative energy
in our poet, we have only to observe that six pub-

lished plays and one unpublished were produced in seven years, besides four volumes of lyrics. The first, *Joan of Arc*, appeared in 1909; the last, *King Monmouth*, came out in 1916; the other four, *Mary Queen of Scots, Manin, Marcus Aurelius* and *Belisarius*, belong (with the lyrics) to the intervening years. Moreover, these plays are all fully developed and of elaborate structure. Being poetic and historical drama, perhaps it is natural that they should follow the Shakespearean model, though their dependence on tradition is a curious fact at this time of day. *Joan of Arc* and *Mary Queen of Scots* are both of five-act length, and the rest are of four acts. Numerous characters are introduced and a great deal of material is handled : incident is plentiful, situations vary and scenes change with some frequency ; while underplot and cross-action bring in interests which are additional to, though subserving, the main theme.

Looking at the work thus, and noting its mass and general character, one is constrained first to pay a tribute to the fertility of the genius from which it springs, and to the strength and staying power of the dramatic impulse which impels it. But we soon find that this is reinforced by other remarkable qualities. There is what one may call a comprehensive intelligence, ranging wide-eyed over the fields of history and gathering material in many places. There is selective power in a discriminating choice from so much diversity; and a fine constructive gift patiently building up, fitting together, organizing and articulating the form of the work. Selection acts constantly and with rigour; proportion is generally—though not always—true; and a noble spirit and a manner at once gracious and dignified give the work distinction.

However, all that is little more than to say— here is a genuine artist working conscientiously in a given medium. It does not go far towards a relative estimate of the work as pure drama. Only a detailed critical analysis could do that adequately; though one may perhaps try to indicate two or three of the prominent features of the plays. Thus in *Joan of Arc* we meet at once certain qualities which become in the later plays definitely characteristic. There is, for example, a conception of the theme which stresses the element of spiritual conflict, and draws upon it for dramatic inspiration. That is a primary fact in all this work; and in four of the five plays it is implied in the very name of the protagonist. *Joan, Manin, Marcus Aurelius* and *Belisarius* are synonyms for the purest spirituality of which human nature is capable. They suggest, before a page of this poetry has been turned, that

265

the conflict out of which drama always springs is in this case largely a matter of invisible forces—of principles and ideas. And they point to a type of dramatic art which, trending to fine issues, deals inevitably in quiet effects.

There is, in fact, in the extreme grandeur of these four characters, a possible source of weakness to the plays, as actual drama. There is a danger that Joan may be too good a Christian, Marcus Aurelius too austere a stoic, Manin or Belisarius too absolute an idealist, to put up a strenuous fight against destiny. It is a criticism which does not hold against the latest play, *King Monmouth*, just because of the mixed elements of Monmouth's character; but in the final impression of the earlier plays one is aware of a vague touch of regret that the protagonist is not a better fighter; and although that may arise from one's own pugnacity, one suspects the existence of a good many other imperfect humans who will share it. From which it may be inferred that the weakness inherent in the subject has not been entirely overcome. I doubt whether it would be possible to overcome it altogether; and by the same token I salute the power which has evoked profoundly moving and stimulating drama out of themes like these.

Nevertheless, the poet knows well how to use

John Presland

the human elements of a story to make the stirring
scenes through which the spiritual crisis is reached.
Thus Joan, in the fundamental struggle of her soul
for the soul of France, is brought into external
conflict which fills out the plot with incident. It
belongs, of course, to the historical setting of her
life, that that conflict is one of actual warfare;
but we are bound to admire the art which has
placed her as the central figure of those warring
factions—the invading English, the army of the
Duke of Burgundy, the Church, and Charles the
Dauphin. Out of that come the events through
which the action proceeds and by which the incomparable beauty of her character is revealed.

It is the struggle of Joan's enthusiasm with the
apathy and indolence of Charles which gives rise
to one of the finest scenes in the play. It occurs
in Act I, the whole of which is skilfully designed to
set the action moving, while indicating so much of
the political situation as ought to be known, and
the weakness in Charles' character which is the
ultimate cause of Joan's downfall. A premonitory
note is struck in the opening dialogue. A little
story is told by la Tremoille, who is Joan's chief
enemy, of how he had just whipped a ragged
prophet in the street and caused him to be stoned.
It has a double purpose—to introduce Joan, the

prophetess of Domrémy, as the subject of conversation; and, by reminding us of her own end, to awaken the sense of tragic irony through which we shall view the subsequent action. The talk turns to Joan, who is awaiting audience; and la Tremoille proposes the trick of the disguise. Charles agrees to it, and goes out to put on the dress of a courtier, while his absence is filled out by a lively dialogue which glances lightly from point to point of court life. When Charles and his train re-enter and Joan is brought in, the scene rises strongly to its climax. Joan recognizes the Dauphin through his disguise and announces her divine mission—

> I do declare to you
> That I, no other,—neither duke, nor prince,
> Nor captain,—no, nor learned gentlemen,
> But I alone, a girl of Domrémy,—
> Am sent to save you.

By means of a flexible blank-verse, plain diction, and free and nervous phrasing, dialogue runs with an easy vigour. It is fired by strong and quickly changing emotion—the incredulity of Charles, the base hostility of la Tremoille, the indignation of Joan's friends, or the amazement and curiosity of the courtiers. But for the most part it remains strictly dramatic poetry; that is to say, raised by several degrees above the level of prose, yet closely fitted to personality. When, however, Joan begins to tell about her life, her quiet country home, and the divine command which bade her save her country, the note deepens. The verse becomes lyrical, burning with the mystical passion which possesses her—a flame, like the grand simplicity of her own nature, white and intensely clear.

> JOAN.   Sire, it was in the spring; one afternoon
> When I was in a meadow all alone,
> Lying among the grasses (over head
> The scurrying clouds were like a flock of sheep,
> Chased by a sheep-dog); then, all suddenly,
> I heard a voice—nay, heard I cannot say,
> There *was* a voice took hold upon my sense,
> As if it swallowed up all other sounds
> In all the world; the birds, the sheep, the bees,
> The sound of children calling far away,
> The rustling of the rushes in the stream,
> Were only like the cloth, whereon appears
> The gold embroidery, the voice of God.
> ARCHBISHOP.   Did you see aught?
> JOAN.   Yea, see!   Our earthly words
> Cannot express divinity, but like
> Small vessels over-filled with generous wine,
> They leave the surplus wasted.   If I say,
> I saw, or heard, that seems to leave untouched
> The other senses; but indeed, my lords,
> All of my body seemed transformed to soul.

269

So I should say I *saw* the voice of God,
And *heard* the light effulgent all around,
Nay, heard, and saw, and felt through all of me
The radiance of the message of the Lord.

Passages like that bring home to us the poetical character of this drama. True, they may remind us that in such a form of the art action is bound to lag sometimes : that its movement is apt to be impeded, as toward the end of *Joan of Arc*, by lyrical speeches. On the other hand, they emphasize the peculiar virtue of this kind of drama ; the twofold nature of its appeal, and the fact that the two elements are often found concentrated at their highest degree in single scenes of great power. With genius of this type (if genius may be classified in types !), when the dramatic imagination is most vividly alight, it will inevitably kindle poetry of the finest kind.

Thus, in the last act of *Marcus Aurelius*, we get the force of the whole drama, and all the incidence of the directly preceding scene moving behind and through the Emperor's speech from which I shall quote. The play has shown the complicity of Faustina in the plot to depose her husband : we know that she is a wanton and a traitress. But Marcus is ignorant of the truth, and generously unsuspecting. After the death of Cassius, the chief

John Presland

conspirator, Marcus orders an officer to bring all
the dead man's papers to him. It is necessary to
examine them for the names of accomplices. They
are brought in while he is chatting with Faustina ;
and she knows that they contain certain incrimi-
nating letters that she had written. Exposure is
imminent—disgrace and probable death for her
await the opening of the letters. She tries every
ruse that a bold and cunning mentality can suggest
to prevent her husband from reading them. She
seems about to succeed, but her insistence faintly
warning Marcus, she fails after all. He takes up
the package and goes away to open it quietly in his
tent, and Faustina, believing that in a few minutes
he will know all her treachery, drinks poison and
dies. Unconscious of this catastrophe, the Emperor
is sitting alone in his tent, with the package of
letters on a table before him.

> . . . . Here, beneath my hand,
> Are laid the hidden hearts of many men.
> What shall I read therein ? Ingratitude,
> Lies, envy, spite, the barbed and venomous word
> Of those that called me Emperor, I called friend ;
> . . . Break the seal, and read
> Which of our subjects, of our intimates,
> Our friends of many years, are netted here.
> How thickly fall the shadows in the tent !
> Almost I fancied, with my tired eyes,

271

I saw Faustina there . . . Faustina, you!

. . . . . .

                        If I should find
Her name among the friends of Cassius?
Ah no, Faustina, not such perfidy!
The gods must blush at it! Am I grown grey
And learnt no wisdom? Though it should be so—
Though yet it cannot be—what's that to me?
Am *I* wronged by it? Yet it cannot be,
With that frank brow. I've loved you faithfully;
It could not be so. . . .

                 . . . I will not know
More than I must of unprofitable things,
Lest they should, in the garden of my soul,
Nourish rank weeds of hate and bitterness;
I will not hate that which I cannot change.
                (*He drops the papers into a tripod.*)
Burn! Go into oblivion! The gods
Permit themselves to pity good and bad,
Giving to each the sunshine and sweet rain,
And hiding all things in the mist of years.
May I not do as gods do? Burn away,
Consume all hate and evil into smoke!
I will not know of them; assuredly
For me such ills exist not——
          (*The body of Faustina is brought in.*)

The same combination of dramatic elements will
be found in the crucial scenes of *Manin* and *Belisarius*. In *Manin* it is especially notable, because
of the curious nature of the crisis. This would

seem, on the face of it, almost calculated to inhibit the dramatic impulse : to tend to negative the dynamic properties of character and circumstance. Manin, the defender of Venice, has held his city against the Austrian enemy by sheer force of character. His courage and confidence and determination have heartened the Venetians to continue their resistance ; and his statesmanship has been diligent in trying to secure the intervention of France or England, or military aid from Kossuth. But help is refused from every quarter ; the garrison is small and weak; the people are starving, and ravaged by disease. Nevertheless, inspired by their leader, they are willing and eager to resist to the end, although they know that this must bring on them the hideous penalties with which the Austrians notoriously punished that kind of patriotism.

The crux of the drama lies in the problem thus presented to Manin. It is essentially a spiritual struggle : between wisdom on the one hand and patriotic ardour on the other ; between foresight and courage ; between the long, weary, unattractive processes that make for life and the blind impetuosity that makes for death ; between, in his personal career, a prospect of humiliation in exile and the glory of a hero's end. Given the character of Manin, victory in the conflict was bound to lie with reason against passion, with sagacity against recklessness ; but the victory in this case meant defeat—physical and apparently moral. It would mean to the world, and even to his own people, that, with the surrender of the town, he yielded up the very principles for which he stood. Therein, of course, lies the unusual nature of this crisis. The dramatic instinct has somehow to vitalize a dead weight of failure. To see how that is done— and it *is* done, finely—one must turn to the scene in Act III, which is the core of the play. There the poet creates an external conflict between Manin and the people which embodies, as it were, the spiritual struggle ; and, translating it into action, visibly reveals Manin as a conqueror. Quotations hardly do justice to the poet here, but there are two speeches, one before and one after Manin has won the people to the proposed surrender, which indicate the skill of the art at this point.

The first expresses the agony of failure in Manin's mind, resulting from his decision to yield to the enemy. It is in answer to his faithful friend and secretary, Pezzato, who has been trying to comfort him with a prediction that the freedom of their city and their land is only deferred, that it must ultimately come. Manin replies :

274

John Presland

> I shall not see it.
> I shall be blind beneath my coffin lid
> There in a foreign land; I shall not see
> The glory and the splendour of St. Mark's
> When our Italian flag salutes the sun;
> I shall be deaf, and never hear the peal
> Of our triumphant bells, and volleying guns;
> I shall be dumb, I shall be dumb that day,
> And never say, "My people, for this hour
> I saved you when I sacrificed you most."

The second passage burns with the fire of triumph, tragical but prophetic, which has been kindled in Manin by his struggle with the opposing will of the people and his victory over it:

> Of this one thing be sure. A little time,
> A little hour, in the span of years
> That history devours, we submit
> To bow before the flail of tyranny;
> Ay, it may strike us down, and we may die
> With Europe passive round our Calvary;
> Yet that for which we stand, for liberty,
> For equal justice, and the right of laws
> Purely administered, can never die,
> Being of the nature of eternity;
> Nor all the blood that Austria has shed
> Mar the indelibility of truth;
> Nor all the graves that Austria has dug
> Bury it deep enough; nor all the lies
> That coward hearts have bandied to and fro,
> And coward hearts received to trick themselves,
> Smother the face of it.

275

Contemporary Poets

There remains to be particularly noted the poet's gift of realizing character. It is seen at its best in *Mary Queen of Scots*, where the unhappy Queen is very strikingly re-created. Out of the diverse and stormy elements of her nature she is made to live again with a complex unity and completeness which are amazing. That is largely the reason why this play is the most powerful of the six, from the point of view of pure drama. Its theme is unerringly chosen, for drama inheres in Mary's being. The seeds of tragedy lurk in her contrasted weakness and strength, excess and defect, nobility and baseness. And, because she has been so brilliantly studied, this play moves at every step to the majestic truth that character is destiny.

The broad lines of Mary's personality are established in the first act, revealing at once the springs of action. The sensuous basis of her nature, her strong will and quick temper, may be seen to set in motion the forces which will presently overwhelm her. Her widowed state is irksome—therefore she will marry. She hates authority—therefore she will make her own choice in the matter of a husband. And finer threads already begin to complicate the issues. She is really fond of Darnley, but that motive is intricately mixed with the satisfaction of insulting Elizabeth through him;

John Presland

while her ready wit gives a spice to her malice
which, in dialogue at least, is very refreshing.
When she enters the audience-chamber she calls
Darnley to her side and, with a gesture towards
the gloomy faces of the disaffected nobles, says in
merry mockery :

> . . . . look you there
> On these good gentlemen, all friends of ours,
> The earls of Morton, Ruthven, and Argyll :
> For friends they are—upon their countenance
> We see it written.

She turns to the English ambassador :

> . . . Here's Sir Nicholas.
> What news of our dear cousin ?   Has she come
> At last to give that virgin heart away
> Into another's keeping, that brave Archduke,
> Who'd bite your hand, they say, as soon as kiss it—
> Such manners are in Austria—or Charles,
> My dear French brother, who is well enough,
> And only fourteen years her junior ?
> Not yet the happy moment ?   Patience, then,
> Another day you'll have that news for us.

Sir Nicholas states formally Elizabeth's objections
to Darnley, who interjects :

> By my beard !

MARY.   No ! No !
> Not by your beard, dear Henry, or your oath
> Is emptier than a prince's promises—

277

Some princes we have heard of, we would say,
Though cannot think it truth.   Nay, let me hear
What is it that my sister Princess wills
Out of the largeness of her heart for me?

The complexity of Mary's character is well
brought out.   There is, for instance, the little
scene with Mary Beaton at the beginning of Act
II.   Here the Queen, discovering Darnley's infidelity, passes rapidly through half a dozen moods
—from satirical bitterness to a fury of pride, and
then to tears in which humiliation, gratitude, and
tenderness are mingled.   Mary Beaton has just
said that the people pity their Queen :

MARY.   . . . . On my life,
    I'll not be pitied : pity is a chafe
    On open wounds of pride.   To pity me
    Makes me a beggar—dare you pity me?
BEATON.   Sweet lady, I would not, but must perforce!
MARY.   Nay, would you have me weep?   What thing
        am I
    That three soft words should drive the tear drops forth
    Like floods in winter?   Nay, nay, good my girl,
    This is my body's weakness, not my soul's.

The gentleness of that gives place at the entrance
of Darnley to intense scorn, changing to indignation
when he compels her to answer him, and to provocative coquetry at his insult to Rizzio.   But the

John Presland

finest achievement of this portrayal is that which shows the Queen conscious of her infatuation for Bothwell, and perceiving the tragedy which it is preparing, yet incapable of stemming the flood that is carrying her away. Intelligence remains acute : reason holds as clear a light to consequence as ever it did, but both are ineffectual against the storm of instinct. Here is a passage from the end of Act III in which Bothwell after a rebuff has protested his love for the Queen :

MARY.   Nay, swear nòt ; nay, I know you what you are—
    Hotter than flame in your desires ; false—
    Falser than water.
BOTHWELL (*embracing her*).   Be a salamander,
    To live for ever in the midst of fire.
MARY.   Oh, Bothwell !   Oh, my love !   I am bewitched
    To love you so.   You are a deadly poison
    That's crept through all my veins ; you are the
      North,
    And I the needle ; I must turn to you
    From every quarter of the hemispheres.
              . . . I am yours
    Utterly, wholly ; when I walk abroad,
    Jewelled and brocaded, I feel all men's eyes
    Can see me naked, and, from head to foot,
    Branded in red-hot letters with your name.
BOTHWELL.   This is indeed love !
MARY.   You may call it so !
    It is not that which most men mean by love—

A moment's idle fancy.   No, this love
Is like a dragon, laying waste the land
Of all my life; it is a deadly sickness,
Of which we both shall die; it is a sin,
Of which we both are damned, the saints of God
Not finding mercy; there's no pleasure in it,
But dust in the mouth and saltness in the eyes.

One would like to indicate further the truth
with which the character is studied through the
last two acts, providing the material as it does
for scenes of great power and range of effect.
Particularly one would wish to convey some idea
of the final tragedy, broadly conceived against a
background of the angry Edinburgh populace, and
throbbing with the defiance of the Queen.   Psychological imagination here is no less than brilliant,
and one could cull perhaps half a dozen passages
to illustrate it.   But a single extract must suffice;
and that is chosen for the additional reason that
its closing sentences contain the very root of the
tragedy.   It is from Act IV, and the scene, following upon Mary's marriage to Bothwell, is designed
to show her last desperate struggle against him
and against herself.   Already she is remorseful,
disillusioned, and bitter; she knows the marriage
to be hateful to her people, and she has found
Bothwell cruel and treacherous.   Before the nobles,

who are assembled to receive them, she taunts
Bothwell that he is not royal; flouts him for
Arthur Erskine; declares that she will never wear
jewels again; and at last provokes from Bothwell
angry abuse and threats of violence. The nobles
interpose to protect her, and beg her to let them
save her from him. It needs but one word of
assent to be rid of him for ever. She is almost won;
she takes a few steps towards them, and actually
gives her hand to one of them. Then she hesitates,
turns, and looks at her husband:

MARY. I am yours, Bothwell.
BOTHWELL.   Will you go with me?
MARY. Ay, to the world's end, in my petticoat.
BOTHWELL. Let go her hands, my lord.
MORTON.   Ay, let them go,
    And let *her* go, for naught can save her now.
    Not ours the fault.
MARY.   Not yours, nor his, nor mine.
    'Tis not the fault of floods to drown, nor fire
    To burn and shrivel—no, nor beasts to bite,
    Nor frosts to kill the flowers—not the fault,
    Only the property. There's something here
    That's stronger than our wishes and our wills.
    There is no going back; our course is laid,
    And we must keep it, though it lead to death.
    Good-bye, my lords. My husband, let us go.

James Stephens

ONE does not put a poet like Mr Stephens into a group—it cannot be done. If you try to do it, weakly yielding a wise instinct to mere intelligence, one of two things will happen. You will return to your careful group the moment after you thought you had made it, to find either that Mr Stephens has vanished or that the others have. Either he has broken away from the ridiculous frail links which bound him, and is already disappearing on the horizon with a gleeful shout, or his unfortunate companions have vanished before so much exuberance.

That is why this poet was not included in the Irish chapter where, if the thing were possible at all, one would have hoped to catch him. There are racial strands out of which you would think a net could be woven; and they appear to enmesh an Irishman and an Irish poet. We think we recognize that eye, critical and appreciative, for a woman—or a horse. We believe we know that wit, with a touch of satire and another touch of merry malice. We are surely not mistaken in that adoration of beauty and its converse hatred of ugliness; while we have no doubt whatever about that passion for liberty.

282

James Stephens

But the true poet will transcend his nation, as he does his manhood, at times of purest inspiration; and Mr Stephens has those happy seasons—happy, surely, for those to whom he sings, though, doubtless, each with its own agony to him. In many of the slighter poems, however, all of them good and most of them quite beautiful, the signs of nationality are obvious. They are comically clear, in fact, proceeding as they do directly from the quick, keen perception of the Comic Spirit itself. Only a blessed simpleton whose name was Patsy, could see the angel who walks along the sky sowing the poppyseed. The word ' Sootherer ' sounds like English ; and indeed individuals of the species are not unknown in this country. But they, like the word, are native to the land of the born lover. Has anybody heard of a Saxon who could fit names like these to his sweetheart—Little Joy, Sweet Laughter, Shy Little Gay Sprite ? or who could woo her with such a ripple of flattery—

> . . . You are more sweetly new
> Than a May moon : you are my store,
> My secret and my treasure and the pulse
> Of my heart's core.

But, on the other hand, no mere English boy could hope to match the glib rage of spite in this disappointed youth—

> You'll go—then listen, you are just a pig,
> A little wrinkled pig out of a sty ;
> Your legs are crooked and your nose is big,
> You've got no calves, you have a silly eye,
> I don't know why I stopped to talk to you,
> I hope you'll die.

Again, no Jack Robinson, though the dull smother
that he would call his imagination were fired by
plentiful beer, could ever have conceived of " What
Tomas an Buile Said in á Pub " ; or could have
accompanied Mac Dhoul on his impish adventure
into heaven, to be twitched off God's throne by
a hand as large as a sky, and sent spinning through
the planets—

> Scraping old moons and twisting heels and head
> A chuckle in the void. . . .

These outward marks are unmistakable ; and so,
too, are certain qualities in the essence and texture
of the work. His lyric moods may be as tender
and fanciful, though always more spontaneous, than
those of Mr Yeats. And one may find the arrowy
truth, the rich earthiness and the profound sense of
tragedy of a Synge. But the filmy threads which
seem to stretch between Mr Stephens and his
compatriots have no strength to bind him. They
are, indeed, only visible when he is ranging at
some altitude that is lower than his highest reach.

James Stephens

When he soars to the zenith, as in "The Lonely God" and "A Prelude and a Song," their tenuity snaps. He has gone beyond what is merely national and simply human ; and has become just a Voice for the Spirit of Poetry.

Nevertheless the affinities of this poet with what is best in modern Irish literature would make a fascinating study. Foremost, of course, there is imagination. You will find in him the true Hibernian blend of grotesquerie and grandeur, pure fantasy and shining vision. But each of these things is here raised to a power which makes it notable in itself, while all of them may sometimes be found in astonishing combination in a single poem. In the book called *Insurrections*, which is dated 1909, and appears to represent Mr Stephens' earliest efforts in verse, there is the piece which I have already named, "What Tomas an Buile Said in a Pub." Already we may see this complex quality at work. Tomas is protesting that he saw God ; and that God was angry with the world.

> His beard swung on a wind far out of sight
> Behind the world's curve, and there was light
> Most fearful from His forehead . . .
>
> .   .   .   .   .
>
> He lifted up His hand—
>   I say He heaved a dreadful hand

Over the spinning Earth, then I said " Stay,
You must not strike it, God ; I'm in the way ;
And I will never move from where I stand."
He said " Dear child, I feared that you were dead,"
  And stayed His hand.

You will see—a significant fact—that there is no
nonsense about a dream or a transcendent waking
apparition. In the opening lines Tomas says, with
anxious emphasis, that he saw the ' Almighty Man '
—and that is symbolical. It has its relation to the
mellow tenderness with which the poem closes ; but
apart from that it is a sign of the way in which the
creative energy always works in this poetry. It
seizes upon concrete stuff ; and that is fused, ham-
mered and moulded into shapes so sharp and clear
that we feel we could actually touch them as they
spring up in our mental vision. This is not peculiar
to Mr Stephens, of course. It would seem to be
common to every poet—though to be sure they are
not many—in whom sheer imagination, the first
and last poetic gift, is pre-eminent. Mr Stephens
has many other qualities, which give his work
depth, variety and significance ; but fine as they
are, they take a secondary place beside this ardent,
plastic power.

We quickly see, even in the early poem from which
I have quoted, the mixed elements of this gift. Now

the grotesquerie which seems to lie in the fact that Tomas tells about the majesty and familiar kindliness of God 'in a pub,' may be apparent only. It probably arises from one's own sophistication and painful respectability. We have lost the simplicity which would make it possible to talk about such a subject at all; and as for doing it in a pub. . . . !

Yet there is something truly grotesque in this work. That is to say, there is a juxtaposition of ideas so violently contrasted that they would provoke instant mirth if it were not for the grave intensity of vision. Sometimes, indeed, they are frankly absurd. We are meant to laugh at them, as we do at Mac Dhoul, squirming with merriment on God's throne with the angels frozen in astonishment round him. But generally these extraordinary images are presented seriously, and often they are winged straight from the heart of the poet's philosophy. Then, the driving power of emotion and a passion of sincerity carry us safely over what seems to be their amazing irreverence. There is, for instance, in the piece called "The Fulness of Time," a complete philosophic conception of good and evil, boldly caught into sacred symbolism. The poet tells here how he found Satan, old and haggard, sitting on a rusty throne in a distant star.

Contemporary Poets

All his work was done ; and God came to call him
to Paradise.

> Gabriel without a frown,
> Uriel without a spear,
> Raphael came singing down
> Welcoming their ancient peer,
> And they seated him beside
> One who had been crucified.

It is not irreverence, of course, but the audacity
of poetic innocence. Only an imagination pure of
convention and ceremonial would dare so greatly.
And the remarkable thing is that this naïveté is
intimately blended with a grandeur which sometimes
rises to the sublime. The noblest and most complete expression of that is in " The Lonely God."
That is probably the reason why this poem is the
finest thing that Mr Stephens has done—that, and
the magnitude of its central idea. There is, indeed,
the closest relation here between the thought and
the imagery in which it is made visible. But,
keeping our curious scrutiny fixed for the moment
on the changing form of the imaginative essence
of the work, let us take first the opening lines of
the poem :

> So Eden was deserted, and at eve
> Into the quiet place God came to grieve.
> His face was sad, His hands hung slackly down
> Along his robe . . .

James Stephens

> . . . All the birds had gone
> Out to the world, and singing was not one
> To cheer the lonely God out of His grief—

There follow several stanzas of exquisite reverie as the majestic figure paces sadly in Adam's silent garden and pauses before the little hut

> Chaste and remote, so tiny and so shy,
> So new withal, so lost to any eye,
> So pac't of memories all innocent. . . .

Then, reminiscent of the dear friendliness of those banished human souls, desolation comes upon the solitary Being. He remembers that he is eternal and ringed round with Infinity. He sends thought flying back through endless centuries, but cannot find the beginning of Time. He ranges North and South, but cannot find the bounds of Space. He is most utterly alone—save for his silly singing angels—in the monotonous glory of his heaven.

> . . . Many days I sped
> Hard to the west, a thousand years I fled
> Eastwards in fury, but I could not find
> The fringes of the Infinite. . . .
> —till at last
> Dizzied with distance, thrilling to a pain
> Unnameable, I turned to Heaven again.

And there My angels were prepared to fling
The cloudy incense, there prepared to sing
My praise and glory—O, in fury I
Then roared them senseless, then threw down the
   sky
And stamped upon it, buffeted a star
With My great fist, and flung the sun afar :
Shouted My anger till the mighty sound
Rung to the width, frighting the furthest bound
And scope of hearing : tumult vaster still,
Thronging the echo, dinned my ears, until
I fled in silence, seeking out a place
To hide Me from the very thought of Space.

There was once a reviewer who compared the genius of this poet to that of Homer and Æschylus. Now comparisons like that are apt to tease the mind of the discriminating, to whom there instantly appear all the gulfs of difference. But, indeed, this poet does share in some measure, with Æschylus and our own Milton and the unknown author of the Book of Job, a sublimity of vision. His conceptions have a grandeur of simplicity ; and he makes us realize immensities—Eternity and Space and Force—by images which are almost primitive. Like those other poets too, whose philosophical conceptions were as different from his as their ages are remote, he also has made God in the image of man. But the comparison does not touch

what we may call the human side of this newer
genius ; and it only serves to throw into bolder
relief its perception of life's comedy, its waywardness,
and its mischievous humour. This aspect, strongly
contrasted as it is with the poet's imaginative
power, is at least equally interesting. It is apparent, in the earlier work, in the realism of such
pieces as " The Dancer " or " The Street." There
is a touch of harshness in these poems which
would amount to crudity if their realism were an
outward thing only. But it is not a mere trick
of style : it proceeds from indignation, from an
outraged æsthetic sense, and from a mental courage
which attains its height, rash but splendid, in
" Optimist "—

> Let ye be still, ye tortured ones, nor strive
> Where striving's futile.   Ye can ne'er attain
> To lay your burdens down.

This poet is not a realist at all, of course—far
from it. But he loves life and earth and homely
words, he is very candid and revealing, and he has
a sense of real values. His humanity, too, is deep
and strong, and often supplies his verse with the
material of actual existence, totally lacking factitious
glamour. Thus we have " To the Four Courts,
Please," in which the first stanza describes the

Contemporary Poets

deplorable state of an ancient cab-horse and his driver. Then—

> God help the horse and the driver too,
> And the people and beasts who have never a friend,
> For the driver easily might have been you,
> And the horse be me by a different end.

This humane temper is the more remarkable from being braced by a shrewd faculty of insight. There is no sentimentality in it ; and that the poet has no illusions about human frailty may be seen in such a poem as " Said The Old-Old Man." It is ballasted with humour, too ; and has a charming whimsicality. Hence the lightness of touch in " Windy Corner "—

> O, I can tell and I can know
>   What the wind rehearses :
> " A poet loved a lady so,
> Loved her well, and let her go
>   While he wrote his verses."
>
> .   .   .   .   .
>
> That's the tale the winds relate
>   Soon as night is shady.
> If it's true, I'll simply state
> A poet is a fool to rate
>   His art above his lady.

Returning, however, to the larger implications of this poetry, one may find a passion for liberty in it, and a courageous faith in the future of the race.

292

James Stephens

Here we have, in fact, a pure idealist, one of the invincible few who have brought their ideals into touch with reality. One does not suspect it at first—or at least we do not see how far it goes—largely for the reason that it is so deeply grounded. The poet's hold on life, on the actual, on the very data of experience, is unyielding : his perception of truth is keen and his intellectual honesty complete. And then the way in which his imagination moulds things in the round, as it were, leaves no room to guess that there is a limitless something behind or within. True, we have felt all along what we can only call the spiritual touch in this poetry. It is always there, lighter or more commanding, and sometimes it will come home very sweetly in a comic piece, as for instance when " The Merry Policeman," appointed guardian of the Tree, calls reassuringly to the scared thief :

> . . . " Be at rest,
> The best to him who wants the best."

We have observed, too, a faculty of seeing the spirit of things—a habit of looking right through facts to something beyond them. But still we did not quite understand what these signs meant ; and if we tried to account for them in any way, we probably offered ourselves the all-too-easy explanation

293

that this was the playful, fanciful, Celtic way of looking at the world. Well, so it may be ; but that charming manner is, in all gravity, just the outward sign of
an inward grace. And if anyone should doubt that
it points in this case to a clear idealism, he may be
invited to consider this little poem which prefaces the
poet's second volume, called " The Hill of Vision " :

> Everything that I can spy
> Through the circle of my eye,
> Everything that I can see
> Has been woven out of me ;
> I have sown the stars, and threw
> Clouds of morning and of eve
> Up into the vacant blue ;
> Everything that I perceive,
> Sun and sea and mountain high,
> All are moulded by my eye :
> Closing it, what shall I find ?
> —Darkness, and a little wind.

Now it must not be inferred that Mr Stephens
is an austere person who propounds ideals to himself as themes for his poetry. We should detect
his secret much more readily if he did—and it may
be that we should not like him quite so well. Hardly
ever do you catch him, as it were, saying to his
Muse : " Come, let us make a song about liberty,
or the future." The very process of his thought,
as well as the order of his verse, seems often to be

James Stephens

by way of an object to an idea.   He takes some bit
of the actual world—a bird, a tree, or a human
creature; and tuning his instrument to that, he is
presently off and away into the blue.

Once, however, he did sing directly on this subject
of liberty, and about the external, physical side of it.
It was, of course, in that early book; and there may
also be found two studies of the idea of liberty in its
more abstract nature. They both treat of the woman
giving up her life into the hands of the man whom she
marries. And in both there is brought out with ringing clarity the inalienable freedom of the human soul.
Thus "The Red-haired Man's Wife," musing upon
the inexplicable changes that marriage has wrought
for her—on her dependence, and on the apparent loss
of her very identity, wins through to the light—

> I am separate still,
>   I am I and not you :
> And my mind and my will,
>   As in secret they grew,
> Still are secret, unreached and untouched and not
>   subject to you.

Thus, too, "The Rebel" finds an answer to an
importunate lover—

> You sob you love me—What,
> Must I desert my soul
> Because you wish to kiss my lips,

.   .   .   .   .

295

Contemporary Poets

I must be I, not you,
That says the thing in brief.
I grew to this without your aid,
Can face the future unafraid,
Nor pine away with grief
Because I'm lonely. . . .

It is, however, in " A Prelude and a Song " that
this ardour of freedom finds purest expression.
Not that the poem was designed to that end. I
believe that it was made for nothing on this earth
but the sheer joy of singing. How can one describe
this poem ? It is the lyrical soul of poetry ; it is
the heart of poetic rapture ; it is the musical spirit
of the wind and of birds' cries ; it is a passion of
movement, swaying to the dancing grace of leaves
and flowers and grass, to the majesty of sailing
clouds ; it is the sweet, shrill, palpitating ecstasy
of the lark, singing up and up until he is out of
sight, sustaining his song at the very door of heaven,
and singing into sight again, to drop suddenly down
to the green earth, exhausted.—And I have not
yet begun to say what the poem really is : I have
a doubt whether prose is equal to a definition. In
some degree at any rate it is a pæan of freedom :
delighted liberty lives in it. But we cannot apply
our little distinctions here, saying that it is this or
that or the other kind of freedom which is extolled ;
296

because we are now in a region where thought and feeling are one ; in a golden age where good and evil are lost in innocency ; in a blessed state where body and soul have forgotten their old feud in glad reunion.

One hesitates to quote from the poem. It is long, and as the title implies, it is in two movements. But though every stanza has a lightsome grace which makes it lovely in itself—though the whole chain, if broken up, would yield as many gems as there are stanzas, irregular in size and shape indeed, but each shining and complete—the great beauty of the poem is its beauty as a whole. It would seem a reproach to imperil that. Yet there is a culminating passage of extreme significance to which we must come directly for the crowning word of the poet's philosophy. From that we may take a fragment now, if only to observe the reach of its imagination and to win some sense which the poem conveys of limitless spiritual range.

> Reach up my wings !
> Now broaden into space and carry me
> Beyond where any lark that sings
> Can get :
> Into the utmost sharp tenuity,
> The breathing-point, the start, the scarcely-stirred
> High slenderness where never any bird
> Has winged to yet !

297

> The moon peace and the star peace and the peace
> Of chilly sunlight : to the void of space,
> The emptiness, the giant curve, the great
> Wide-stretching arms wherein the gods embrace
> And stars are born and suns. . . .

There follows hard upon that what is in effect a confession of faith. It is not explicitly so, of course. Subjective this poet may be—is it not a virtue in the lyricist ?—but he does not confide his religion to us in so many words. He has an artistic conscience. But the avowal, though it is by way of allegory and grows up out of the imagery of the poem as naturally as a blossom from its stem, is clear enough. And is supported elsewhere, implicitly, or by a mental attitude, or outlined now and then in figurative brilliance. There can be no reason to doubt its strength and its sincerity—and there is every reason to rejoice in it—for it reveals Mr Stephens as a poet of the future.

One pauses there, realizing that the term may mean very much—or nothing at all. It may even suggest a certain technical vogue which, however admirable in the theory of its originators, has not yet justified itself in the creation of manifest beauty. Our poet has no association with that, of course, except in that he shares the general forward impulse of the spirit of his generation. That is,

James Stephens

quite clearly, to escape from the tyranny of the past in thought and word and metrical form; and therein he is at one with many of the poets in this book. We may grant that it is an important exception: that the movement which is indicated here may be the sober British version of its more daring Italian counterpart. Yet there remains still a difference wide enough and deep enough to disclaim any technical relationship.

The root of the matter lies there, however. In Mr Stephens what we may call the poetic instinct of the age works not merely to escape from the past, but to advance into the future—and it has become a conscious, reasoned hope in human destiny. It does not with him so much influence the form of the work as it directs the spirit of it. And that spirit is an absolute and impassioned belief in the future of mankind. Therein he stands contrasted with many of the younger English poets, and with his own compatriots. With many of his compeers the escape has been into their own time, and the noblest thing evolved from that is a grave and tender social conscience. Some, of course, have not escaped at all, and have no wish to do so. Their work has its own soft evening loveliness. But whilst Mr Yeats lives delicately in a romantic past, whilst poor Synge lived tragically in a sardonic present, this

poet stands on his hill of vision and cries to the
world the good tidings of a promised land.   Here
it is, from the closing passage of " A Prelude and a
Song " :

> There the flower springs,
> Therein does grow
> The bud of hope, the miracle to come
> For whose dear advent we are striving dumb
> And joyless : Garden of Delight
> That God has sowed !
> In thee the flower of flowers,
> The apple of our tree,
> The banner of our towers,
> The recompense for every misery,
> The angel-man, the purity, the light
> Whom we are working to has his abode ;
> Until our back and forth, our life and death
> And life again, our going and return
> Prepare the way : until our latest breath,
> Deep-drawn and agonized, for him shall burn
> A path : for him prepare
> Laughter and love and singing everywhere ;
> A morning and a sunrise and a day !

Margaret L. Woods

ABOUT one half of the poetry in Mrs Woods' collected edition is dramatic in character. There are two plays in regular form, tragedies both. One, *Wild Justice*, is in six scenes which carry the action rapidly forward almost without a break. The other, called *The Princess of Hanover*, is in three acts, which move in a wider arc through the rise, cumulation and catastrophe of a tragic story. These two dramas, which are powerfully imagined and skilfully wrought, are placed in a separate section at the end of the book —quite the best wine thus being left to finish the feast.

Fine as they are, however, the plays do not completely represent the poet's dramatic gift. And when we note the comic elements of two or three pieces which are tucked away in the middle of the volume, we may admit a hope that Mrs Wood may be impelled on some fair day to attempt regular comedy. There is, for instance, the fun of the delightful medley called " Marlborough Fair." Here are broad humour and vigorous, hearty life which smells of the soil ; little studies of country-folk, incomplete but vivid ; scraps of racy dialogue, and the prattle of a child, all interwoven with the

grotesquer fancies of a fertile imagination, endowing
even the beasts and inanimate objects of the show
with consciousness and speech. Hints there are
in plenty (though to be sure they are in some cases
no more than hints) that the poet's dramatic sense
would handle the common stuff of life as surely
and as freely as it deals with tragedy. In this
particular poem, of course, the touches are of the
nature of low comedy ; the awkward sweethearting
of a pair of rustic lovers ; the showman, alter-
nating between bluster and enticement ; the rough
banter of a group of farm lads about the cokernut-
shy, and the matron who presides there—

> Swarthy and handsome and broad of face
> 'Twixt the banded brown of her glossy hair.
> In her ears are shining silver rings,
> Her head and massive throat are bare,
> She needs good length in her apron strings
> And has a jolly voice and loud
> To cry her wares and draw the crowd.

> —Fine Coker-nuts ! My lads, we're giving
> Clean away ! Who wants to win 'em ?
> Fresh Coker-nuts ! The milk's yet in 'em.
> Come boys ! Only a penny a shot,
> Three nuts if you hit and the fun if not.

The effects are broad and strong, the tone cheery.
But in another piece where the dramatic element
enters, "The May Morning and the Old Man,"

Margaret L. Woods

the note is deeper. There is, indeed, in the talk of
the two old men on the downland road, a much
graver tone of the Comic Spirit. One of them has
come slowly up the hill and greets another who is
working in a field by the roadside with a question.
He wants to know how far it is to Chillingbourne ;
he is going back to his old home there and must
reach it before nightfall.

> First Old Man.   It bean't for j'y I taäk the roäd.
> But, Mester, I be getten awld.
> Do seem as though in all the e'th
>   There bean't no plaäce,
> No room on e'th for awld volk.
> Second Old Man.   The e'th do lie
> Yonder, so wide as Heaven a'most,
>   And God as made un
> Made room, I warr'nt, for all Christian souls.

It is, however, through the medium of tragedy
that the genius of Mrs Woods has found most
powerful expression. Not her charming lyrics, not
even the contemplative beauty of her elegiac poems,
can stand beside the creative energy of the two plays
to which we must come directly. But the best
of the lyrics are notable, nevertheless ; and two
or three have already passed into the common
store of great English poetry. Of such is the
splendid hymn, " To the Forgotten Dead," with

303

its exulting pride of race chastened by the thought
of death.

> To the forgotten dead,
> Come, let us drink in silence ere we part.
> To every fervent yet resolved heart
> That brought its tameless passion and its tears,
> Renunciation and laborious years,
> To lay the deep foundations of our race,
> To rear its mighty ramparts overhead
> And light its pinnacles with golden grace.
> To the unhonoured dead.

> To the forgotten dead,
> Whose dauntless hands were stretched to grasp the rein
> Of Fate and hurl into the void again
> Her thunder-hoofed horses, rushing blind
> Earthward along the courses of the wind.
> Among the stars along the wind in vain
> Their souls were scattered and their blood was shed,
> And nothing, nothing of them doth remain.
> To the thrice-perished dead.

It will be seen that the lyric gift of the poet
moves at the prompting of an imaginative passion.
It is nearly always so in this poetry. Very seldom
does the impulse appear to come from intimate
personal emotion or individual experience ; and the
volume may therefore help to refute the dogma
that the poetry of a woman is bound to be

Margaret L. Woods

subjective, from the laws of her own nature. Occasionally, of course, a direct cry will seem to make itself heard—the most reticent human creature will pay so much toll to its humanity. And it is true that in such a spontaneous utterance the voice will be distinctively feminine—life as the woman knows it will find its interpreter. Thus we see austerity breaking down in the poem " On the Death of an Infant," mournfully sweet with a mother's sorrow. Hence, too, in " Under the Lamp " comes the loathing for " the vile hidden commerce of the city "; and accompanying it a touch of the feminine bias (yielding in these late days perhaps to fuller knowledge and consequent sympathy) which inclines to regard the evil from the point of view of the degradation of the man rather than that of the wrong to the woman. Or again, there is " The Changeling," perhaps the tenderest of the few poems which may, in a certain sense, be called subjective. Through the thin veil of allegory one catches a glimpse of the enduring mystery of maternal love. The mother is brooding over the change in her child : she has not been watchful enough, she thinks ; and while she was unheeding, some evil thing had entered into her baby and driven out the fair soul with which he began.

305

Perhaps he called me and I was dumb.
Unconcerned I sat and heard
　　Little things,
　Ivy tendrils, a bird's wings,
　　　A frightened bird—
Or faint hands at the window-pane ?
And now he will never come again,
The little soul.　He is quite lost.

　She tries to woo him back, with prayer and incantations ; but he will not come ; and when at last she is worn out with waiting, she seeks an old wizard and begs him to sell her forgetfulness for a price.　But it is too hard a thing that she asks : it needs a mighty spell to make a woman forget her son ; and the mother has to go without the boon.　She has not wealth enough in the world to pay the Wise Man's fee.　But afterwards she is glad that she was too poor to pay the price :

Because if I did not remember him,
My little child—Ah ! what should we have,
He and I ?　Not even a grave
With a name of his own by the river's brim.
Because if among the poppies gay
On the hill-side, now my eyes are dim,
I could not fancy a child at play,
And if I should pass by the pool in the quarry
And never see him, a darling ghost,
Sailing a boat there, I should be sorry—

Margaret L. Woods

If in the firelit, lone December
I never heard him come scampering post
Haste down the stair—if the soul that is lost
Came back, and I did not remember.

Such poetry reveals the woman in the poet,
and is precious for that reason : it brings its own
light to the book of humanity. But it is not
especially characteristic of Mrs Woods' work, for
much more often it is the poet in the woman who
is revealed there. Powers which are independent
of sex—of imagination, of sensibility, and of
thought, have gone to the making of that which
is finest in her verse. They are not equally present
here, of course. Imagination overtops them, lofty
and keen, achieving at will the complete objectivity demanded of her art. Thought is a degree
less powerful, perhaps. It is brooding, museful,
and retrospective, tinged with a melancholy that
may be wistful or passionate ; and though it
commonly revolves the larger issues of life within
the canons of authority, it is clear enough to see
beyond them, and even, upon occasion, to pierce
a way through. But it is not always sufficiently
strong to control completely the flight of imagination ; and there is no acute sense of fact to
reinforce it with truth of detail. Instead of
watching, recording, analyzing, this is a mind

307

which leans lovingly toward the past, and has a sense, instinctive as well as scholarly, of historic values : while, for its artistic method, it passes all the treasure that fancy has gathered, and even passion itself, through the alembic of memory. So is created a softer grace, a serener atmosphere, and a richer dignity than the realist can achieve —and we will not be churlish enough to complain if, at the same time, the salt of reality is missing.

I should think that "The Builders: A Nocturne in Westminster Abbey," most fully represents this poet's lyrical gift. Individual qualities of it may perhaps be observed more clearly elsewhere ; but here they combine to produce an effect of meditative sweetness and stately, elegiac grace which are very characteristic. The poem is in ten movements, of very unequal length and irregular form. It is unrhymed, and stanzas may vary almost indefinitely in length, as the verse may pass from a dimeter, light or resonant, up through the intervening measures to the roll of the hexameter. But this originality of technique, leaving room for so many shades of thought and feeling, was happily inspired ; and below the changeful form runs perfect unity of tone. The creative impulse is subdued to the

308

Margaret L. Woods

contemplative mood induced in the mind of the
poet as she stands in the Abbey at night and broods
upon its history. Her thought goes far back, to the
early builders of the fabric whose pale phantoms
seem to float in the shades of the 'grey ascending
arches.'

> When the stars are muffled and under them all the
>   earth
> Is a fiery fog and the sinister roar of London,
> They lament for the toil of their hands, their souls'
>   travail—
>   "Ah, the beautiful work!"
> It was set to shine in the sun, to companion the stars,
> To endure as the hills, the ancient hills, endure;
>   Lo, like a brand
> It lies, a brand consumed and blackened of fire,
>   In the fierce heart of London.

Or, like Dante, this poet will follow the old
ghosts to a more dreadful region, and bring them
news of home—

>   Fain would my spirit,
> My living soul beat up the wind of death
> To the inaccessible shore and with warm voice
> Deep-resonant of the earth, salute the dead:

> .   .   .   .   .   .

>   I also would bring
> To the old unheeded spirits news of Earth;
> Of England, their own country, choose to tell them,

And how above St. Edward's bones the Minster
Gloriously stands, how it no more beholds
The silver Thames broadening among green meadows
And gardens green, nor sudden shimmer of streams
  And the clear mild blue hills.
Rather so high it stands the whole earth under
Spreads boundless and the illimitable sea.

The steps of the sentry, pacing over the stones which cover the great dead below, remind her of those other builders who lie there, makers of Empire.

Over what dust the atom footfall passes !
Out of what distant lands, by what adventures
  Superbly gathered
To lie so still in the unquiet heart of London !
Is not the balm of Africa yet clinging
About the bones of Livingstone ? Consider
The long life-wandering, the strange last journey
Of this, the heroic lion-branded corpse,
  Still urging to the sea !
And here the eventual far-off deep repose.

This poem is characteristic, as well in the choice of its materials as in its treatment and its literary flavour. One may note the opulent language, enriched from older sources, the historical lore and the allusive touch so fascinating to those who love literature for its own sake. But the poet can work at times in a

Margaret L. Woods

very different manner. There is, for instance, another piece of unrhymed verse, " March Thoughts From England," which is a riot of light and colour, rich scent and lovely shape and bewitching sound— the sensuous rapture evoked by a Provençal scene ' recollected in tranquillity.' Or there is " April," with the keen joy of an English spring, also a glad response to the direct impressions of sense. Imagination is subordinated here ; but if we turn in another direction we are likely to find it paramount. It may be manifested in such various degrees and through such different media that sharp contrasts will present themselves. Thus we might turn at once from the playful fancy of " The Child Alone " (where a little maid has escaped from mother and nurse into the wonderful, enchanted, adventurous world just outside the garden) to the thrice-heated fire of " Again I Saw Another Angel." Here imagination has fanned thought to its own fierce heat ; and in the sudden flame serenity is shrivelled up and gives place to passionate despair. In a vision the poet sees the awful messenger of the Lord leap into the heavens with a great cry—

> Then suddenly the earth was white
> With faces turned towards his light.
> The nations' pale expectancy
> Sobbed far beneath him like the sea,

311

But men exulted in their dread,
And drunken with an awful glee
Beat at the portals of the dead.

I saw this monstrous grave the earth
Shake with a spasm as though of birth,
And shudder with a sullen sound,
As though the dead stirred in the ground.
And that great angel girt with flame
Cried till the heavens were rent around,
" Come forth ye dead ! "—Yet no man came.

But from the intensity of that we may pass to the
dainty grace of the Songs, where the poet is weaving
in a gossamer texture. Or we may consider a love-
lyric like " Passing," a fragile thing, lightly evoked
out of a touch of fantasy and a breath of sweet pain.

With thoughts too lovely to be true,
With thousand, thousand dreams I strew
The path that you must come. And you
Will find but dew.

.   .   .   .   .

I break my heart here, love, to dower
With all its inmost sweet your bower.
What scent will greet you in an hour ?
The gorse in flower.

In the plays there are lyrics, too, delicately
stressing their character of poetic drama, and giving
full compass to the author's powers in each work.
Indeed, the combination of lyric and dramatic

312

elements is very skilfully and effectively managed. There is a ballad which serves in each case to state the *motif* at the opening of the play : not in so many words, of course, but suggested in the tragical events of some old story. And snatches of the ballad recur throughout, crooned by one of the persons of the drama, or played by a lutist at a gay court festival. But always the dramatic scheme is subserved by the lyrical fragments. Sometimes it will fill a short interval with a note of foreboding, or make a running accompaniment to the action, or induce an ironic tone, or, by interpreting emotion, it will relieve tension which had grown almost too acute. But, fittingly, when the crisis approaches and action must move freely to the end, the lyric element disappears.

" The Ballad of the Mother," which precedes " Wild Justice," creates the atmosphere in which the play moves from beginning to end. It prefigures the plot, too, in its story of the dead mother who hears her children weeping from her grave in the churchyard ; and, after vainly imploring both angel and sexton to let her go and comfort them, makes a compact with the devil to release her.

" Then help me out, devil, O help me, good devil ! "
" A price must be paid to a spirit of evil.
Will you pay me the price ? " said the spirit from Hell.

" The price shall be paid, the bargain is made."
.   .   .   .   .

Boom ! boom ! boom !
From the tower in the silence there sounds the great
    bell.
" I am fixing the price," said the devil from Hell.

The mother in the play is Mrs Gwyllim, wife of
a vicious tyrant. For twenty-one years she had
borne cruelty and humiliation at his hands. She
had even been patient under the wrongs which he
had inflicted on her children : the violence which
had maimed her eldest son, Owain, in his infancy ;
which had hounded another boy away to sea and
had driven a daughter into a madhouse. But at the
opening of the play a sterner spirit is growing in
her : meekness and submission are beginning to break
down under the consciousness of a larger duty to
her children. We find that she has been making
appeals for help, first to their only accessible relation ; and that failing, to the Vicar of their parish.
But neither of these men had dared to move against
the tyrant. They live on a lonely little island off
the coast of Wales, where Gwyllim practically has
the small population in his power. He had built a
lighthouse on the coast ; and at the time of the
action, which is early in the nineteenth century, he
is empowered to own it and to take toll from passing

vessels. Thus he controls the means of existence of the working people ; and the rest are deterred, by reasons of policy or family interest, from putting any check upon him.

In the first scene the mother announces to her daughter Nelto and her favourite son Shonnin the result of her appeal to the Vicar. His only reply had been to affront her with a counsel of patience, though Gwyllim's misconduct is as notorious as his wife's long-suffering. We are thus made to realize the isolation and helplessness of the family before we proceed to the second scene, with its culmination of Gwyllim's villainy and the first hint of rebellion. He comes into the house, furious at the discovery of what he calls his wife's treachery. Owain, the crippled son, is present during part of the scene ; and Nelto passes and repasses before the open door of an inner room, hushing the baby with stanzas of the ballad which opens the play. In the presence of their children, Gwyllim raves at his wife, taunts her with her helplessness, boasts of his own infidelity, and flings a base charge at her, of which he says he has already informed the parson ; while Nelto croons—

> The angels are fled, and the sexton is sleeping,
> And I am a devil, a devil from Hell.

The mother does not answer ; but Owain is

goaded to protest. This only excites Gwyllim
further, and he strikes Owain as he sits in his
invalid chair ; while Shonnin, coming in from the
adjoining room, brings the scene to a climax by
asking of his father the money that he needs to go
away to school. Gwyllim replies, taking off his coat
meanwhile, that there is a certain rule in his family.
When a son of his is man enough to knock him down
he shall have money to go out into the world ; but
not before.   He invites Shonnin to try his strength :

> GWYLLIM. . . . Come on. Why don't you come
> on ? I'm making no defence.
> SHONNIN. Mother ?
> GWYLLIM. Leave her alone. Strike me, boy. I
> bid you do it.
> SHONNIN. Then I will ; with all my might, and
> may God increase it !
> OWAIN. There is no God.

Shonnin strikes three times ; and is then felled
by a blow from his father, who goes out, shouting
orders to wife as he retreats. The scene closes in
a final horror. Nelto, a pretty, high-spirited girl,
has hitherto taken little part in the action. Her
character, however, has been clearly indicated in one
or two strong touches. We realize that she is
young, impulsive, warm-hearted ; keenly sensitive to
beauty, wilful and bright ; thrilling to her finger-

tips with life that craves its birthright of liberty and joy. But we see, too, that with all her ardour she is as proud and cold in her attitude to love as a very Artemis. And when she declares that she also has reached the point of desperation, and that sooner than remain longer in the gloom and terror of her home she will fling herself into a shameful career, we feel that the climax has indeed been reached.

In the third scene the plan of wild justice is formulated. It had originated in the mind of Owain, who had fed his brooding temper on old stories of revenge. To him the dreadful logic of the scheme seemed unanswerable. No power on earth or heaven could help them ; either they must save themselves, or be destroyed, body and soul. He puts his plan before Shonnin—to lure their father by a light wrongly placed, as he rows home at night, on to the quicksands at the other side of the island. But Shonnin, if he has less strength of will than Owain, is more thoughtful and more sensitive. He is appalled at the proposal. Owain reminds him of their wrongs ; asks him what this monster has done that he should live to be their ruin. And Shonnin, seeing the issues more clearly, replies

> . . . Nothing ;
> But then I have done nothing to deserve
> To be made a parricide.

But Nelto has been listening, and hers is a nature of a very different mettle. Besides, as she has put the alternative to herself, it means but a choice between two evils; and this plan of Owain's seems at least a cleaner thing than the existence she had contemplated. She declares that she will be the instrument of the revenge.

The rest of the play is occupied with the execution of the plan. Scene IV shows us Nelto going on her way down to the sea at night with the lantern that is to lead Gwyllim on to the sands. She is trying not to think; but the very face of nature seems to reflect the horror that is in her soul—

> . . . Down slips the moon.
> NELTO. Broken and tarnished too? Now she hangs motionless
>   As 'twere amazed, in a silver strait of sky
>   Between the long black cloud and the long black sea;
>   The sea crawls like a snake.

The figure of a woman suddenly appears in the path. It is her mother; she has overheard their plans, and for a moment Nelto is afraid that she has come to frustrate them. But Mrs Gwyllim has a very different purpose: she intends to take upon herself the crime that her children are about to commit—

Margaret L. Woods

All's fallen from me now
But naked motherhood. What ! Shall a hare
Turn on the red-jawed dogs, being a mother,
The unpitying lioness suckle her whelps
Smeared with her heart's blood, this one law be stamped
For ever on the imperishable stuff
Of our mortality, and I, I only,
Forbidden to obey it ?

But Nelto sees that she is too frail and weak for
the task ; and entreats her mother to return to
the house. Time is slipping, and her father is
waiting for the boat.

Mrs. Gwyllim.   Ellen, you are too young ;
 You should be innocent—
Nelto.   Never again
 After this night. Come, mother, I am yours ;
 Make me a wanton or an avenger.
Mrs. Gwyllim.   Powers
 That set my spirit to swing on such a thread
 Over mere blackness, teach me now to guide it !
Nelto. Mother, the moon dips.
Mrs. Gwyllim.   Go, my daughter, go !
 And let these hands, these miserable hands,
 Too weak to avenge my children, let them be
 Yet strong enough to pull upon my head
 God's everlasting judgment ! All that weight
 Fall on me only !

We see what follows in the closing scenes as
a fulfilment of that prayer. Nelto takes the boat

319

to meet Gwyllim, intending to row him over to the false light that she herself has placed. When he has stepped ashore she is to push off instantly, and leave him either to stride forward into the quicksand, or to be drowned by the tide. Owain and his mother peer from their window through the darkness, trying to follow Nelto's movements by the light on her boat. They have locked Shonnin in his room that he may not know what they are doing and interfere. But he manages to awaken a sleeping child in the next room, and is released in time to discover what is afoot. He seizes another lantern and rushes down to the bay to signal a warning to his father. Meantime Mrs Gwyllim and Owain search the opposite shore with a telescope ; they see the light on the boat approach it, stop for just so long as a man would need to clamber out, and then move away. For a few seconds they distinguish the swaying light that Gwyllim carries, and then it disappears. To their strained imagination it seems that they hear his terrible cry as he reaches the quicksand ; and at the same time they are horrified to see that Nelto's boat is returning to him. She also has heard the cry, and has gone back to try to save her father. The light moves forward, slowly at first and then more quickly, as Nelto seems to spring ashore. A moment afterwards it too goes out.

Margaret L. Woods

No other sign comes to the watchers, for when they turn their glasses to the nearer shore Shonnin also has disappeared. They keep their dreadful vigil till dawn ; and then the mother, pitifully hoping against hope, goes out to seek her children.—She returns with Nelto's shawl.

MRS. GWYLLIM.   Where are my children, if they are
    not there ?
    They cannot both be—Owain, where are they ?
OWAIN [*Makes a gesture towards the sea*] Mother,
    May God have mercy on us !
MRS. GWYLLIM.   No, not both,
    Not both ! She's somewhere in the house. Come,
      Ellen !
    She is afraid to come. Come, Nelto, Nelto !
    Shonnin, my heart's adored, Shonnin, my love,
    Do not be angry with me, answer, Shonnin,
    Shonnin ! Not dead—not dead !
OWAIN.   O hush—hush—hush !

In a summary of this kind it is impossible to indicate all the dramatic values of the work. One cannot show, for instance, how the characters come to life, and by touches bold or subtle, develop an individuality out of which the conflict of the drama springs. Even the conflict itself can hardly be suggested, for an outline of the story gives only the physical action ; whilst there is a spiritual struggle in the minds of at least two of the characters which

321

is infinitely more tragical. And neither can one hope to convey any sense of the force with which the play takes possesssion of the mind. That is of course, its chief artistic excellence ; and on a moment's consideration it is seen to be a remarkable achievement. For although the poet is working towards a catastrophe very remote from ordinary experience, and in a poetic medium deeply stamped with the marks of an earlier age, she has succeeded in evoking a powerful illusion of reality. Here and there, indeed, are signs that the handicap she has imposed upon herself is almost too great. There is, perhaps, exaggeration in the portraiture of Gwyllim ; or, to put it in another way, the author has not taken an opportunity to balance what is extraordinary in this character with the relief which would have suggested a complete personality. And now and then there is a hint of incongruity in the use of a rich Elizabethan diction, even for Owain, who is supposed to be steeped in the literature of that age.

Those are not radical defects, however, for they do not interrupt the enjoyment of the drama : they only emerge as an afterthought. If the incompleteness of Gwyllim disturbed our conviction of his villainy, the whole plot would be weakened. Whereas we are profoundly convinced that the wrongs of his family are intolerable, and the revolt a natural consequence. Similarly, if the exuberant Elizabethan language were really unfitted to the spirit of the work, I imagine that it would be barely possible to read the drama through, so irritating would be its ineptitude. But, as a fact, the language wins upon us somehow as the right expression for these people. We are probably satisfied, subconsciously, that human creatures who have been thrust back to an almost elemental stage of passion and thought, might talk in some such way. In any case the emotional force of that old style, with its vivid imagery and metaphor and its copious flow, does somehow suit the intensity and gloomy grandeur of this play.

I am not sure that it suits *The Princess of Hanover* quite so well—which is curious, considering that we have, in the royal theme of this drama, a subject which might be supposed to require an ornate style. But in treating the tragic love-story of Sophia of Zell the poet was bound to reproduce something of the atmosphere of the Hanoverian Court, with its intrigues and indecencies and absurd conventionality. And at such points poetry lends too large a dignity. In those scenes, however, where as in " Wild Justice," the author comes to deal with naked passion and with turbulent thought that is driving some person of the drama to disaster, the instrument is admirably fitted to its purpose. Thus, in the second half of the play, when the unfortunate Princess at last yields to her lover, Königsmarck, and plots with him to escape from her sottish husband, there are moments when it seems that no other medium would serve. There is, for example, the crucial scene in the second act when the endurance of the Princess finally gives way. The action turns here directly towards its tragic culmination ; for the Princess, who had hitherto saved her honour at the cost of her love, suddenly breaks down at an insult from the old Electress. The revulsion of feeling as she flings restraint away carries her to an ecstatic sense of liberty. As the Electress goes out and she is left alone with her lady-in-waiting, she laughs bitterly and declares that she is now free for ever from the House of Hanover.

LEONORA.   Weeping, dear lady,
  Will balm our misery better than laughter.
PRINCESS.   Misery ?   I am mad with all the joy
  Of all my years, my youth-consuming years'
    Hoarded, unspent delight.
    Say, Leonora,
  Where are my wings ? Do they not shoot up radiant,
  A splendour of snowy vans, swimming the air
  Just ere the rush of rapture ?

One might quote a dozen such passages, in which

a rush of emotion seems to overflow most naturally
into poetical extravagance, There is the rhapsody
of the Electress—significantly, upon the theme of
Queen Elizabeth. There are the love-scenes, passionate or tender, between Königsmarck and the
Princess; and the fierce moods—of sheer avidity or
hatred or remorse—of the courtesan who contrives
their downfall. But the only other illustration
which need be given is taken from the last scene
of the play; and has a further importance which
must be noted. I mean the tragic irony which
underlies it, and, running throughout the scene,
closes the play on a note of appalling mockery.

The scene is in the Electoral Palace at night, or
rather very early morning, when the grey light is
slowly coming. The Princess and Leonora have
come into the outer hall of their apartments to
burn certain papers in the fireplace there. Their
plans are all made for flight with Königsmarck on
the following day; and as they kindle the fire they
talk, the Princess eagerly and Leonora with more
caution, about their chances of escape. But on the
very spot where they stand, Königsmarck had been
secretly assassinated less than an hour before. And
at this moment, while they are talking, his body
is being hastily bricked into a disused staircase
leading out of the hall. Faint sounds of the work

Contemporary Poets

reach the ears of the ladies as they begin their task ;
but though Leonora is disquieted, the Princess will
not listen to her fears. She is on the crest of a
mood of exaltation—

PRINCESS.　　　　　　The night is almost over,
Soon will the topmost towers discern the'day.
The day ! The day ! O last of all the days
I have spent in extreme penury of joy,
In garish misery, unhelped wrong,
And in unpardonable dishonour. . . .

.　　.　　.　　.　　.

Up lingering dawn !
Why dost thou creep so pale, like one afraid ?
I want the sun ! I want to-morrow !
LEONORA.　　　　　　Madam,
There was a hand on the door. What can these
　builders
Be doing here at this hour ?
PRINCESS.　　　　　Why, they're building.
What does it matter ?　Let them build all night,
I warrant they'll not build a wall so high
Love cannot overleap it.

John Drinkwater

EARLY in the third year of the Great War
I went to Birmingham. The outlook at
that time was dark; and national vitality,
drained by the long struggle, burnt low. The
high ideals for which England had seized the sword
had flickered and almost faded. The whirling
futilities of war-service seemed driven solely by
the force themselves had generated; and that was
blind and feverish, a mad rotation in a gloom of
hatred, jealousy, suspicion and greed.

But in Birmingham there were lights burning—
one from the Art Gallery, and another from the
Repertory Theatre of John Drinkwater. The
pictures of Burne-Jones shone upon something
which a citizen of Cosmopolis could but be re-
freshed to find—a homogeneity, a clear type bred
fine and true in Midland folk. They illuminated
the source from which their own inspiration had
been drawn, showed whence had come to the
painter his vision of a marriage of physical grandeur
with spiritual grace, and revealed it as the essential
thing about these dwellers in the heart of England.
But while throwing into relief that union, making
it seem almost typical and characteristic, the
pictures stressed another aspect of the truth in

327

their austerity. For, interpreting and interpreted by the life around them, they showed that though imperfect humanity could, after all, arrive but seldom at the perfect union of body and soul, and though modern industrialism might work sad havoc with that fine physique, yet it was possible—difficult but possible—for the spirit to survive that ravage. And the survival of the spirit was perhaps the clearest ray that those pictures threw over Birmingham city, evoking kindred colour in its busy Midland life.

At that moment the other light I spoke of, the Repertory Theatre of John Drinkwater, was known to me in a quite different sense. Its art was life; an escape from the death-in-life in which all the world was furiously whirling. Only within its walls could one get out of the gloom cast by dead hopes, dead ideals and dead men. Only there, or so it seemed, could one breathe a living air and feel the healthful sunlight and join in the energies of sane living. It spoke no special message, at the time; but it was a place of robust vitality, where one went in the intervals of seemingly futile labour, and drank up draughts of life. That was all, then. But in retrospect, and with fuller knowledge, one salutes its beam also as the light of the conquering spirit, and sees it for a

John Drinkwater

symbol of the same union of which the art of Burne-Jones had spoken.

But it is here that Mr Drinkwater's work comes in. One had known of him before the war, of course, as a lyrical poet, as the author of *Cromwell*, and as the writer of at least one successful play for the Pilgrim Players of Birmingham. He was already recognized by his compeers, and familiar to a certain public; for it was impossible to mistake the paternity of lines like these:

> Come tell us, you that travel far
>   With brave or shabby merchandise,
> Have you saluted any star
>   That goes uncourtiered in the skies?
>
> .   .   .   .   .
>
> If the grey dust is over all,
>   And stars and leaves and wings forgot,
> And your blood holds no festival—
>   Go out from us; we need you not.
>
> But if you are immoderate men,
>   Zealots of joy, the salt and sting
> And savour of life upon you—then
>   We call you to our counselling.
>
> And we will hew the holy boughs
>   To make us level rows of oars,
> And we will set our shining prows
>   For strange and unadventured shores.

329

Contemporary Poets

Where the great tideways swiftliest run
We will be stronger than the strong,
And sack the cities of the sun,
And spend our booty in a song.

Apollo is their undoubted father; and yet,
somehow, one did not pay much heed. I think
the reason (apart from one's own sheer dullness)
might have been that this poetry was too poetic.
It had almost too fine a point upon it. That seems
a heresy, and would be one in truth if it implied
that a poet ever dare neglect the form of his art.
But there is such a thing as undistinguished perfection, and the earlier work of Mr Drinkwater was
rather like that. Not really perfect, nor quite
undistinguished, of course, but regular with an
immobile regularity in which the primal fire was
apt to burn low. The fault did his verse a double
injury, hiding from the indifferent its thought
content, and from its admirers the nature of that
content. It was therefore a comprehensible judgment five or six years ago (though perhaps not an
intelligent one) to say that Mr Drinkwater was
living in his time but was not of it : that writing
contemporaneously with others of his own generation, he was yet not a contemporary poet. So
little did he bear the mark of the spirit of the time,
and so placid were the features of his Muse.

330

John Drinkwater

In 1914 Mr Drinkwater published a volume into
which he had gathered all the poems prior to that
date which he wishes to preserve, except *Cromwell* ;
and perhaps one might date from that time the
change. But I prefer to herald it in a poem called
" The Fires of God," first published about 1912.
This appears to be a piece of spiritual autobiography ;
but whether or not it be a record of actual experience, it remains the most succinct statement that
we possess in poetry of the modern position in
religion and philosophy. In it Mr Drinkwater is
sealed a poet of his own time by the spirit of his
time. Weighing at once the arrogant claims and
the profound abasements of the old philosophies,
cleaving a middle way between the Heaven and
Hell of the old religions, he takes his stand on the
good earth and sees himself neither as demi-god
nor devil, but as an integral member of a unity, all
the multitudinous parts of which are singing together
for delight in the beauty of the whole :

As I beheld—

With a new wisdom, tranquil, asking not
For mystic revelation—this glory long forgot,
This re-discovered triumph of the earth
In high creative will and beauty's pride
Establishèd beyond the assaulting years,
It came to me, a music that compelled
Surrender of all tributary fears,

Full-throated, fierce, and rhythmic with the wide
Beat of the pilgrim winds and labouring seas,
Sent up from all the harbouring ways of earth
Wherein the travelling feet of men have trod,
Mounting the firmamental silences
And challenging the golden gates of God.

That is his hymn of ecstasy in the revelation; but it is characteristic of this poet that ecstasy should be touched to further ends than simple joy in itself. And one is arrested by the fact that the end of exultation here—this being, as would appear, the record of a spiritual crisis—is the act of walking out into the street and shouldering his bit of humanity's burden there:

Henceforth my hands are lifted to the touch
Of hands that labour with me, and my heart
Hereafter to the world's heart shall be set
And its own pain forget.

That is a passage whose significance bears both on the man and his age. One has seen the same symbolic act in other contemporary poets. But beyond observing that the humanitarianism of this poet is a conscious principle, one ought not to stress it, just because the artistic impulse has forbidden him to give a prominent place to anything so abstract in his work. Artistic integrity is strong in him, and is leading him now more and more

332

John Drinkwater

towards Drama for vivid and concrete expression.
It is the destined path of the poets, the inevitable
sequence by which the lyrical intensity of youth is
succeeded by a more critical, observant and reflective faculty, operating in a larger world of experience. It is not for nothing that Mr Drinkwater is
a poet of Warwickshire, of delight in life, of keen
sense-impressions and swift response to them, of
gentle and homely scenes of nature, of hearty
country folk, of friendship and of extravagant
passion. He is an inheritor, and this fair body of
his verse came out of the heart of England. Its
qualities are specifically English. It has dignity,
sweetness and nobility, but it has also pith, vigour
and clarity. Its imagination is sunny : there are
no mystical shadows haunting it, and it does not
ever fly high enough nor deep enough to reach the
outer darkness. Its imagery is bright and clear, so
that even a thought of " Symbols " is given the
shape and stir of life :

> I imagined measureless time in a day,
> And starry space in a wagon-road,
> And the treasure of all good harvests lay
> In the single seed that the sower sowed.
>
> My garden-wind had driven and havened again
> All ships that ever had gone to sea,

333

And I saw the glory of all dead men
In the shadow that went by the side of me.

And even an idea so abstract as the eternal lament
for the passing of beauty is caught, half playfully,
into a series of shining figures :

> Lord Rameses of Egypt sighed
>   Because a summer evening passed ;
> And little Ariadne cried
>   That summer fancy fell at last
> To dust ; and young Verona died
>   When beauty's hour was overcast.
>
> Theirs was the bitterness we know
>   Because the clouds of hawthorn keep
> So short a state, and kisses go
>   To tombs unfathomably deep,
> While Rameses and Romeo
>   And little Ariadne sleep.

So one thinks of this poetry as of a healthy body
ruled by a serene mind : its temper sane, its manner
gracious, planned on noble lines which are shaping
toward perfection by a rigorous discipline. And
one likes to believe it peculiarly English. But there
is something else ; and in the strength and persistence of that other quality one seems to come
still closer to its origin in the Puritan spirit of
mid-England. Recall the work by which Mr
Drinkwater is popularly known—his most con-

John Drinkwater

siderable poem, *Cromwell*, and his most successful
play, *Abraham Lincoln*. The mere names will give
the clue to the outstanding thing about their author.
The fact that he chose those two men from all others
for commemoration and the worship of his art is
significant enough. But when one remembers the
impression which those works leave upon the mind,
the thing which stays after the sonorous music has
passed and the action is done, one salutes again the
same survival of the spirit which shone as a beacon
in Birmingham during the Great War.

The *Cromwell* poem is lyrical in essence and
largely so in form. It is designed to tell in twelve
movements or episodes of the rising of Cromwell
and his Ironsides, the battles in which the king's
armies are defeated, the trial and execution of
Charles, the final victory of the Puritan cause,
and the death of Cromwell. There are five interludes between the principal episodes, where the
poet, after the manner of a Greek chorus, muses
upon the event and its significance. A prologue
nobly states the theme in blank verse, and an
epilogue lightens the tragic intensity of the finished
tale in a lyrical finale.

A great charm of the poem is the variety of
measure used. The narrative pieces are not all, as
one would expect, in blank verse ; and of the three

or four episodes related in this form, no two are quite in the same manner. So with the rhymed pieces : a different measure has been made for each, to fit its own mood or circumstance ; and even stanzas which have a superficial resemblance will be found to vary in rhyme or rhythm, in the number or length or stress of the verses.

One might attempt a short selection, to give an idea of the changeful form and constant spirit of this poem. Thus, the prologue tells that the theme is to be of " stern and memorable days " and

> Of one who watched the shadows folding in
> All beautiful goings in the lives of men,
> And heard the arrogant mastery on the lips
> Of spoilers of the spirit's husbandry.

Then one might cut a fragment from the first interlude, to illustrate a thought which often preoccupies this poet. The interlude is written in praise of great men ; but it comes back to the sense of human frailty which underlies also the poet's reading of the character of Lincoln—the perception that these Titans are but earth-born after all :

> We are men, and godhead is far, and it shall not be
> That men as gods without flaw shall travel to death,
> Yet a rumour of stars is with us, the light of a sea
> No ship has ventured. . . .

336

John Drinkwater

" The Call " finds Cromwell in " the middle watches of his days " :

> Oliver Cromwell, keeper of the gate
> Of one proud temple yet inviolate,
> Looked upwards to the stars and prayed that then
> He might not be unworthy among men
> To serve. . . .
>
>   . . . " Lord, might I avail
> But as the meanest of the men whose laws
> Are Thine alone, Thy peace their sole estate ;
> My sword, my will, my love are consecrate
> Unto Thy cause, my God, unto Thy cause."

In " The Coming " Cromwell answers the call and realizes that the issue is " Charles, King of England " :

> O place of man, high on the windy scar
> That o'ertops desolation and the void ;
> O heart of man that knoweth not the end
> Of all thy pride though fiery witnesses
> Are all about thee, loud in prophecy.

In " Edgehill " the king's army, merry and gaily dressed, goes followed by the " great silent shadow " of Cromwell's men. There is a notable portrait of Charles here :

> Rode Charles the king, dreamer of twisted dreams,
> Hearing all counsels, speaking all men fair,
> Prey to all bidders for a kingly pledge,

Yet governed ever by one sovran rule—
The tattered sway of his own motley heart.

Then comes " The Gathering of the Ironsides," a
swinging battle-song :

From the north to the south he travelled, and out to the
east and west,
And cried as a fiery prophet in lands where the heathen
rest,—
" The God of Battles calls you, and the service of God is
best."

The varying fortunes on " Marston Moor " close in
victory for the cause of freedom ; and in the " Idyll "
which follows, Cromwell the warrior is seen com-
passionately caring for the widow of a Royalist
enemy :

A quiet man mid quiet men
He was ; he took her from the place,
Not courtly was his hand, no grace
Of word mocked consolation then,
Yet as he helped her helplessness
A strong and wonderful gentleness
Was on him. . . .

There is the issue of " Naseby," when Ireton's line
is routed, and defeat of the Parliamentarians seems
imminent :

But in that hour when exultation rose
In a great shout along the prevailing ranks

John Drinkwater

A sudden blast smote back the waves of war,
As once it had so smitten on the day
Of Marston field . . .
 . . . till the noonday sun
Looked down upon the legions of the king
Scattered and stark, a memory—no more.

In the fourth interlude, "Of War," the ideal
spectator muses on the cause and motive of war.
To put right a great wrong a man may be compelled to raise his hand to kill his enemy; but to
deal in death as a trade is the last iniquity:

So signed is your cause? Do you dare to steer
So rotten a ship on so stern a stream?

The soldiers of Cromwell's army come to London
to weigh their cause against the defeated king:

And well the curlèd king may frown,
And well the queen in her scented gown,
 For twenty thousand men are marching
Along the streets of London town.

Charles is tried at Westminster in the bitter winter
weather, and judgment is passed on him:

Hushed were the judges then; the men-at-arms
Stood motionless as graven soldiery
In some old woven fable, and no sound
Was heard save winter's trouble in the air.

The fifth interlude muses upon tyranny. It is
not the tyrant alone who sins, but every man

339

who bears tyranny patiently and strikes no blow for freedom :

> By these things suffered in your fatherland,
> By Milton's word and Cromwell's winnowing hand,
> By your green ways and shining leagues of foam,
> By England's name, by Athens and by Rome
> Let tyrants bear their brand,
> Rise up and strike your spoilers and strike home.

" Dunbar " is fought and won : at " Worcester " the " Ironside sword is sheathed " ; and now Cromwell comes to the end of all fighting :

> Thy loving-kindness has been great,
> And great Thy blessing of the sword,
> Thy hand has prospered my estate,
> I was not worthy, Lord.
>
> . . . .
>
> Not any worth of mine I trust,
> Nor love that I have given Thee,
> But Thy sweet spirit in my dust,
> Thy love that is in me.
>
> . . . .
>
> From travel in the dusty ways,
> From strife of speech and sounding sword,
> I come undaunted of the days
> Into Thy keeping, Lord.

Such a selection, of course, does violence to the poet's design ; but it does at least indicate what one has figured as the fine union of body and soul in this work. Generous emotion, sensitiveness and

John Drinkwater

acute perception of beauty are shaped patiently
into noble form, but the living breath in it is the
breath of the spirit, and the spirit is that of Puritan
England. Now I am not suggesting any theological
connotation here. Mr Drinkwater frequently uses
the word 'God,' even where there is no dramatic
urgency, as one of those earlier Puritans might have
named it. There is, too, a characteristic humility
which is religious in its basis ; and the hymn on
which Cromwell's life closes is the essential music
of the Christian religion. But the spirit of this
work cannot be narrowed to any theology : it is
as much bigger than that as those old Puritans were
bigger than their reputed creed. One aspect of it
is seen in the piece called " Challenge " :

> You fools behind the panes who peer
> At the strong black anger of the sky,
> Come out and feel the storm swing by,
> Aye, take its blow on your lips, and hear
> The wind in the branches cry.

It is seen in a fierce love of freedom, in the interlude
" Of Tyranny " which shames a coward patience,
in " The Fires of God," burning up self-pity and
bidding a man to service. It is seen, too, in the
courage of the short play called $X = O$, acted at
Birmingham during the war, in which the poet
cries out against War's madness and hideous waste.

341

Contemporary Poets

Again it is seen in the profounder courage of the enigma called *The God of Quiet*; and in the conception of the character of Alice in the play called *The Storm*.

I do not know anything in modern poetry more true and lovely than this little play : though it is pitiful truth and sorrowful loveliness. Dramatically, too, it seems to me the best thing that Mr Drinkwater has done, in spite of the fact that there is little action in it. Its substance is, indeed, of actual *inaction*—of waiting, of taut suspense.

The scene is a shepherd's cabin on the Welsh hills at night, with a furious storm raging outside. The shepherd had gone out hours before, and has not returned : he is lost somewhere in the storm. His wife is waiting in intense anxiety. She has sent out searchers with lanterns and has built up the fire to prepare hot water against her husband's return. Her young sister and an old neighbour-woman keep her company ; and while the old woman reiterates with the relentless realism of age that the shepherd must by this time have died from the storm's violence, the wife vehemently denies that her husband can be dead.

I said that there was practically no action in the play ; but indeed the action is fierce and continuous. It is, however, on the spiritual plane. It is

John Drinkwater

a heart-breaking struggle between age and youth,
between illusion and reality, between love and
despair, between hope and an inescapable logic.
And this against a consciousness of that other
imagined struggle out on the hills, between a man
and the immense force of the elements:

ALICE.   You know that he's not dead—
          I know that too—if only that dark rage
          Howling out there would leave tormenting me.

The character of Alice is very nobly imagined,
and she is presented with great force and subtlety.
Under her passionate denial of the truth the conviction of it grows, creeping into her distraction and
fear, and leaping out when in the lull of an un-
guarded moment she turns to her young sister:

ALICE.   . . . My little Joan,
          Do you know at all what a man becomes to a woman?
                    . . . A woman takes a mate,
          And like the patient builder governs him
          Into the goodman known through a country-side,
          Or the wise friend that the neighbours will seek out,
                    . . . And when he is dead
          It comes to her that the strength she has given him
          To make him a gallant figure among them all
          Has been the thing that has filled her, and she lonely
          Or gossiping with the folk, or about the house.
SARAH.   When he is dead.

343

ALICE.   Why should I think of that?
I am crazed, I say, because of the madness loosed
And beating against the panes.   He is not dead—

It is a fine stroke of tragic irony by which there
breaks upon the scene at this point a young stranger,
taking refuge from the storm; and it serves the
dramatist to complete his presentment of Alice.
The young man is exhilarated by his fight with the
wind, and ecstatic in his relief at escaping from it.
Ignorant of their trouble and blinded by his own
exuberance, he praises the god of the storm in a
lyrical rapture to the silent women.   Nor does he
cease when Alice, controlling herself and seeking to
check him, interposes quietly that the storm is no
thing for praise, but a treacherous fury.   Again he
launches on a flight of exaltation.   And then Alice,
the agony of her suspense tearing at her courtesy,
turns upon him:

                    Stranger, I'd give
Comely words to any who knocks at the door.
You are welcome; but leave your praising of this
    blight.
You safely gabbing of sly and cruel furies,
Like a child laughing before a cage of tigers.
You with your fancy talk of lords and gods
And your hero-veins—young man, do you know this
    night
Is eating through my bones into the marrow,

John Drinkwater

And creeping round my brain till thought is dead,
And making my heart the oldest thing of any?
Do you see those lights?
THE STRANGER. They seemed odd moving there
In a storm like this.
ALICE. A man is lost on the hills.
THE STRANGER. That's bad. But who?
ALICE. My man is lost on the hills.

It must not be supposed, however, that because this poetry is always serious that it is therefore always solemn. It is true that Mr Drinkwater knows how to handle tragedy, and has often a beautiful gravity of manner. It is also true that sometimes his sonority is a little pompous, that there is an occasional redundance of phrase and rhetorical emphasis. But his Muse is riant and bountiful as Warwickshire meadows. It is sweetened by laughter and fellowship. It does not love twilight and melancholy and mysticism, as does the Celtic Muse; and charm of that kind does not therefore distinguish it. It is not contemplative in its attitude or subtle in its expression. It belongs to the cheerful day, is vital and vivid and is in touch with the source of comedy. And if the idea of "Holiness" is a familiar one to this poet, it is of a special kind such as he has made this song about:

If all the carts were painted gay
And all the streets swept clean,

345

Contemporary Poets

And all the children came to play
    By hollyhocks, with green
    Grasses to grow between,

If all the houses looked as though
    Some heart were in their stones,
If all the people that we know
    Were dressed in scarlet gowns,
    With feathers in their crowns,

I think this gaiety would make
    A spiritual land.
I think that holiness would take
    This laughter by the hand,
    Till both should understand.

Michael Field

*Katharine Harris Bradley and
Edith Emma Cooper*

W E all know now that the name of Michael
Field spells tragedy, and that it covers
the story of two lives which burned in
a single flame of creative ardour right up to the
gates of death. But it is a veiled history; and
although we may some day know more about its
poignant joy and pain, I imagine that the veil will
never be completely rent. It has been lifted once
or twice for the fraction of a moment; and now and
then a crumb of knowledge is dropped to the hungry
inquirer. But the story of that unique fellowship
and surpassing love could never be fully told. Yet,
merely to gather the spare morsels of fact gives
warrant of heroic stature, and sustenance to a robust
denial that women are incapable of greatness in art
and comradeship.

The two ladies who used the *nom de plume* of
Michael Field were named Katharine Bradley and
Edith Cooper. They were related as aunt and
niece, though there was not a great disparity of age
between them; and neither of them married.
They lived together and were devoted to each other

347

in a very real sense. They called each other familiarly Michael and Henry, Katharine Bradley, the elder, being Michael. Each was poetically gifted, though with a certain dissimilarity ; and they vowed themselves, early in their career, to literary co-operation. The vow was kept with perfect loyalty. They worked together for upward of thirty years, producing in that time twenty-five poetical dramas, in which it is all but impossible to discover evidence of a double authorship, and seven volumes of lyrics.

Their first two plays—*Callirrhoe* and *Fair Rosamund*, were published in one book in 1884. Their last drama, *In the Name of Time*, came out in the summer of 1919. But before it appeared both poets had died. The younger, Edith Cooper, was attacked by cancer in 1912 ; and while nursing her, Katharine Bradley was also seized by the same disease. The affection between these two friends and their heroic temper may be judged by two facts. Both refused to the end the alleviation of morphia ; and Katharine Bradley, who only survived her niece by less than a year, continued to nurse her till her death, successfully hiding the torture which she was herself enduring from her and from the world. Edith Cooper died in December 1913, and Katharine Bradley nine months

Michael Field

afterwards. She, the fiery-hearted, who had chosen Michael for her patron saint, was buried on St Michael's day, 1914.

It is a story whose depths and heights we can but feebly guess at; and one passes from the personal aspect of it in awe at human magnificence. We are stayed from touching it—except perhaps to note three steps in that *via dolorosa* which the poet herself has marked. Thus there are two poems written by Michael during Henry's illness:

> She is singing to Thee, *Domine!*
>   Dost hear her now?
> She is singing to Thee from a burning throat,
> And melancholy as the owl's love-note;
> She is singing to Thee from the utmost bough
>   Of the tree of Golgotha, where it is bare,
> And the fruit torn from it that fruited there;
> She is singing. . . . Canst Thou stop the strain,
>   The homage of such pain?
> *Domine*, stoop down to her again!

The second poem is called " Caput tuum ut Carmelus " :

> I watch the arch of her head
>   As she turns away from me. . . .
> I would I were with the dead,
>   Drowned with the dead at sea,
> All the waves rocking over me!
>   .   .   .   .   .

Oh, what can Death have to do
With a curve that is drawn so fine,
With a curve that is drawn as true
As the mountains' crescent line? . . .
Let me be hid where the dust falls fine!

To comment on that would be to profane it; and
of this other it is only permitted to marvel at a
wonder—that in the last tortured days of a life so
bereaved the singing spirit could still conquer.

THE ONLY ONE

I think of her
As the fastness of hepatica,
The little fort of blue that held itself so fine,
So lightsome and so sure,
In that garden-plot of mine where the snow spread.
I cannot take anything else, or instead.
I think of her
By the plot where I miss my hepatica.

But there is another aspect of this history which
we may examine a little more closely, partly because
it is a question of art and therefore impersonal;
and partly because the poet herself has raised the
veil by a hair's-breadth here and there, giving a
fleeting glimpse within. They will be found, these
peeps at identity, scattered among the lyrics. It
is only there, of course, that the subjective element
which induces self-betrayal can exist; and even
there it operates but rarely. From this fragmentary

Michael Field

evidence, however, I incline to think that Michael,
the elder of the two women, was the leading spirit :
that her genius was intense, ardent and creative :
that she was the initiator ; and that she was respon-
sible for most of the lyrics, the greater part of the
verse of the tragedies, and the conception of the
protagonist in almost every case. To Henry would
therefore belong the constructive share of the work,
the critical faculty by which it was tested and
shaped, and, of course, a great deal of verse. This
view of the collaboration is indeed supported by
another fact gathered from those who know. But
keeping to internal evidence, I cull three short
passages from the volume entitled *Underneath the
Bough*, published in 1893.

The first is a precious record, being nothing less
than the marriage testament of these two souls :

> It was deep April, and the morn
>   Shakspere was born ;
> The world was on us, pressing sore ;
> My love and I took hands and swore
>   Against the world to be
> Poets and lovers ever more.

The second is a document of great interest to the
student of the art of poetry :

> A girl,
> Her soul a deep wave-pearl

351

> . . . and our souls so knit,
> I leave a page half-writ—
>   The work begun
> Will be to heaven's conception done
> If she come to it.

That passage testifies to complete union and
suggests a powerful originating impulse in the
elder woman which drew the deep affinity of the
other into the fire of her inspiration. It suggests
a great deal, too, about a fine submission of great
gifts, of the role of finisher which Edith Cooper
seems to have played, of a large constructive ability
and of much patient labour.

The third passage which I have chosen is one of
several that reveal the tenderness existing between
the two poets, and the adoration which Michael
gave to the person and the genius of her yoke-fellow.

> When my lady sleeping lies,
>   Her sweet breaths her lips unbar;
> This when King Apollo spies,
>   With dream footfall, not to mar
>   The dear sleep,
>   Through the rosy doors ajar,
> He with golden thoughts doth creep.

Not in any of the lyrics, however, but in one of
the plays will be found a passage which, though
dramatically fitted where it stands, is the ultimate
expression of the love which held these two lives

Michael Field

in union. It occurs in *The Tragedy of Pardon*,
Act III, Scene III :

> There is love
> Of woman unto woman, in its fibre
> Stronger than knits a mother to her child.
> There is no lack in it, and no defect;
> It looks nor up nor down,
> But loves from plenitude to plenitude,
> With level eyes, as in the Trinity
> God looks across and worships.

Now that has great significance, not only in its
personal reference and human charm, but in the
light it throws upon the whole achievement of
these poets. For when we approach a little closer
to the very considerable bulk of their work, we see
that love is its ruling passion. Putting aside for
the moment the theme of religious devotion (where
the very titles of the books—such as *Mystic Trees*
and *Poems of Adoration*—are illuminating) one
finds everywhere breadth and depth and height of
love which are almost infinite. And if, as I sometimes think, one might measure the stature of a
poet by a capacity for loving, then these two are
great indeed. Of course I do not mean only sexual
passion, although that has its place. But it is kept
in its place. *Attila, my Attila!* and the two
dramas founded on the Tristram romance are

353

Contemporary Poets

examples of the delicious frenzy as it is treated, vividly and with great beauty, by Michael Field ; just as Ras Byzance treats the foul, inescapable, jealous shadow of that insanity. But love which is no less powerful because it is also sane, clear-eyed and gentle, has a much larger share in this poetry.

There is, for example, the motherhood of *Julia Domna*, with the astonishing gesture on which the play closes—a miracle of maternal love which, for all our wonder, we feel to be deeply true and psychologically right. The Empress has seen one son murder the other—him who was her best-beloved—in jealous rage. She has turned in wrath upon the murderer, and has forbidden him her touch and her very presence. But presently he returns, worn out from an orgy of slaughter, and falls at her feet, drunk with weariness. She turns slowly from her dead, and says :

> You have need of sleep.
> My son, my living son, you are weary now. . . .
> And the lids close so soft ! Ye blessed gods,
> To see him fall asleep, my living son.

There is the comradeship of *Deirdre* ; the wistful yearning of *The Accuser*, incredulous and inappeasable—*There is such loving in me !*

> You love me . . . stay !
> And Mariamne loved me ? . . . But these words

Michael Field

Are as great victories in lands so far
The distance makes a glory in itself.

There is the variable, gracious loving of *The Tragic Mary* ; the adoration of those amazing lovers, Marcia and Eclectus, for the Emperor Commodus in *The Race of Leaves* ; the love of country in *A Question of Memory* ; and there are many women up and down the plays who, like Fair Rosamund and Brangaena and Anna Ruina, might say with Mercia in *The World at Auction* :

> And yet the gods for many thousand years
> Have loved by blessing : it is so I love.

One might continue to give examples ; but the thing is so much of the essence of this poetry that it seems ridiculous to try to illustrate—as though one should bottle samples of the air to prove that one were living. But that is the point. The passion which informs this poetry is its nature, the breath of life in it, the power which lights its imagination and stirs its multiform sympathy and sharpens its inner sight till it darts like lightning to the secret of psychological truth. So that while it is possible to select at ease one quotation out of many where love is the explicit theme, it is only by breathing the atmosphere of the whole work

355

Contemporary Poets

that one can come at the pervasive, embracing ether which is the soul of it.

Honoria, in *Attila, my Attila!* is the fullest embodiment of sensuous passion in this work. So one may take from her lips one explicit example :

> . . . Love makes life so whole,
> Fills up all hollow spaces, enters in
> All gaps of solitude : it is the vigil,
> The fasting, and the ecstasy in one.

And another, of a different aspect, from Emma, in *Canute the Great*:

> . . . Oh, this love
> Is a diviner power than holiness ;
> It puts all evil past imagining.

But when we seek for some phrase which shall make visible the deep source from which this poetry draws its life, we have a more difficult task. Yet I think there is at least one passage which reveals it. It is to be found in *Ras Byzance*, at the end of Act II. Menelik the Emperor is thinking of the crime into which Ras Byzance has stumbled, of innocent lives crushed and nobility and greatness brought low :

> We are here together
> As men among the boulders in sheer darkness :
> And we may fall and hurt each other, fall
> And hurt ourselves.

356

Michael Field

There, as it were in a tear, is reflected the tenderness, the large charity, the comprehending pitifulness which is the soul of Michael Field.

But, if you please, this poetry is by no means sentimental. Neither, by the same token, is it or ever was it decadent; though this last charge a writer has dared to suggest against the earlier work, in zealous joy that these two ladies were converted, toward the end of their career, to the Church of Rome. Of that conversion, what has one the right to say? Nothing—except that if it brought them the grace of beauty and the solace of comfort in the last bad years, the world owes it a debt of gratitude. But . . . comfort! When for the sake of their religion they suffered unnecessary torture: when Michael, to the day she died, rose each morning at seven o'clock to be carried to Mass!

Is the protest unfair? Perhaps. The martyr brings to his religion so much more than he takes from it. And these two poets brought their heroic temper, nurtured on love and disciplined by many years of labour at their art. Not the Church, but their own splendid humanity, inspired and supported those acts of noble folly; and we small critical people, zealous for a theology (or *no*

357

theology) can but peer up at the colossus and wonder at life.

So the influence of religion may be put aside, save to observe that it probably restrained the poets from publishing work which now seems their finest. Art has a quarrel there too fierce to be taken up at this moment. But one has a right to be indignant at the suggestion of decadence. Have people no eyes? Can they not see truth when it is clear as the sun at noon? The austere heroism in which the lives of these two poets closed was of their fibre from the beginning: all their work is touched with it, making of gentleness a sword and rooting tenderness in adamant.

But what, then, can be the meaning of this word decadent, if indeed it is not wholly irresponsible? Is it used simply as a label for the epoch when they began to write? when to be drunk and disorderly is said to have been a poet's favourite sport? But these two ladies lived blameless lives. Or is the grumble directed at the fact that much of the material of the plays is drawn from decadent periods of history, and the lives of great sinners—Herod and Borgia and Attila, Mary and Conchobar and Commodus? But to be great in sin is to be greatly human; and inevitable tragedy. And Michael Field is a tragic poet. She has herself quoted from

358

Michael Field

the *Antigone—Nothing that is vast enters into the life of man without a curse*; and the vast forces, with their attendant curse, had an invincible attraction for her. One sees why. Deep called to deep, and a great capacity for life stretched out eager hands to pluck life wherever it was most vivid and intense. Inherent in those vast forces are the struggle and defeat which make tragedy; and she was drawn as by a magnet to that conflict.

Hence every one of the twenty-five dramas is a tragedy; but come a very little closer and it will be seen that ruined lives have been breathed upon by triumph, and through perverse lives is revealed fundamental rightness: that sweetness has strength, and sympathy inexorable justice, and pardon cleansing tears.

One pauses a moment on that, because below it lies the primary significance of the work we are considering. It is a vast charity, sending its roots down to the heart of life and planted ineradicably there in essential truth. There are those who doubt its stability; and it is conceivable that the luxuriant, plastic graciousness of this tree of life may hide from a superficial glance the iron grip it keeps upon the rock below. Which is to say that genius of a certain grandeur is exposed to misunderstanding by its own largesse. Hence it has been possible for even a sympathetic reviewer to speak of this work as " the Ethic of Anarchy," probably because he was not regarding it in the whole. It may be admitted at once that, taken piecemeal, there is audacity enough to frighten the timid. Michael Field had an immense love of liberty, and hatred of every kind of bondage. She had an understanding of youth and its wilfulness. She had no reverence for mere custom and consistency, but adored the changefulness which is the very process of life.

Let us look at some of these daring passages. The most provocative are those which condemn family ties ; but here it is important to remember that it is the tie which has lost the sanction of love that she censures. Affection gone, the bond, become cruel, automatic and mechanical, is thereby cancelled. So Honoria, her young exuberance thwarted and her person held a prisoner, exclaims :

> You have no relatives ?
> How fortunate !
>
> .   .   .   .   .
>
> I have hated
> My family for more than fourteen years.

And Pulcheria replies :

> Oh, that is nothing, all the saints do that.

Michael Field

So Rothsay, in Act II of *The Father's Tragedy*, rebels against the cold austerity in which his father insists on wrapping his life :

<pre>
                    Old men
    Will answer for the sins that they have done
    Across the years to those in backward Time's
    Most lovely season.
        .   .   .   .   .

                            Lording it
    Over the wretched body and crushed soul ?
    Then is paternity a monstrous crime
    Blind justice cannot see.
</pre>

It may be said that that is dramatic logic : that it belongs inalienably to its setting of character and circumstance. True ; but the frequent recurrence of the idea, and its emphasis, give warrant to a statement that the poet had deep sympathy with the youthful rebel. It is, of course, but additional evidence to a prevailing love of freedom, which takes many forms and is apparent everywhere. It may appear as political liberty, in the theme of a play or the ruling motive of a character : as physical liberty in the agony of imprisonment or the rapture of escape : as delight in untrammelled initiative, or sheer joy in unfettered movement. All forms of external liberty are thus seen to be precious in the eyes of this poet : while for spiritual freedom she has a passion only second to the love which we have found to be the soul of her genius. Is it second, indeed ? One sees it rather as coequal, the proud intellectual partner of that fellowship. But just because it is thus of the mental texture of the work, one needs to know all the work to feel its full weight. Quotation will hardly serve it, and in attempting a selection one can only hope that it will not actually dis-serve. Thus Honoria, in youthful optimism :

> . . . All life is simple and we want
> No masters in it, if we will but live.

Thus Canute, shaking off the bondage of the old pagan religion :

> To myself this new,
> Unsettled energy within my brain
> Is worth all odds.

And thus Carloman, who is the supreme symbol of freedom for this poet, as he is the supreme creation of her art, cries when he is accused of being a rebel:

> I am, I am, because I am alive—
> And not a slave who sleeps through Time.
>   .   .   .   .   .
> I am free !   I prove it, acting freely.
>   .   .   .   .   .
> We must give our natures to the air,

Michael Field

To light and liberty, suppressing nothing,
Freeing each passion.

.   .   .   .   .   .

We must escape
From anything that is become a bond,
No matter who has forged the chain.

It is from Carloman, in the tragedy of *In the Name of Time*, that one gathers the poet's philosophy, and sees it to be a philosophy of change serving a religion of life. And here, too, the independence and breadth of her thought are liable to misunderstanding. I do not, of course, use the word philosophy in its technical sense, though it would seem that in this department of humane learning, as well as others, she was a careful student. But it had become a reproach to her because its laws operated to frustrate the vital impulse : it ran counter to her religion of life. In *The Race of Leaves*, Fadilla, the daughter of Marcus Aurelius and Faustina, is made to say :

. . . Philosophy,
That smiles on life, till life is made ashamed,
And sunders from each end for which it throbs.

I think, therefore, that we are forbidden to consider *In the Name of Time* as a philosophic argument, or to refer it to any system, Bergsonian or

363

other. It is much more of the nature of a creed, though too big and glowing to fit into any formula. Theologies dwindle beside it ; and if one does not assert that it is a triumphant attack upon the Church of Rome, that is only because it has too much of greatness, moral and artistic, to be anything so polemical. One can see, however, why publication was delayed till after the poet's death. But, theological reasons apart, the human instinct which withheld this her finest work is comprehensible and touching. For there are things in it which throw a challenge, not to priests alone, but to all the multitude which puts an eternal faith in an ephemeral morality. And, courageous as this poet was, one feels that her deeply religious spirit could not have borne the accusation of irreligion.

Nevertheless there is here a philosophy of life. It is indeed the chief import of all the tragedies and the problems they involve, notwithstanding that dramatic power makes their artistic value very high indeed. But it is more just to the poet's thought and method to approach her meaning through her art : that is to say, to watch the actual movement of the drama, to observe the logic of its events, and to accept the fragmentary, suggestive and often complex wisdom which is struck out of the conflict, as it is struck out of life, in fleeting

364

sparks. And the fact that one has to reach her philosophy in this way is of course a tribute to her art.

It follows that much of the significance of *In the Name of Time* is only apparent in reviewing the action, which there is not space to do here. We can but note its prime movement—that Carloman, desiring to " possess the great reality," puts off his royal state and seeks God in the cloister. But he finds that in renouncing fellowship with his kind he has renounced God. He is plunged into the misery and loneliness of bondage, out of which he ultimately wins, though only in dying, through the benediction of human love. And his last words, answering those first words, " I will possess the great reality," across the vehement action of the drama are :

> I for myself
> Deep drink to life here in my prison cell.
>
> .   .   .   .   .
>
> *Fellowship, pleasure,*
> *These are the treasure—*
> So I believe, so in the name of Time. . . .

If, therefore, one is at all justified in attempting a definition for Michael Field's philosophy—or religion—it is surely a worship of life, a belief in the joy of fellowship, and a vision of change as the vital principle of living. Thus Carloman, in Act I :

> There is no vanity in life ; life utters
> Unsparing truth to us,—there is no line
> Or record in our body of her printing
> That stamps a falsehood.   Do not so confound,
> Father, life's transience and sincerity.

Again, in Act III :

>   . . . Time
> Is God's own movement, all that He can do
> Between the day a man is born and dies.
>   . . . Think what the vines would be
> If they were glued forever, and one month
> Gave them a law—the richness that would cease,
> The flower, the shade, the ripening.   We are men,
> With fourscore years for season, and we alter
> So exquisitely often on our way
> To harvest and the end. . . .

And in Act IV :

> The God I worship.   He is just *to-day*—
> Not dreaming of the future,—in itself,
> Breath after breath divine !   Oh, He becomes !
> He cannot be of yesterday, for youth
> Could not then walk beside Him, and the young
> Must walk with God : and He is most alive
> Wherever life is of each living thing.

So, too, with the fellowship which this poet

Michael Field

adores. It is not a thing of ties, by blood or otherwise : it will have no dealings with anything that hurts or hinders life. Carloman, hearing the confession of his wife's lover, refuses to bind her freedom :

> You wrong her—
> Not yours nor mine.   Earth's wisdom will begin
> When all relationships are put away
> With their dull pack of duties, and we look
> Curious, benignant, with a great compassion
> Into each other's lives.

It is, in brief, simply the freedom of love. And we come back to the beginning, and close the circle, in that " great compassion." Boniface, the gentle Christian missionary, has come to visit Carloman in his prison. He exclaims as he enters—*Beloved!* and Carloman stops him :

> No more !   Dear voice, end with that word :
>   . . . Go to your heathen lands
> With that great lay of love.

Thomas Hardy

I HAVE observed a special gleam in the eyes of thoughtful people when they talk about Thomas Hardy. There is a certain inflection of the voice, too, and a lingering smile, which mean nothing if they do not mean affection. So that, in thinking of the veteran poet among his contemporaries, a word of his own darts into the mind and insists upon defining him—Hardy the Well-beloved.

Now that is rather curious when one notes the fact that generally Mr Hardy's work has few of the more attractive poetic graces. The qualities in a poet which capture one unawares are not his: simple winsomeness his poetry very seldom has. Besides, he seems in a sense too big for familiar affection, too austere a thinker, ruled too often by a satiric mood; and too close an observer of all one's faults and follies.

If it is not, therefore, for charm of manner that this poet holds his place in the heart of his time, it must be for something in the material of his thought. And the instant we turn our eyes in that direction we see at a glance that it is the modernity of Hardy which enshrines him. He is pre-eminently a modern poet, and this despite the fact that he is twice as old as the most modern of his contem-

Thomas Hardy

poraries. But Hardy has escaped the doom of age to harden and grow dull. His thought remains young, alert, flexible, sensitive; and that angry indictment of the old men made by so many generous young ones from the days of Sophocles' Creon onward has no force here. It is, indeed, splendidly refuted. For instead of a mind wearily falling back upon reaction as some tired body upon a down bed, or at best rigidly maintaining a philosophy which has ceased to be true, here is a thinker who, from the accumulated data of many patient years, begins to utter his explicit message tentatively—a word here and a word there; and formulates it fully (in the *Dynasts*) only after long and concentrated effort. But still finality has not been reached. There is no such thing as finality here; and the latest poems of Hardy show his thought to be still a living and growing thing, marching abreast of its time with the youngest and boldest there.

It is for this reason especially that we have cause for thankfulness that Hardy did not stay his hand after he had written his novels. We should not then have known him. We might have made imperfect guesses. It would have been possible, perhaps, for a rare mind of scope almost equal to his own to deduce from the novels the philosophy of life which is implicit there. But for most of us

369

he would have remained only half known—the teller of a good story, the shaper of a moving tragedy out of the chaos of existence, a lively and ironical writer, but suspected of pessimism, and, despite a real tenderness, almost harsh in manner.

But with the *Dynasts* and the two later volumes of lyrics before us, our view is not only very much greater but vastly different. We see now something so grand that it is almost too big to grasp; and so sensitive that it must of its very nature be profoundly tragical. And we know that in it is crystallized all the elements which the artistic consciousness of a lifetime has gathered, tested, and passed through the crucible over and over again.

Hardy's method, indeed, is avowedly scientific and is but another aspect of his modernism. In the preface to *Poems of the Past and the Present*, he alludes to the fragmentary and unassimilated condition of much of his material, and vindicates his use of it. "Unadjusted impressions," he says, "have their value, and the road to a true philosophy of life seems to lie in humbly recording diverse readings of its phenomena as they are forced upon us by chance and change."

Hence we see him at work, patiently experimenting, observing and recording in the true manner of the scientist. It is a method which has its weakness for the purposes of the poet; but it has ultimately justified itself so well to Hardy that we are free to note where it occasionally fails, and to see where the man of science does violence to the poet. Thus one sometimes finds him heaping up records apparently for their own sake, without reflection or feeling; so that many of the shorter lyrics are but data in verse. Curious facts, grotesque people and extraordinary incidents are dressed out in jolly rhyme and metre. They trip and tinkle merrily, and do their utmost to be poetry, but they succeed only in appearance. They are ill at ease in their fine dress. They seem conscious of being "unadjusted impressions," and to be ruefully wishing that the poet had left them in their native garb of prose, tucked away in a commonplace book. Occasionally they are so absurd that we suspect him of poking fun at us; sometimes so bizarre that they have but the frailest link with reality. A thing which might just conceivably happen, but which could surely never happen twice, may throw its unique beam on the path to a philosophy of life, but it is too alien to win its way into that happy region of belief and acceptance where only poetry can live. So a piece like " Royal Sponsors," where the corpse of a baby is christened, merely revolts us; one like " The Caged Goldfinch " makes us

perversely laugh ; and " The Statue of Liberty,"
with its strong flavour of a sailor's yarn and its
" long arm of coincidence," compels an irreverent
ejaculation about the Marines.

The truth is, of course, that in such pieces the
poet has not sufficiently played his part. He has
ceded the first place to the recorder of data, and
has contented himself with arranging the record
in a pretty pattern. He has thought about the
incident very much, but he has felt it hardly at all.
Hence materials which are unpromising in themselves, and which could only become poetry by
complete fusion in the poetic consciousness, remain
as mere fragments, very carefully chipped and
polished, it is true, but hard and rather clumsy
fragments nevertheless.

That, however, is only one aspect of Hardy's
scientific method, and it is not the most important.
To watch the application of the method to the
form of the work is much more interesting, as he
constantly tries new shapes and fresh combinations
and intricate rhyme tunes ; as he presses everything into the service of his diction, even ugly,
forcible and commonplace words ; and continually
experiments with rhythm until he succeeds in an
exquisitely happy lilt like that of " Timing Her,"
or a tender elegiac one such as that of " Afterwards."

Thomas Hardy

And to watch it amassing material in the *Dynasts*, checking, co-ordinating, and constructing, is to see a function no less wonderful than the selective and recreative power which it nobly serves. Its great triumph lies there, indeed—in providing an instrument so well attuned to the mind of the poet : in forging a sword for his spirit so excellently tempered.

Thus one comes back to the modernism of Hardy, and sees that not only his philosophy but his style and his method are shaped by it, and in their turn express it. His philosophy is a purely intellectual conception of the universe. It is no vindication of the ways of God to man ; but, starting from frank nescience, it is an unwearied search for an explanation, a steady scrutiny of facts, a projection of thought far through space and time, a survey of the fields of cosmic and human history ; and a bold pursuit of Truth, though it threaten to destroy, until a stand is made at last before certain inevitable conclusions. And there the whole process of the universe is seen as a vast unconscious force, a single energy, working blindly and automatically toward some possible goal of ultimate consciousness. So, in the Forescene of the *Dynasts* :

> What of the Immanent Will and Its designs ?
>
> .   .   .   .   .   .
>
> It works unconsciously, as heretofore,

Eternal artistries in Circumstance,
. . . like a knitter drowsed,
Whose fingers play in skilled unmindfulness,
The Will has woven with an absent heed
Since life first was; and ever will so weave.

There is something awful in the grandeur of this
conception as it is worked out from the clash of
tremendous forces in the *Dynasts*. Nevertheless it
is not made into a dogma, and it is not insisted on.
No new creed is formulated, and one finds no claim
to completeness or finality. On the contrary, the
great epic-drama closes on a low, tremulous, un-
certain note—all its magnificence of thought and
imagination stooped to catch a pale gleam which
seems to the poet to come from the future:

Last as first the question rings
Of the Will's long travailings;

.   .   .   .

But—a stirring thrills the air
Like to sounds of joyance there
That the rages
Of the ages
Shall be cancelled, and deliverance offered from the
darts that were,
Consciousness the Will informing, till It fashion all
things fair!

This word of hope on which the epic closes is
nothing impulsive or fleeting. Neither is it a mere

374

palliative. It is amplified in a poem, which by all
the signs was written later, called " The Sleep-
Worker," and which is addressed to Mother Nature
as another figure for the " Immanent Will " of the
Dynasts. The poet resumes the idea (which appears
in other pieces also, notably " A Fragment ") that
the power which informs the Universe will one day
achieve feeling and consciousness. It will understand what it has done, and, looking on the misery
of the human race, it will learn to feel sorrow for
them and horror at itself. But what will happen
when that day comes ?

> Wilt thou destroy, in one wild shock of shame,
> Thy whole high-heaving firmamental frame,
> Or patiently adjust, amend, and heal ?

It is an austere philosophy, but it will carry
solace to all those who, in however small degree,
have seen the problem as the poet faced it—that is
to say, the apparent existence of an evil power in
the scheme of things. To escape from the night-
mare of that possibility is an escape indeed ; and
in winning free from it Hardy has refuted the charge
of pessimism which is often brought against him.
He has discovered once for all that there is no
malicious purpose in the heart of things, and that
the blows which fall on us are not so aimed. As he

symbolizes it in the poem called " The Subalterns,"
the wind which lays waste his garden is but an
instrument, and entirely passive : the elements are
not in league against him.

> We smiled upon each other then,
> And life to me wore less
> That fell contour it wore ere when
> They owned their passiveness.

The relief which that denial of an evil power will
bring is of course proportioned to the acuteness
with which such a power has been apprehended.
One lightly supposes—though it may be, after all,
a much too facile hope—that not many of the
people one meets in the bus would need the solace
of it. But there is a development of Hardy's
philosophy which has positive and universal value.
It advances from the point which the *Dynasts* had
attained—from that stand before inexorable truth
whence the poet had declared that there is no
power in the universe to give us either good or evil,
there is only the Incognizant. " Here, then, is the
truth," he seems to say. " We accept it. But
what then ? Is there no succour anywhere for
humanity ? Surely yes. There is humanity itself,
its love and its brotherliness." So, in the poem
called " A Plaint to Man," Hardy figures the idea
of God complaining to mankind that He has been

created merely to pray to ; but that His day is done, and now He is dwindling in a clearer light :

> The truth should be told, and the fact be faced
> That had best been faced in earlier years,
>
> The fact of life with dependence placed
> On the human heart's resource alone,
> In brotherhood bonded close and graced
>
> With loving-kindness fully blown,
> And visioned help unsought, unknown.

So much it was necessary, very inadequately, to say about Hardy's philosophy, because, after all, it is in the massiveness and the courage of his thought that his greatness consists. But there is a whole region of his work which is very much more delightful to the lover of poetry for poetry's sake.

There are lyrics written since *The Dynasts* which are more spontaneous and more exuberant than any of the earlier poems. They have put off the weight of the world, and are lighter and freer than ever before. It is an amazing thing when one thinks about it, that lyrics so sweet and tender should come to us at this stage of the poet's career, when by all the precedents thought should predominate over feeling and march to a graver measure. But it is only another sign of that youthfulness of spirit

which endears him. Joy almost dances in " Timing
Her," from *Moments of Vision*:

> Lalage's coming:
> Where is she now, O?
> Turning to bow, O,
> And smile, is she,
> Just at parting,
> Parting, parting,
> As she is starting
> To come to me?

And in " Great Things " this poet of an austere
and tragic philosophy, whose view of life is, in
his own words, as a " breast-bared spectacle,"
triumphantly chants the jollity of living and the
sweetness of love. He praises the things that have
given him joy—love and the dance and sweet cider
—and lightly banishes reflection when it tries to
intrude :

> Will these be always great things,
>   Great things to me? . . .
> Let it befall that One will call,
>   " Soul, I have need of thee."
> What then? Joy-jaunts, impassioned flings,
>   Love, and its ecstasy,
> Will always have been great things,
>   Great things to me.

So, too, in many other of these lyrics emotion
conquers, winning also a happier grace of form. It

Thomas Hardy

is not always joy, of course. Sorrow and tender
regret breathe through a whole series of them, as
in " The Going " and " Lament ":

> She is shut, she is shut
> From friendship's spell,
> In the jailing shell
> Of her tiny cell.

And in " The Blinded Bird " there is indignation
and infinite pity :

> So zestfully canst thou sing? . . .
>
>   .   .   .   .
>
> Who hath charity? This bird.
> Who suffereth long and is kind,
> Is not provoked, though blind
> And alive ensepulchred?
> Who hopeth, endureth all things?
> Who thinketh no evil, but sings?
> Who is divine? This bird.

The detachment of the earlier work has gone.
The ironical themes, the satirical attitude, the old
insistence on the unlovely side of character, are all
but banished here. The prevailing mood is one of
tenderness : the attitude one of complete concentration. Thought is not fierce any longer ; tragedy
is less bitter ; sadness is gentler ; and all the poetic
energies are mellowed. So, in the poem " To
an Unborn Pauper Child," the elements of his

379

philosophy are distilled to an exquisite pitifulness ; and in the poem called " Afterwards," where the poet is looking forward to the time when he will take his final departure, the elegiac sweetness is suffused by a sunset glow which warms and softens and brings nearer to us all his greatness :

When the Present has latched its postern behind my
    tremulous stay,
And the May month flaps its glad green leaves like wings,
Delicate filmed as new-spun silk, will the people say,
" He was a man who used to notice such things " ?

.   .   .   .   .

If I pass during some nocturnal blackness, mothy and warm,
When the hedgehog travels furtively over the lawn,
Will they say, " He strove that such innocent creatures
    should come to no harm,
But he could do little for them ; and now he is gone " ?

J. C. Squire

THERE was once a Jester at the Court of
Modern Poetry, and his name was J. C.
Squire. He was a great joy to everybody
who, not being exactly a member of the Court,
could listen to the jingle of his bells from a distance.
One could chuckle safely there over his jibes at
those others. But to his friends he must have
been an *enfant terrible*, and to certain enemies an
abomination.

He was, as the Fool needs must be, a seer; and
because the nature of his seeing was critical, he was
the Censor of the Court as well as its fun-maker.
His jesting was a correction, his satire a purge, and
his laughter had the tonic properties of the Comic
Spirit. He loved to chaff the other poets, and
exercise his wit on their idiosyncrasies and artistic
faults. So he made parodies of them, both of the
living and (for he had no proper reverence) of the
dead. Because he had a gift of mimicry and a very
sharp eye for the ridiculous, the parodies were good
fun; and because he nearly always practised a
justesse of exaggeration, and set nothing down in
malice, they were, to all but their victims perhaps,
most amusing exercises in criticism.

So, though the Jester has done with jesting,

people do not intend to forget that he once wore
motley. He delighted in all manner of fooling,
from the blasphemous vision of the poet Gray com-
posing his " Elegy " among the " lewd forefathers "
in the Spoon River Cemetery, to Sir Rabindranath
Tagore delicately distilling inanity out of " Little
Drops of Water " ; or from the affectionate banter
of Mr W. H. Davies to the Punch-and-Judy knock-
about of the parodies of Mr Masefield. In the last
the Jester for once ran past himself, to use the
expressive vernacular. He broke his almost in-
variable rule of heightening a feature in precisely
the right degree to let loose its potential humour
—and in that degree only. He passes this golden
mean several times in the narrative poem about Flo,
the barmaid of Pimlico, supposed to have been
written by Mr Masefield—not to speak of the version
of " Casabianca " also attributed to that poet ;
and both are rather ugly fooling in consequence.
I quote a mild example. Flo's mother speaks :

If't wasn't for Flo's fifteen bob a week,
  Me and them brats would not know where to turn,
For some of 'em ain't old enough to speak,
  And none of 'em ain't old enough to earn,
  And as for 'er bright merry japes, why, durn
My bleedin' eyes, if we'd no Flo to quirk us,
I'm sure we'd soon be droopin' in the workus.

J. C. Squire

Of course both the Masefield parodies are funny, and so justify their existence. But even if they were not, they would be saved from repulsiveness by the Jester's insight. His art is something more than a trick: it does more than catch the manner of whomsoever he is burlesquing. It is a criticism, small but complete, of form and spirit, of manner, matter and mental outlook. And if he lays about him too roughly in these particular instances, I suspect it is because there is something antithetical to him in the whole genius of the poet he is bludgeoning. Which is not to say that the two may not be very good friends, for indeed one would not thump an enemy in just that way. But the exuberant creative faculty of Mr Masefield and the means by which it hurries to utter itself are sufficiently opposed to the other questioning and fastidious spirit. One would have thought the extreme simplicity of Mr Davies almost as great a contrast, and therefore equally provocative. It makes, indeed, an excellent target, and the Jester "gets the bull's-eye" every time; but its very singleness makes it less vulnerable, partly because fewer points of attack are exposed, and partly because there is a charm about it which disarms the attacker. Here is a stanza from No. 1 :

I saw some sheep upon some grass,
   The sheep were fat, the grass was green,
The sheep were white as clouds that pass,
   And greener grass was never seen ;
I thought, " Oh, how my bliss is deep,
With such green grass and such fat sheep ! "

And I cannot resist taking the whole of No. 2 :

    A poor old man
      Who has no bread,
    He nothing can
      To get a bed.

    He has a cough,
      Bad boots he has ;
    He takes them off
      Upon the grass.

    He does not eat
      In cosy inns
    But keeps his meat
      In salmon tins.

    No oven hot,
      No frying-pan,
    Thank God I'm not
      That poor old man.

That is delicious fooling, and more. Laughter is enriched by something other than mockery, for under the touch of caricature and the heightened colour we recognize a portrait. Through the oddity

J. C. Squire

of manner shines a serene and genial temper. The whole thing is in character. So, too, with the vivacious parody of Mr Belloc :

> At Martinmas, when I was born,
>   Hey diddle, Ho diddle, Do,
> There came a cow with a crumpled horn,
>   Hey diddle, Ho diddle, Do.
> She stood agape and said, " My dear,
> You're a very fine child for this time of year,
> And I think you'll have a taste in beer,"
>   Hey diddle, Ho diddle, Ho, do, do, do,
>   Hey diddle, Ho diddle, Do.

And again with that of Mr Chesterton. The nonsense of it has all the vigour of its original—and some other recognizable features as well. To see Mr Chesterton leaping over Thames bridges one after the other is sport indeed ; and to hear him chanting antitheses about green rain and pink grass has a jolly and familiar ring.

The essence of the Jester's work in this kind is its good temper. One can imagine that when he was working in another vein the people he satirized might have been rather cross with him. But he seems to have had a tender spot in his heart for poets. And even the Very New Ones who are supposed to have written " The Lotus Eaters " have not much to complain about :

385

Work !
Did I used to work ?
I seem to remember it
Out there.
Millions of fools are still at
It,
Jumping about
All over the place. . . .
And what's the good of it all ? . . .
Buzz,
Hustle,
Pop,
And then . . .
Dump
In the grave.

Perhaps they are let off more lightly than they deserve, in view of their tender age. But it was quite another story about Lambeth guardians who proposed to teach pauper children how to realize the war by denying them their breakfast egg on Christmas morning. Still another when " A Living Dean " described conscription as " a step towards the higher life " ; and still another when the editor of *The Spectator* preached a gospel of war as a " biological necessity." Then that indignation which is a holy weapon in the hands of the satirist flashed out and struck without mercy. There is a poem called " The Survival of the Fittest " which is very far from being a jest. It is written in

386

J. C. Squire

memory of three friends dead in the war who had
" clear eyes, strong bodies and some brains," and
who

> Not seeing the war as a wise elimination,
>   Or a cleansing purge or a wholesome exercise,
> Went out with mingled loathing and elation
>   Only because there towered before their eyes
> England, an immemorial crusader. . . .
>
> .   .   .   .   .   .
>
> Tompkins, these died. What need is there to mention
>   Anything more ? What argument could give
> A more conclusive proof of your contention ?
>   Tompkins, these died, and men like you still live.

The anger of that is proportioned to the insane
pseudo-science which it mocks, and to grief for
irreparable loss. The fierce passage of the war has
left its mark on this verse ; and though the poet
survived, it killed the Jester. It would have been
strange if that merry spirit had remained the same :

> For half of us are dead,
> And half have lost their youth,
> And our hearts are scarred by many griefs
> That only age should know.

But in our regret for the passing of so much light-
heartedness, we remember that it is but a part of
the price that we must all go on paying till we die,
and that yet will never be paid in full. But the

change is not a thing to dwell upon. Rather one may be thankful that the poet survived; and that it *is* a cause for thankfulness may be seen by reference to a volume called *Poems: First Series*, published in 1918.

This book contains a selection from the serious verse of Mr Squire; and comprises those pieces which, as he expresses it, he does not wish to destroy. It is a modest way of putting it; but, accepting his own delimitation, there is still enough work in which to watch the developing of a poet of distinction. And the point of first interest is that here, in poetry of a completely different order from that which we have been considering, there are precisely the same forces at work. Leagues of distance separate the parodies from, let us say, the "Ode: In a Restaurant" or "Antinomies on a Railway Station"; yet they are all of the same essence. They are all of the substance of a critical reaction to life. In the gayer work the mood is lighter because the criticism is relatively superficial. It is a matter of the absurdity of Mr Masefield's swear words or Wordsworth's banality. And even though it often includes much more than that, it is still by comparison floating on the surface of the deep In the more serious work the critical spirit sometimes probes questions too profound for answer,

J. C. Squire

and at other times sends its inquisitive beam like the sharp ray of a searchlight into regions immensely dark. So it is in " The Mind of Man," a piece of self-criticism where the ray travels steadily and mercilessly through foul places of which most of us refuse to admit the existence. So it is, again, in " Antinomies," when in that sharp light the poet sees " the delusiveness of change . . . the transparency of form " and watches so curiously that he sees the passing of Beauty herself :

> Flower and leaf and grass and tree,
> Doomed barks on an eternal sea,
> Flit phantom-like as transient smoke.
> Beauty herself her spell has broke,
> Beauty, the herald and the lure,
> Her message told, may not endure.

But Beauty is avenged on him for the impiety of that. So long the supreme goddess of the poets, she will not yield place without extorting a penalty. So she clips his wings and fetters his feet whenever he allows the challenging intellect to take precedence of her. Thus the artist who has had a vision of something beyond Beauty is confounded ; for by that light he cannot attain even to Beauty herself. He gets very far, however. He reaches a clear truth of thought and word which justly expresses reality ; and he presents with courage the

389

Contemporary Poets

fruit that Reason has plucked, no matter how unfamiliar or unpalatable it may be.

Thus, in the " Ode : In a Restaurant " he forces
himself to contemplate the human scene by which
he is surrounded, and to explore it to its recesses.
He plucks himself from a mood of revulsion en-
gendered by the physical aspect of the spectacle—
its greedy feeding, and the heat and noise—to turn
his scrutiny steadily upon human needs, and to pay
his tribute of homage to the body. He thinks of
the ceaseless stream of life flowing through these
men and women who are avidly and untidily eating
and drinking :

> The confused, glittering armies of humankind,
>   To their own heroism blind,
> Swarm over the earth to build, to dig, and to till,
> To mould and compel land and sea to their will . . .
>   Whence we are here eating. . . .
>
>   .   .   .   .
>
> So, so of every substance you see around
>   Might a tale be unwound
> Of perils passed, of adventurous journeys made
> In man's undying and stupendous crusade.
>
> > This flower of man's energies, Trade,
> > Brought hither to hand and lip
> > By waggon, train or ship,
> > Each atom that we eat. . . .

J. C. Squire

It is a noble idea, not inadequately sung; but it is not deeply felt. Perhaps its nature precludes that. It is an intellectual conception taking shape in reaction from a mood of disgust; and is an apt example of the kind of work this poet does when he allows intellect to overrule him. It is shapely, musical, true; but it is not the real thing. The divine spark does not burn in it.

One must hasten to say, however, that this critical faculty is not always allowed to dominate. Concentrated thought often evokes a kindred emotion; and the intellectual passion thus lighted is Apollo's own fire. In the poem called "Starlight," the whole process may be seen in epitome, as though the poet had deliberately made a figure for it—proceeding from the arrogant interrogatory to the sense of wondering adoration, with its ecstasy flashing at once into beautiful form:

> Grass to my cheek in the dewy field,
> I lay quite still with my lips sealed,
> And the pride of a man and his rigid gaze
> Stalked like swords on heaven's ways.
>
> But through a sudden gate there stole
> The Universe and spread in my soul;
> Quick went my breath and quick my heart,
> And I looked at the stars with lips apart.

Mr Squire's most beautiful poems are those in

which there has been this fusion of thought and
feeling. Because the fusion was complete those
poems are lovely in themselves, and are to be en-
joyed simply for their beauty. But there is always
a charm in watching the germ of thought out of
which they flowered; and in observing its nature.
It is often metaphysical, engaged with the riddle
of the Universe. But they are modern meta-
physics: not affiliated to any school, but deeply
individual. Hence we find " A Reasonable Pro-
testation " stating his position and sealing it of his
own time :

> This autumn of time in which we dwell
>> Is not an age of revelations,
>> Solid as once, but intimations
> That touch us with warm misty fingers
> Leaving a nameless sense that lingers
> That sight is blind and Time's a snare
> And earth less solid than the air. . . .

Again one sees in " The Three Hills " the idea
of change and impermanence which so often preoccupies this poet; but the glow of feeling has
wrought it into a lively image. The three hills
have been ravaged by the town-builder until they
are scarred almost beyond recognition; and one
of them is imagined speaking to the others :

J. C. Squire

"Brothers, we stood when they were not,
　　Ten thousand summers past.
Brothers, when they are clean forgot
　　We shall outlive the last.

One shall die and one shall flee
　　With terror in his train,
And earth shall eat the stones, and we
　　Shall be alone again."

And in the poem called "Crepuscular" the
eternal antagonism of matter and spirit is felt in
a twilight mood of melancholy and weariness.
"Mute at her window sits the soul" regarding the
immensity of the material universe :

How quell this vast and sleepless giant,
Calmly, immortally defiant :

How fell him, bind him, and control
With a silver cord and a golden bowl ?

Sometimes, moreover, the critical and reflective
power which checks the creative impulse in this
work, denying to it any large measure of exuberance
and spontaneity, is completely vanquished. That
is when a great emotion strikes directly into the
mind and takes complete possession. There are
examples of this which I forbear to lay hands upon
because they are threnodies—" On a Friend Recently
Dead," " The March," and others. But there is an

393

instance in this kind, " Artemis Altera," with which
one may more permissibly take liberties :

> You hate contempt and love not laughter ;
>   With your sharp spear of virgin will
> You harry the wicked strong, but after,
>   O huntress who could never kill,
>
> Should they be trodden down or piercèd,
>   Swift, swift you fly with burning cheek
> To place your beauty's shield reversèd
>   Above the vile defenceless weak !

But the single, untroubled flame of that is infrequent in this poetry. More often a diffused
light shines here, evoking colour in softened tones.
The subtlety of the mind through which it passes is
reflected everywhere, even in its prosody, where
intricacy of rhythm and rhyme are delicately shaped
to express it. That Mr Squire is rapidly gaining
mastery of a various and significant beauty of
form is readily seen in his more recent work,
notably in poems such as " A House " and
" The Lily of Malud." I quote a stanza from
" A House " to illustrate the distinction of its
metrical scheme, although the fidelity with which
the scheme serves the mood and creates its
atmosphere can only be appreciated in the poem
as a whole :

J. C. Squire

Darkness and stars will come, and long the night will be,
   Yet imperturbable that house will rest,
Avoiding gallantly the stars' chill scrutiny,
   Ignoring secrets in the midnight's breast.

Lastly, I quote from the closing passage of " The Lily of Malud," a poem which tells about the lily which flowered and died in one midnight in the heart of the forest. Absolute beauty is created here :

Something sorrowful and far, something sweet and
      vaguely seen,
Like an early evening star when the sky is pale green,
A quiet silver tower that climbed in an hour,
Or a ghost like a flower, or a flower like a queen.
Something holy in the past that came and did not last.

Contemporary Women Poets

OVER and over again, in those weary years of the War, we had to remind ourselves (when we could snatch a moment to think about it at all) that great literature cannot be created in times of stress.

The truth came home most sharply, of course, to the incurable optimist; for he, forgetting that violence can only destroy, went peering wistfully through the murk for some great epic of the world-conflict. But it did not appear, and it gives no sign of being about to appear. For all that we can see, we may have to wait years before that chaos will begin to shape to intelligible features, and before it will be possible for the events and passions of it to be " recollected in tranquillity " by the poet. Then, if the right mind shall have escaped destruction, we may hope to get genuine poetry of the war, crystallizing the essential meaning of its madness, and the terrible beauty of its heroism. But it depends at last upon the right mind; and that, too, Ares demanded as a sacrifice. One—he who seemed to promise a range of genius and a completeness of humanity greater than his compeers—moulders at Lemnos.

Therefore, since poetry requires peace and leisure for the conditions of its being, we have no right to expect the appearance of supreme work even now. We cannot fairly look for it at any time, or from any society, where those conditions do not exist; and the World War has but given place to disquieting industrial conflict. But in considering especially the work of women, we have to remember that there was another conflict which, for the previous ten years or so, had made poetical work for them difficult almost to impossibility.

The strife that I refer to was, of course, only part of the general agitation of the modern mind which a sharp reawakening had caused. But it roused woman the more abruptly as she had been more soundly sleeping; it implicated her more deeply because she had so much lost ground to recover; and it drove her to an activity all the fiercer because she had not been trained in the gentle art of compromise. So, while there are both men and women poets who have been stimulated by that awakening (and in direct proportion as they are alert and responsive), it is in the work of women that the effects of it may be most clearly seen.

That is not to assert that all contemporary women

poets are making poetry of the new kind.   Just as
there are men who seem to have drifted out of the
current, or who have never been touched by it, so
there are also women who have remained in peace-
ful back-waters.   Let us say at once, that from their
safe anchorage, out of their serene quietude, they
have sent the sweeter and more graceful songs.
They have achieved a completer and more harmonious beauty, dearer far to ear and eye because
it is more familiar.

If, therefore, one would get a clear view of what
the newer poetry is and means, one should place
side by side with this more regular verse certain
contemporaries who are working in a directly contrasted manner.   On the one hand we may put
those women who have not gone down into the
fight at all ; and who, for any sign their poetry
gives, are not even aware that a conflict is going on.
They sing simply for joy, impelled by an instinct
to render into visible beauty some intimate emotion.
Hence their verse has the primary values of spontaneity and exuberance, ease and grace.   It is quick,
light, musical ; flowing unfreighted and unimpeded
by the careful questions of modern life.

On the other hand we must place the women
poets who are actually fighting.   They are engaged
in that battle of ideas which is agitating the awakened

Women Poets

mind everywhere, of which the political status of women is but one phase and one aspect. And if we look at the work of this group with a single eye to beauty, if we judge it from the absolute standard of Art, we shall declare that the turmoil has had an unhappy influence upon it. There will be something strange to us in this verse; something almost harsh in its music, almost halting in its movement. And the unfamiliar rhyme and rhythm will repel us, unless and until we come to accept them as the proper garment of the thought which this poetry is struggling to express.

There is a tiny poem by a member of this group, Anna Wickham, which is apt to every turn of the present point, so I quote it here. It is called " The Singer," and it will readily be seen how the six small lines, while summing up the whole case for modern poetry, exactly illustrate at the same time the austerity of its manner :

> If I had peace to sit and sing,
> Then I could make a lovely thing;
> But I am stung with goads and whips,
> So I build songs like iron ships.
>
> Let it be something for my song
> If it is sometimes swift and strong.[1]

But we are going to glance first at the work of

[1] Anna Wickham, *The Contemplative Quarry.*

two or three women who are making poetry in the old style; and in order to emphasize the difference, we shall select from them only their poems upon old themes. Such themes, however, are characteristic of them; and thus it would not be unfair to take Helen Parry Eden, for example, as representing motherhood; Anna Bunston (Mrs de Bary) to stand for religion; and Olive Custance as the devotee of beauty.

Here the poetic spirit is brooding upon universal and enduring things, such as are a constant source of its inspiration, and which may be found prompting the specifically 'modern' verse as well. But they are more frequent in this verse; and they are regarded in large, clear outline. They are accepted implicitly, in the contours which the centuries have shaped and the colours they have mellowed. And the essential largeness and simplicity of the theme have been matched by a direct and simple treatment only possible to minds which are untroubled by the cross-currents of contemporary thought.

Thus we might gather, from Anna Bunston, fair flowers of the old faith. In her book called *Songs of God and Man*, she sees a snowdrop as " a thought of God " :

> It is so holy,
> And yet so lowly.

Would you enjoy
Its grace and dower
And not destroy
The living flower?
Then you must, please,
Fall on your knees.

Looking at " a primrose by the wayside," humility
trembles into beauty :

Can anything so fair and free
Be fashioned out of clay?
Then God may yet cull flowers from me,
Some holy summer day.

There is a song of the burden of life :

" How far to Calvary,
And when shall I be there,
To hang my bruisèd body
On the heavy tree I bear?"

"Not far to Calvary,
The pilgrimage not long,
For close to holy cities
Are the hills of human wrong."

The Roman Catholic Church has always been the
nursing mother of devotional poetry. From her
ritual, her tradition, her mystery, and her warm
emotional atmosphere, the religious poet draws the
natural food of his soul. I do not know whether
Mrs de Bary is a Roman Catholic, but one has only

to recall three other women poets of our own time
—Alice Meynell and the two ladies who called themselves " Michael Field "—to admit the truth that
the Church of Rome has not failed in this age for
nurture to her children. All their work, varied in
individual character though it is, owns its parentage
by indubitable signs, not of outward affiliation only,
but of graciousness of spirit and a delicate fervour
of adoration. Thus again from Anna Bunston,
in " Mingled Wine," these two fragments. The
first is a moment of happy vision :

> God will come home to His saints,
>   Come home to them every one,
> As down to puddle, and pool, and blot
>   Comes home the infinite sun.

And the second is from a song of passionate thanksgiving :

> For strength of youth, and charity of age ;
> For this life's myrrh and euphrasy,
> For those ' sublime attractions of the grave '—
>   Gloria Tibi Domine !

But leaving religion now for the second of these
universal themes of poetry, we shall find in the verse
of Olive Custance a complete devotion to beauty,
and no other concern at all. Here the spirit of
poetry drinks the loveliness of the world through
every sharpened sense. It revels in light and colour

Women Poets

and warmth. But that mere sensuous delight goes haunted by its own inescapable shadow; and into these bright tapestries dark threads have crept. The irresponsibility of Art for Art draws down Nemesis. Lacking a soul, there is here, ultimately, not beauty at all, but only prettiness. And one soon wearies of such verse.

There are brilliant hues in this poetry; but one sees them the more strikingly through the author's more sombre moods. There, too, we shall find the prevailing artist-joy happily making picturesqueness out of its own sadness. So it is in " Grief " :

> Night has become a temple for my tears . . .
>   The moon a silver shroud for my despair,
> And all the golden forests of the spheres
>   Have showered their splendours on me leaf by leaf
> Till men that meet me in the sunlight stare
>   To see the shining garment of my grief!

In " Life," again, the poet is clearly taking pleasure in shaping a graceful song out of a mood of melancholy :

> Sometimes my soul is as fierce and mad
>   As a winter sea :
> Sometimes my soul is brave and glad,
>   And the hours are good to me,
> But often enough it is tired and sad,
>   Poor waif of eternity.

Again, from the *Inn of Dreams* one takes " The Autumn Day " for its pensive sweetness, where the lines are touched with the tenderness of a caress :

> How delicately steps the autumn day
> In azure cloak and gown of ashen grey
> Over the level country that I love . . .
>
> And how my heart that all sweet things beguile
> Goes laughing with her for a little while . . .
> And then turns homeward like a weary dove.

Sweetness is, indeed, a virtue of all three members of this group, though sometimes it becomes almost a fault by its very excess. It is distilled at leisure, from quiet thoughts and pleasing fancies ; and it is poured out in a ripple of rhythm and a tinkle of rhyme which quickly captivate the ear.

In the work of Helen Parry Eden, however, a more bracing element has been added. There is no vacuity here, where a soul should be ; but there is, especially in the second volume, *Coal and Candle-light*, a deep sense of social responsibility. There is, too, a tang of humour, sign of a vigilant mental eye. All the deep and tender feeling for the small child who is enshrined in this poetry is lightly held in check ; and no sentimentality weakens it. The verse trips along gaily, in its own very individual and attractive measure, smiling at the self-imposed curb, and poking gentle fun at itself in quaint and homely phrasing.

The intensity of the poetry which we have just been considering has therefore given place to a more refreshing charm : a piquancy which invites one to enjoy its gaiety, while hinting all the time at deeper things. A good example of this will be found in the author's first volume, entitled *Bread and Circuses*. The piece is called, with characteristic humour, " To Betsey-Jane, on her Desiring to go Incontinently to Heaven."

> My Betsey-Jane, it would not do,
> For what would Heaven make of you :
> A little, honey-loving bear,
> Among the Blessèd Babies there ?
>
> Nor do you dwell with us in vain
> Who tumble and get up again
> And try, with bruisèd knees, to smile—
> Sweet, you are blessèd all the while
>
> And we in you : so wait, they'll come
> To take your hand and fetch you home,
> In Heavenly leaves to play at tents
> With all the Holy Innocents.

Another is " The Third Birthday," from the same volume :

> Three candles had her cake,
> Which now are burnt away ;

We wreathed it for her sake
With currant-leaves and bay
And the last graces
Of Michaelmas Daisies
Pluckt on a misty day.

.   .   .   .

Three candles lit her state;
Dimmed is their golden reign—
Leaves on an empty plate,
Petals and tallow stain;
Nor will she
Nor the candles three
Ever be three again.

Perhaps the most engaging of all the lyrics in this book is one to the same small child, called " A Song in a Lane," from which, however, I must quote only the last stanza :

When the Wind comes up the lane
And you go down—
Your tresses, for a gusty space,
Discover all your merry face
And the Wind drops with pinioned grace
To kiss the small white forehead place
Above your summer brown ;—
When the Wind comes up the lane
And you go down.

While, to conclude reluctantly this greedy pilfering from the " Betsey " poems, I cannot refrain from quoting one in a very different mood. It is from the author's second volume, *Coal and Candlelight*; and was therefore published later than those we have already considered. The date is indeed significant, for the poem was written at the beginning of the Great War, when over all English mothers and children hung the shadow of threatened invasion. This piece is called "The Admonition—to Betsey":

> *Remember, on your knees,*
> *The men who guard your slumbers—*
>
> And guard a house in a still street
> Of drifting leaves and drifting feet,
> A deep blue window where below
> Lies moonlight on the roof like snow,
> A clock that still the quarters tells
> To the dove that roosts beneath the bell's
> Grave canopy of silent brass
> Round which the little night winds pass
> Yet stir it not in the grey steeple;
> And guard all small and drowsy people
> Whom gentlest dusk doth disattire,
> Undressing by the nursery fire
> In unperturbèd numbers
> On this side of the seas—
>
> *Remember, on your knees,*
> *The men who guard your slumbers.*

A poem like that, and many of the others in this second volume, is essentially of our time. So that

407

it might serve as a link between the older manner and the new, if one were searching for some arbitrary sign. But that is not of our purpose for the moment : and we turn directly from the general features of the poetry we were considering earlier in this study to work which is more truly representative of our time.

It is like going out from a warm old garden to watch the dawn from a breezy hill. The prospect is grey and cold by comparison. You may be buffeted by the wind and stung by showers and wrapped in chilly mist long before the sun will rise. And perhaps it will never rise—for you ; though that depends entirely upon the state of your own vision. For, however veiled by storm-clouds, there is no doubt that the sun is coming. It may be seen, by those who have eyes for it, in the work of a dozen men and women who have wakened to the call of the Time-spirit. Through them the light is struggling ; and if its rays are sometimes broken and obscured, that is all the surer promise of a fair day to follow.

So, in our pendant group, we shall put three of the women poets who, going out in the daybreak, have girt themselves to encounter wind and weather. They are clad in homespun and shod with stout leather, and armed with the austere energy of

morning. Of keen sight and clear brain is this
modern Muse: alert and eager, with a line of
thought between the brows, satire and sympathy
chasing quick smiles upon the lips, indignation
hastening the step, a hand steady and strong for
service, and most compassionate eyes. She strides
along in the eastern light, young, immature, imperfect; with gravity for the old grace, truth for
the old lures, responsibility for the old sweetness,
and knowledge for the old illusions.

No wonder that the unaccustomed ear is startled
at this music, and that even the critical person
hardly knows what to make of it. Listening ever
so hopefully, one is doubtful at first; and even
when the true harmony of it has been caught, one
finds in its complexity a most difficult thing to
define. For it is not possible to classify this poetry
as—by a stretch—we were able to do with the work
of our first group. The themes in themselves are
not so simple, and they are not so simply handled.
They are much more varied, and more subtle;
introducing aspects of life which are new subjects
for poetic treatment, and questions which are
freshly agitating the modern mind. A wider range
is thus taken; but at the same time there is a closer
hold on fact and a closer scrutiny of it. Ideas,
tentative or daring, bring a challenge to old forms

and ways of thought. Conventional technique
goes the way of traditional themes; and Beauty,
suddenly perceived in strange places and things, is
evoked in forms that are equally strange.

> Only a starveling singer seeks
> The stuff of songs among the Greeks.
>
> .   .   .   .   .
>
> We are outwearied with Persephone:
> Rather than her, we'll sing Reality.

Thus Anna Wickham, in her *Contemplative Quarry*,
puts into a snatch the impulse and the meaning of all
this poetry.   Two principles will be found to govern
it.   It is a revolt; but it is also a new allegiance.   It
is angrily breaking down the old limits and the old
lies; but it is building with equal passion, from
Reality thus perceived, a new Heaven and a new
Earth.   So Anna Wickham again:

> Thank God for war and fire
> To burn the silly objects of desire,
> That from the ruin of a church thrown down
> We see God clear and high above the town.

Who will dare to say that the spirit of a piece
like that is less religious, in the true sense of the
word, than that of the poetry at which we were
looking a minute or two ago?   And so with this,
called " Sehnsucht ":

410

Because of body's hunger are we born,
And by contriving hunger are we fed;
Because of hunger is our work well done,
And so are songs well sung, and things well said.
Desire and longing are the whips of God—
God save us all from death when we are fed.

There is a world of difference between the intensity and sweetness of that other verse and the keen fire of this; a difference which does but measure, of course, the forward leap that the mind has taken. One sign of the distance travelled in this subject of Religion may be seen in " Genuflection "; and here, as elsewhere, one perceives that the mental struggle involved in attaining to a new aspect of truth has had an influence upon the form of the verse, making it terse and incisive almost to severity:

I most offend my Deity when I kneel;
I have no profit from repeated prayers.
I know the law too perfect and too real
To swerve or falter for my small affairs.

There is the same profound change in the treatment of the theme of Motherhood. Who shall say that the feeling which prompts such a poem as " To a Young Boy " is less deep and tender because it looks so resolutely at the truth of human imperfection? I am sure that the love for him is as strong

411

as that for Betsey-Jane. Or, on the question of technique, can one affirm that the irregularity of this measure is not suited to its subject equally with the grace of the Betsey lyrics ?

> Poor son of strife—
> Child of inequality and growth—
>
> .　　　.　　　.　　　.　　　.　　　.　　　.
>
> You will find no steady virtue :
> You will live sometimes with holy ecstasy, sometimes
> 　　with shoddy sin.
>
> You will keep no constant faith,
> But with an agony of faithful longing you will hate a lie.

Feminist questions, narrowly so called, do not much occupy this poetry ; but that does not mean that the larger implications of the Women's Movement are not deeply realized. So this author, thinking of the freedom of soul which cannot be bartered away except at the soul's own peril, sings :

> For the work of my head and hands I will be paid,
> But I take no fee to be wedded, or to remain a maid.

And again :

> We ask our freedom.　In good sooth,
> We only ask to know and speak the truth.

And, thinking of the artificiality which makes the lives of many women a mere pretence of living :

412

Women Poets

> Poor body that was crushed in stays
> Through many real-seeming days,
> You are free in the grave.
>
> .   .   .   .   .
>
> Poor bodies crushed in stays,
> Think of the rotting-days!

Or, of the need to brace the will which has grown feeble under such restraint :

> God send us power to make decision
> With muscular, clean, fierce precision.

Sometimes the new verse does treat directly of the political questions involved in the movement. There is, for example, a poem by Eva Gore Booth in *The Egyptian Pillar*, the theme of which was suggested by a great meeting of women's trades on the Embankment. The Prime Minister of the day, replying to the franchise deputation, had exhorted the women to " have patience " ; and the poet is here associating his words with the memories of old wrong suggested by the pillar of Cleopatra's needle, past which the women are marching :

> Where the Egyptian pillar—old, so old—
>   With mystery fronts the open English sky,
> Bearing the yoke of those who heap up gold,
>   The sad-eyed workers pass in silence by.

413

Heavily hewing wood and drawing water,
   These have been patient since the world began—
Patient through centuries of toil and slaughter,
   For patience is the ultimate soul of man.

    .   .   .   .   .   .

Long has submission played a traitor's part—
   Oh human soul, no patience any more
Shall break your wings and harden Pharaoh's heart,
   And keep you lingering on the Red Sea shore.

In " The Street Orator " there lives a literal
record of the fight which is valuable on that account :

    At Clitheroe from the Market Square
       I saw rose-lit the mountains gleam,
    I stood before the people there
       And spake as in a dream.

    At Oldham of the many mills
       The weavers are of gentle mind ;
    At Haslingden one flouted me,
       At Burnley all the folk were kind.

    .   .   .   .   .

    Oh, I have friends at Haslingden,
       And many a friend in Hyde,
    But 'tis at little Clitheroe
       That I would fain abide.

One is glad to have that record, for the quiet
triumph of its gentleness ; just as one welcomes a
piece like " The Good Samaritan," revealing the

synthetic vision which can see events in their
relation to the larger issue ; and a poetic instinct
to embody truth in a familiar allegory :

> Robbed and wounded, all the day
> The great cause by the roadside lay.
> The Rich and Mighty in their pride
> Passed by on the other side.
> With smiling lips indifferent
> On their way the statesmen went.
> At evening in the sunset-flame
> Out of the mill the winders came ;
> She who with four great looms weaves
> Found Justice fallen among thieves,
> Stone-breakers resting from their toil
> Have poured out wine and oil.
> The miner hurrying from the mine
> Has seen a flash of light divine,
> And every tired labourer
> Has given a helping hand to her.

In pieces like that, which, however, are rare
examples, the poet is treating a single definite aspect
of modern thought, and one which had become
familiar. That fact in itself may have helped her
to the greater smoothness of her verse. But usually
the new poetry is engaged upon ideas which are not
yet in common circulation, and many of which are
the subject of controversy. It would be possible,
if there were space for it, to illustrate an acute

interest in and original thought upon such provocative questions as the penal laws, marriage, the relation between the sexes, eugenics, property, prostitution, ethics, or the conventions of our civilization—all of which are in addition to the primary things which in the past have completely absorbed the poet. Those primary things are less prominent now. Love, in the sense of romantic passion, has only a small place here ; but comradeship is honoured. Sensuous delight ranks second to the joy of mind and spirit. And always there is the mental honesty which will not cry peace when there is no peace ; the courage to take up arms in a just cause, and generous devotion to the service of humanity.

In the volume of poems by Margaret Maitland Radford, which is the most recent of all that I have quoted, there is what one may call—almost literally—the last word of the poetic spirit as it is getting itself uttered by the women of our time. A significant fragment from her lines " To a Poet " will indicate over again the modern attitude to Reality. She calls the poet " Night-watchman for the Truth," and says :

> But I will take a stone up from the dust
> And give it thee. . . .
> At last, oh poet,—the dust is starry stuff.

Women Poets

And another fragment from " Lovers of Men " puts
into a symbol the spiritual unrest which troubles the
heart of the poet of our day :

> Alas for us, who know we are but lost
> Unless we run the streets and cry out as in wrath,
> " Your cold is not kept out with cloth—
> Wood fires can never melt this frost,
> Nor will this bread of flour appease your hunger ! "

Consider, too, the compassion born of larger
knowledge in these last two stanzas of " To a Girl
who was on the Streets," from the same volume :

> You are dying, dying, dear—
> > You knew it must mean this ;
> No friend will come—there's none but me
> > To give you your last kiss.
>
> Along the white beds now
> > Comes the sad morning sun ;
> Man, man, what hast thou done
> > To this little one ?

In a piece like that, tenderness conquers the diffi-
culty which is inherent in a theme at once so strange
to poetry, and so frankly handled. But, generally
speaking, this difficult newness puts the modern
poet at a disadvantage, from the point of view of
making charming verse. And no effort is made
merely to charm.

417

Contemporary Poets

Thus contemporary poetry—of men as well as women—appears at times to be almost raw and crude. And when to this is added the sense of struggle against customary thinking; when, too, the poet is found to be worshipping a new ideal, exalting reality in place of pleasant illusions, and rightness of thought in place of fine technique, we shall not wonder at what seems irregular, awkward, or unfinished in this verse.

But inasmuch as we know that there is ultimately no conflict between Truth and Beauty, we shall look forward to the time when the new thought, growing deeper, stronger, and more comprehensive, shall inevitably find perfect expression. Perhaps the lines which follow, also from Margaret Radford's book, may give us leave to hope that we are already on the way to that happy goal:

> Run to my heart: I know the worst of thee;
> For each scar on thy soul, the soul in me
> Has one as hot, as old;
>
> .   .   .   .   .   .
>
> How many leaves whirled down in last night's wind?
> How many young have sinned?
> I am as wild as thee, as desperate, as weak—
> Come, slip down to my heart,
> Though the tears are on thy cheek.

William Butler Yeats

UNHAPPY Ireland is at least happy in her laureate. The poet of dreams, of patriotism and proud humility, of old legend and song, of sweet sorrow and bitter joy, of a land and a people beyond the world—this is indeed the poet of Ireland ; and it does not matter if no hand has ever set the wreath upon his brow, for he was crowned before his birth.

The fact is perhaps too obvious and too seeming-simple, that W. B. Yeats incarnates the poetic spirit of his country. Yet to the lover of Ireland there is a delight, not unmixed with irony, in contemplating the manner of the incarnation ; while to the lover of poetry there appears (and the more the closer he looks) a sufficient complexity in that which had seemed so simple. For the spiritual identity is complete, and the outward likeness so close that friend and foe are both satisfied. But while the one will tell over joyfully the features of resemblance, the other will seize precisely those points and make a count of them on which to indict the whole race of Irishmen. The one will cry, " Behold the dreamer," holding that word to be the highest ; and in the meantime, the other, holding up deprecating hands, mutters in a very different sense—

"Dreams! Dreams! Dreams!" The one will salute a tentative and wavering philosophy for the very changefulness which is its growing; and the other will groan—"Always, always, unstable as water." And while the one will see an unregarding and extravagant spiritual passion as the austere soul of Ireland herself, that enemy will fling at it his first and last reproach—"Unpractical."

But the enemy is, of course, a Philistine, and one need not much concern oneself with him and his views, except as an ironic spice. It is certainly with no bid for his favour that one notes first of all a cardinal fact of Mr Yeats's artistic career, in that he did, at the outset, deliberately dedicate himself to his country's service. Most people know at this time of day that he has laboured for upward of twenty years in the re-birth of Irish literature; and they do not therefore need to be told that all his plays are to be judged, as he himself says, " as part of an attempt to create a national dramatic literature in Ireland." That is a bit of literary history which will one day be national history too. But so that there might be no doubt about the matter, and so that all the world who cared might know that this genius which is Irish in fibre and essence was solemnly vowed to Ireland, he made the declaration in a poem called " To Ireland in the Coming

Times." There is a passage here which by implication sums up all that is involved in that inborn affinity and conscious avowal, giving a glimpse through what would seem to be the welding of the two into " a beautiful and perfect whole," down to a region where elements too complex and too diverse for fusion are at war. There the ancient spirit of poetry which is his birthright, free and shy and proud, must needs rebel against that more careful modern spirit which would try to fetter it with a purpose.

> Know, that I would accounted be
> True brother of that company,
> Who sang to sweeten Ireland's wrong,
> Ballad and story, rann and song;
> Nor be I any less of them,
> Because the red-rose-bordered hem
> Of her, whose history began
> Before God made the angelic clan,
> Trails all about the written page.

Once more the enemy would provide sauce to our reflection, if we would but admit him, reminding us of what was to happen to the patriotic devotion of Mr Yeats in these latter days, and of a verse of a poem written in 1913:

> Romantic Ireland's dead and gone.

But indeed we have no need of the enemy in this

case, for the poet himself has served us, and one has only to turn to his " Ideas of Good and Evil " for an ironical commentary. There he says : " In my heart of hearts I have never been quite certain that one should be more than an artist, that even patriotism is more than an impure desire in an artist." Of course : one might have known it. Sober purposefulness must needs be subdued to that other beautiful tyrant. That it should become conscious at all in such a poet is a measure of its power, and the indubitable sign of the spirit of the time upon him. But there, in his own words, is enunciated the second cardinal fact of his life's work—that she of the red-rose-bordered hem has triumphed, and that it is in laborious service of her that the poet has served his country. And if it should be objected that there is inconsistency here, one may reply first in a paraphrase of Emerson, that with a superficial consistency the poet has nothing whatever to do ; and then—that the Spirit of Poetry which is his mistress is no less than the Spirit of Ireland too.

It follows that one is bound first to think of Mr Yeats as the patient and laborious artist, resolutely putting aside for the moment the image of his work that is in our mind as of a thing so delicately lovely that it must have quietly grown up in a night,

fostered by moonbeams and dew. Hear his own
protest against any silly fancy of that kind:

> I said, " A line will take us hours maybe;
> Yet if it does not seem a moment's thought,
> Our stitching and unstitching has been naught.
> Better go down upon your marrow-bones
> And scrub a kitchen pavement, or break stones
> Like an old pauper, in all kinds of weather,
> For to articulate sweet sounds together
> Is to work harder than all these, and yet
> Be thought an idler by the noisy set
> Of bankers, schoolmasters and clergymen
> The martyrs call the world."
>
> .   .   .   .   .   .
>
> I said, " It's certain there is no fine thing
> Since Adam's fall but needs much labouring."

That is vigorous enough to be convincing, in all
conscience; and incidentally one observes that it
is written in the more nervous style of his later
satiric mood. One hardly need produce all the
other evidence to " an infinite capacity for taking
pains "—which is just as well, seeing that the proofs
would demand a volume to themselves, so fast do
they multiply as one reads essay and preface, appen-
dix and revision. Indeed, one begins to have a fear
that that passion for polishing has become a malady:
that no line he has ever written is final; and that
some day something dreadful may happen to certain

perfect lyrics. It might be advisable, as a measure of precaution, to remove those lyrics to a place of safety. The poet would resist, of course; but in that event force would certainly be justified, since the poems of which I am thinking, among which are "The Lake Isle of Innisfree," "Down by the Salley Garden," and "To an Isle in the Water," are no longer his own. They are the personal possession of every one who loves them; and it is all very well for Mr Yeats to say:

> The friends that have it I do wrong
> Whenever I remake a song
> Should know what issue is at stake:
> It is myself that I remake.

But there is a point beyond which one refuses to have an old friend remade.

One fact may, however, be noted about this process of refining in its verbal and metrical aspects. It is not a blind impulse; but, like the poet's instinct for selection, it has been strictly directed along a certain path. He has tried always, even in his subtlest effects, to attain a perfection of simplicity; and he has chosen his material almost invariably from national legend and folk-lore. The same principle is at work in the making of his plays: native themes are made articulate in a native idiom. Even in his love-songs—though to be sure there is a

William Butler Yeats

sense in which it is true that all this poet's lyrical work is love poetry—he often slips on the singing robes of an old Irish bard. Thus " Aedh Hears the Cry of the Sedge " :

> I wander by the edge
> Of this desolate lake
> Where wind cries in the sedge :
> *Until the axle break*
> *That keeps the stars in their round*
> *And hands hurl in the deep*
> *The banners of East and West*
> *And the girdle of light is unbound,*
> *Your head will not lie by the breast*
> *Of your beloved in sleep.*

For the material of his art Mr Yeats is constant in acknowledging his debt to Lady Gregory's translations of Irish myth and legend. So we find that the one-act play in blank verse called *On Baile's Strand* is a tragedy from the life of the legendary hero Cuchulain, which is to be found in Lady Gregory's *Cuchulain of Muirthemne*. *The Golden Helmet*, another play about Cuchulain, in which this hero beloved of gods and men offers up his life for his country, is based on stories from the same source to which the poet has given a characteristic turn. Deirdre the sorrowful, who is Celtic and Irish in her very essence, also comes to us through Lady Gregory. *The Countess Cathleen* was found

425

by the poet in a book of Irish folk-lore which had been translated from a French author, who in turn had gathered the tale from children in the streets of Cork and Dublin. And *Cathleen ni Houlihan,* that supreme symbol of the old and ever-young spirit of Ireland, came to the poet quite literally in a dream ; but indeed it was a dream which seems to be an ever-present vision before the eyes of Irish folk. So the proud and pitiful old woman, mysteriously wandering the country-side, has come to rest for a moment by the peasant's fireside :

OLD WOMAN. Sometimes my feet are tired and my hands are quiet; but there is no quiet in my heart. When the people see me quiet, they think old age has come on me and that all the stir has gone out of me. But when the trouble is on me, I must be talking to my friends.

BRIDGET. What was it put you wandering ?

OLD WOMAN. Too many strangers in the house.

BRIDGET. Indeed you look as if you'd had your share of trouble.

OLD WOMAN. I have had trouble indeed.

BRIDGET. What was it put the trouble on you ?

OLD WOMAN. My land that was taken from me.

PETER. Was it much land they took from you ?

OLD WOMAN. My four beautiful green fields.

No doubt this choice of material, which is legendary and specifically national, is to a great extent

William Butler Yeats

instinctive, like the fastidiousness which never is content, but must persistently alter and remake. This is a backward-looking mind, which loves to dwell in regions of remote time, amongst old gods and heroes. But again one comes back to the fact that always, whether in choosing a theme or in adorning it, a deliberate path has been taken to a definite goal. In one place Mr Yeats asks himself: " How can I make my work mean something to vigorous and simple men ? " and in other places he tells of a patient effort to attune his poetic instrument to the speech of Irish country folk. The reward of that is coming, and is already promised in the comedy scenes of his later plays. And the people who regret that his lyrical period is over may at least take heart from dialogue which is flexible, racy, and telling. For if spring cannot last for ever and a silence must fall upon the bird-note at high summer-tide, it is at least something to be thankful for that the music of humanity is beginning to take its place. In that progression he but follows where great ones have gone before him, when illusion and romance have faded in the light of noonday, and the poet has been compelled to regard with a keener eye a larger, more urgent, and more crowded world.

With that future, however, except as a happy

hope, the student of Mr Yeats's accomplished work is not concerned. He has to do with a romantic poet and a self-conscious artist : one who knows himself so well that he is quite innocent of the Saxon virtue (or is it a vice ?) of mock-modesty. He has taken command of himself, and has known how to follow the trend of his temperament—following, but at the same time directing, with absolute mastery. It has been called a pose, this attitude of mind so tenderly fostered ; but so far from being a thing artificial or alien, it is but insistence on himself, hardened to a habit.

Hence the mystical quality of his imagination is given free rein along that bridle-path. It finds constant expression, busying itself now with faery fancies, now with an idea more abstract and remote, now with some aspect of unhappy love. It gives an austerity to all his work, as though it were steeped in moonlight ; so that even his love poetry, shaken with passion though it sometimes is, goes delicately stepping in filmy white garments. Not that there is any puritanical denial of happiness in it ; but the strident sun and his joy of life never enter, being too virile and too fierce for this pale region that is dim with dreams and glimmering with faery feet. The music of that sphere would challenge too loudly the sorrow of ancient tragedy and

428

William Butler Yeats

the twilight peace in which the poet sits to meditate
upon the face of beauty.

> Red Rose, proud Rose, sad Rose of all my days!
>
> . . . . . .
>
> Come near, that no more blinded by man's fate,
> I find under the boughs of love and hate,
> In all poor foolish things that live a day,
> Eternal beauty wandering on her way.

The 'Rose' poems of Mr Yeats are the itera-
tion of his creed : his act of adoration at the shrine
of Beauty. It is a rite to which he returns again
and again, as though it were not enough to worship
the goddess in " dusty deeds," having given his life
to her service, but that he must go apart from time
to time to contemplate and adore. So he sings to
"The Rose of Battle" :

> Rose of all Roses, Rose of all the World!
> You, too, have come where the dim tides are hurled
> Upon the wharves of sorrow, and heard ring
> The bell that calls us on ; the sweet far thing.
> Beauty grown sad with its eternity
> Made you of us, and of the dim gray sea.

And thus to "The Rose of Peace," when Michael
had sheathed his sword in looking upon her face :

> And God would bid His warfare cease,
> Saying all things were well ;
> And softly make a rosy peace,
> A peace of Heaven with Hell.

Contemporary Poets

So, too, he sings of "The Rose of the World":

> Bow down, archangels, in your dim abode:
> Before you were, or any hearts to beat,
> Weary and kind one lingered by His seat;
> He made the world to be a grassy road
> Before her wandering feet.

And finally, thinking perhaps of death and its mystery, and of how all ecstasy and striving is stilled at last, he sings "To the Secret Rose":

> Far-off, most secret, and inviolate Rose,
> Enfold me in my hour of hours; where those
> Who sought thee in the Holy Sepulchre,
> Or in the wine-vat, dwell beyond the stir
> And tumult of defeated dreams; and deep
> Among pale eyelids, heavy with the sleep
> Men have named beauty. . . .

There is no need to analyse the peculiar quality of these poems in order to feel that they are an expression of what this poet calls the Celtic Spirit. Now there has been so much blether about the word Celtic that one is almost afraid to use it. Yet it does mean something, and the special significance of it, defined with more or less precision by Mr Yeats himself in passages up and down his works, is just that which one inevitably comes back to after any study of his own poetry. It is a sense of

430

William Butler Yeats

infinite longing, of something remote and unattainable, of wistfulness and melancholy, of a sort of homesickness of the soul. Of that spirit his poetry is the final incarnation: it is his own realm, and there he is king. Perhaps its loveliest expression is "The Lake Isle of Innisfree"; and the rightness of the poem, its faithful echo of that spiritual nostalgia, have been tried and proved by a very severe test. For it has been parodied with great cleverness, and remains unscathed; and whether one regards it simply as the lament of any exile for his native land, or calls up the flock of unhappy associations which waits upon the thought of an exile from Ireland; whether one listens a little closer for "the very inmost voice of Celtic sadness and of Celtic longing for infinite things," or imagines in its mournful music the soul of all humanity like a lost child crying, it remains a supremely beautiful song.

I will arise and go now, and go to Innisfree,
And a small cabin build there, of clay and wattles made,
Nine bean rows will I have there, a hive for the honey bee,
And live alone in the bee-loud glade.

And I shall have some peace there, for peace comes dropping slow,
Dropping from the veils of the morning to where the cricket sings;

Contemporary Poets

There midnight's all a glimmer, and noon a purple glow,
And evening full of the linnet's wings.

I will arise and go now, for always night and day
I hear lake water lapping with low sounds by the shore;
While I stand on the roadway, or on the pavements gray,
I hear it in the deep heart's core.

Bibliography

LASCELLES ABERCROMBIE

Interludes and Poems. John Lane. 1908.

The Sale of St Thomas. Published by the Author. (Out of print.) 1911.

Emblems of Love. John Lane. 1912.

Deborah. John Lane. 1913.

Contributions to *New Numbers,* February, April, August, December, 1914. (Out of print.)

EVA GORE BOOTH

The Three Resurrections and *The Triumph of Maeve.* Longmans. 1905.

The Agate Lamp. Longmans. 1912.

The Sorrowful Princess. Longmans. 1907.

The Egyptian Pillar. Maunsel. 1907.

The Perilous Light. Erskine Macdonald. 1915.

RUPERT BROOKE

Poems. Sidgwick & Jackson. 1911.

1914 and Other Poems. Sidgwick & Jackson. 1915.

Contributions to *New Numbers.* (See ABERCROMBIE.)

ANNA BUNSTON (Mrs de Bary)

Mingled Wine. Longmans. 1909.

Songs of God and Man. Herbert & Daniel. 1912.

433

Contemporary Poets

JOSEPH CAMPBELL
> *The Mountainy Singer.* Maunsel. 1909.
> *Irishry.* Maunsel. 1913.
> *Earth of Cualann.* Maunsel. 1917.

PADRAIC COLUM
> *Wild Earth.* (Out of print.) 1907.
> *Wild Earth.* Maunsel. 1916. (A different vol. from
> the preceding.)

JAMES COUSINS
> *The Quest.* Maunsel. 1906.
> *Etain the Beloved.* Maunsel. 1912.
> *Straight and Crooked.* Grant Richards. 1915.

OLIVE CUSTANCE
> *Rainbows.* John Lane. 1902.
> *The Inn of Dreams.* John Lane. 1911.

WILLIAM H. DAVIES
> *The Soul's Destroyer.* Alston Rivers. 1906.
> *New Poems.* Elkin Mathews. 1907.
> *Nature Poems.* A. C. Fifield. 1908.
> *Farewell to Poesy.* A. C. Fifield. 1910.
> *Songs of Joy.* A. C. Fifield. 1911.
> *Foliage.* Elkin Mathews. 1913.
> *The Bird of Paradise.* Methuen. 1914.
> *Collected Poems.* A. C. Fifield. 1916.

Bibliography

WALTER DE LA MARE
    Songs of Childhood. Longmans. (Out of print.)
      1902.
    Poems. Murray. 1906.
    The Listeners. Constable. 1912.
    A Child's Day. Constable. 1912.
    Peacock Pie. Constable. 1913.
    Motley. Constable. 1918.

JOHN DRINKWATER
    Cromwell. David Nutt. 1913.
    Poems (1908 to 1914). Sidgwick & Jackson.
    Olton Pools. Sidgwick & Jackson. 1916.
    Abraham Lincoln. Sidgwick & Jackson, 1918.
    Loyalties. Sidgwick & Jackson. 1919.

HELEN PARRY EDEN
    Bread and Circuses. John Lane. 1914.
    Coal and Candlelight. John Lane. 1918.

MICHAEL FIELD (Katharine Bradley and Edith Cooper)
    Calirrhoë and Fair Rosamund. J. Baker & Son.
      1884.
    Canute the Great. G. Bell & Sons. 1887. *
    Attila, my Attila! Elkin Mathews. 1896.
    The World at Auction. Hacon & Ricketts. 1898.
    Poems of Adoration. Sands & Co. 1899.
    Anna Ruina. David Nutt. 1899.

MICHAEL FIELD—*continued*

Borgia. Sidgwick & Jackson. 1905.

Wild Honey. T. Fisher Unwin. 1908.

Mystic Trees. Eveleigh Nash. 1913.

Deirdre. Poetry Bookshop. 1918.

In the Name of Time. Poetry Bookshop. 1919.

WILFRED WILSON GIBSON

Urlyn the Harper and *The Queen's Vigil.* Elkin Mathews (Vigo Cabinet Series). 1900.

On the Threshold. Samurai Press. 1907.

The Stonefolds. Samurai Press. 1907.

The Web of Life. (Out of print.) 1908.

Akra the Slave. Elkin Mathews. 1910.

Daily Bread. Elkin Mathews. 1910.

Womenkind. David Nutt (Pilgrim Players Series). 1911.

Fires. Elkin Mathews. 1912.

Borderlands. Elkin Mathews. 1914.

Thoroughfares. Elkin Mathews. 1914.

Battle. Elkin Mathews. 1915.

Whin. Macmillan. 1918.

THOMAS HARDY

The Dynasts. Macmillan. 1910.

Satires of Circumstance. Macmillan. 1914.

Moments of Vision. Macmillan. 1917.

Collected Poems. Macmillan. 1919.

Bibliography

RALPH HODGSON

    Eve. " At the Sign of Flying Fame." (Out of print.) 1913.

    The Bull. " At the Sign of Flying Fame." 1913.

    The Mystery. " At the Sign of Flying Fame." 1913.

    The Song of Honour. (Out of print.) 1913.

    (All the above reissued by The Poetry Bookshop.)

    Poems. Macmillan. 1917.

FORD MADOX HUEFFER

    Collected Poems. Max Goschen. 1914.

ROSE MACAULAY

    The Two Blind Countries. Sidgwick & Jackson. 1914.

JOHN MASEFIELD

    Salt Water Ballads. Grant Richards. 1902. (Out of print.) (Reprinted by Elkin Mathews.) 1913.

    Ballads. Elkin Mathews. (Out of print.) 1903.

    Ballads and Poems. Elkin Mathews. 1910.

    The Everlasting Mercy. Sidgwick & Jackson. 1911.

    The Widow in the Bye-Street. Sidgwick & Jackson. 1912.

    Dauber. Wm. Heinemann. 1913.

    Daffodil Fields. Wm. Heinemann. 1913.

    Philip the King. Wm. Heinemann. 1914.

    The Faithful. Wm. Heinemann. 1915.

    Lollingdon Downs. Wm. Heinemann. 1917.

Contemporary Poets

ALICE MILLIGAN
> *Hero Lays.* Maunsel. 1908.
> *Sons of the Sea Kings.* M. H. Gill & Son. 1914.

SUSAN L. MITCHELL
> *The Living Chalice.* Maunsel. 1913.
> *Aids to the Immortality of Certain Persons in Ireland.*
> Maunsel. 1913.

HAROLD MONRO
> *Judas.* Sampson Low. 1908.
> *Before Dawn.* Constable. 1911.
> *Children of Love.* Poetry Bookshop. 1914.
> *Trees.* Poetry Bookshop. 1915.
> *Strange Meetings.* Poetry Bookshop. 1917.

SAROJINI NAIDU
> *The Golden Threshold.* Wm. Heinemann. 1905.
> *The Bird of Time.* Wm. Heinemann. 1912.

SEUMAS O'SULLIVAN
> *Poems.* Maunsel. 1912.
> *An Epilogue.* Maunsel. 1914.
> *The Rosses.* Maunsel. 1918.

JOHN PRESLAND (Mrs Skelton)
> *The Marionettes.* T. Fisher Unwin. 1907.
> *Joan of Arc.* Simpkin Marshall. 1909.
> *Mary Queen of Scots.* Chatto & Windus. 1910.

438

Bibliography

JOHN PRESLAND—*continued*

    The Deluge. Chatto & Windus. 1911.

    Manin. Chatto & Windus. 1911.

    Marcus Aurelius. Chatto & Windus. 1912.

    Songs of Changing Skies. Chatto & Windus. 1913.

    Belisarius. Chatto & Windus. 1913.

    King Monmouth. Chatto & Windus. 1916.

    Poems of London. Chatto & Windus. 1918.

MARGARET MAITLAND RADFORD

    Poems. G. Allen & Unwin. 1915.

J. C. SQUIRE

    Imaginary Speeches. Stephen Swift & Co. 1912.

    The Survival of the Fittest. G. Allen & Unwin. 1916.

    Tricks of the Trade. Martin Secker. 1917.

    Poems. (First Series.) Martin Secker. 1918.

JAMES STEPHENS

    Insurrections. Maunsel. (Out of print.) 1909.

    The Hill of Vision. Maunsel. 1912.

    Songs from the Clay. Macmillan. 1915.

    Green Branches. Maunsel. 1916.

    Reincarnations. Macmillan. 1918.

ANNA WICKHAM

    The Contemplative Quarry. Poetry Bookshop. 1915.

    The Man with a Hammer. Grant Richards. 1916.

Contemporary Poets

Mrs Margaret L. Woods
 Collected Poems. John Lane. 1914.

W. B. Yeats
 Collected Edition. Shakespeare Head Press. 1908.
 Poems. T. Fisher Unwin. 1912.
 Responsibilities. Cuala Press. 1914.
 Reveries over Childhood and Youth. Cualá Press. 1915.
 The Wild Swans at Coole. Cuala Press. 1917.

Ella Young
 Poems. Tower Press Booklets. 1906.

Note.—The lists do not, in every case, include all the author's works, the principal object being to give the books mentioned in the studies.